141048

DAILY LIFE IN
PAPAL ROME

THE DAILY LIFE SERIES

DAILY LIFE IN
PAPAL ROME
in the Eighteenth Century

Maurice Andrieux

Translated by
Mary Fitton

THE MACMILLAN COMPANY

Library of Congress Catalog Card Number: 69-11589

First American Edition 1969
Translated from the French *La Vie Quotidienne Dans La
Rome Pontificale,* © Hachette, Paris, 1962

THE MACMILLAN COMPANY

Printed in the United States of America

To My Friend, Jules Antonini

FOREWORD

An old country past its prime, pleasant and peaceful, basking in a warm caressing glow—there is about Rome in the eighteenth century something of a beautiful autumn sunset. Dark clouds gathering over the rest of Europe were to reach the Roman sky, but she was oblivious of danger until the very eve of tempest. In that matter-of-fact century of reason and dialectic she alone, elevated above current realities, clung faithfully to a golden view of life, her people serenely incurious and immune from all surprise. The paternal old men who were her rulers had never been so liberal, so kind or so considerate. They instigated no reforms, for fear of unsettling the happy beneficiaries of abuse. *'Far dolce,'* one of them told an artist working on his portrait, *'sono pastore dei popoli,'*[1] and his words sound the keynote of the Roman Settecento. That famous *douceur de vivre,* vaunted elsewhere so often and so often causelessly, was here found at its best and most extensive. Rome had been at many other periods greater in art or in the craft of politics; at no time was she so engaging or so tranquil. For these hundred years she was a smiling city.

[1] 'Make it a nice one; I am the people's pastor.'

CONTENTS

ILLUSTRATIONS

CHAPTER ONE

THE SETTING

THE PLACE

The study of eighteenth-century Roman life demands a clear picture of its setting and of the background which gave colour to events; otherwise it will lack substance and foundation. Change, we know, is the law of all life and Rome in obeying it has seen many of her characteristic features sacrificed to modern development. But enough of the old papal city still stands, actual and evocative, for us to trace its broad outline and lesser details in Rome today.

The ancient Aurelian wall, so many of whose fragments are preserved, still marked the perimeter in the eighteenth century. But the town which sheltered over two million people at the height of the Empire now counted no more than 140,000,[1] a reduced population lost in the huge area of the antique city and occupying in fact only a fifth of it. They crowded together between the Porta del Popolo, the old Forum Boarium, the district of Trastevere, the crook of the Tiber, the Baths of Diocletian and the slopes of the Quirinal. Beyond these limits lay only waste tracts, vineyards and gardens, with now and then some patrician villa to display a magnificence of park and architecture among the desolation. The country was invading the city proper; great oxen with spreading horns would lie beside the obelisks, flocks of goats graze in and out the ruins. Vines overgrew the fallen column-shafts. In winter a thatch of branches was laid on the houseroofs to cover them. The courtyards were henruns and sometimes cowhouses. There were noble buildings everywhere and the finest churches in the world, but even the busiest quarters retained a country look and often a country smell. Pastoral and epic intermingled in the most ancient Roman tradition, and this union of the formal and the rustic was not the least of the charms of *Vecchia Roma*.

The whole look of the town had changed a great deal during

[1] The census figure for 1709 is 138,568, excluding the Jews who numbered about 5,000. The population rose to 165,000 in 1790.

the preceding century. The world of fashion, concentrated at the Renaissance on and about the Via Giulia, had moved in part to the Corso but mainly to the Quirinal, where the popes elected to live and where many of the prelates had built houses and created superb gardens. The Quirinal was the setting for nearly all the papal plans for urban improvement in the Settecento, ill-advised and ineffectual as these were. The proposed quays along the Tiber, for instance, were everlastingly postponed so that the riverside districts, instead of being the most open and airy in the city, remained darker and filthier than any. When Clement XII in 1735 found himself, by happy chance, possessed of sufficient funds to remedy the evil, he weighed the long-pending embankment against the restoration of the façade of St John Lateran. Deciding for the façade, he left us instead its fifteen monumental statues, the Doctors of the Church who stand, 'preaching to the clouds', above the portico of that ancient basilica.

The most crowded and lively district was still the Campo Marzio in the great bend of the Tiber. Side by side with palaces, convents and churches in its labyrinth of narrow streets stood other, modest dwellings, run up just as the fancy took their small-citizen builders, unplanned, unregulated and often wildly out of line. Yet their haphazard appearance had the sort of charm that exists in the muddle of a painter's studio; none seemed a mere block of masonry, but had its own character and formed a distinct composition. They could—they still can—be looked at individually, each offering some interest or picturesque appeal. The door may stand half-open on a pretty courtyard with bushes of clipped box, sometimes an ornamental statue and often a fountain playing. The spaces left between the larger buildings had been filled by the little houses of the people, narrow houses of perhaps a window's width, with a dark staircase at the end of a damp alley leading to the upper floors. At ground level were burrowlike shops giving directly on the public way, with the food-sellers performing their more malodorous jobs outside, cutting up meat, cooking vegetables and frying fish in the open street.

Workmen, too, moved their less convenient tasks out of doors and this sort of thing was not conducive to tidiness. The roads in the poorer parts were repellently dirty and there were many reasons why nothing could be done about it. First, being quite unpaved, they were thick with dust in fine weather and mud when it rained. Soon after 1730 Pope Clement XII began surfacing them *al modo nuovo*, with small cobble stones and also laid pavements beside the busiest main roads. But the work went on so slowly that it was still far from finished when the French financier Bergeret visited Rome with Fragonard in 1773. He found few roads 'passable' and noted that pavements were so rare and full of gaps that it was rather hard to see what use they were. The Dominican Father Labat, an informed and by no means unsympathetic contemporary observer, has a terse word to say on highway cleansing: 'They have no idea of what it is,' he states. Nor indeed could an occasional sweep by 'primitive and impractical watering machines' —carts loaded with barrels—through streets where the Pope was likely to pass and nowhere else, really count as highway cleansing. It was a period, too, when the residents cared nothing for the state of the thoroughfare and, defying their city Governor's regulations against the unsavoury practice, piled all their refuse at the door and threw the ordure out of the window. Theoretically this garbage was collected in wagons three times a week and emptied into the Tiber and some, certainly, was removed by gardeners in search of good manure; but in the intervals between these sporadic and unreliable forays the gutters stayed choked with rubbish and footloose pigs grubbed for food in mounds of excrement. It was strictly forbidden to let these creatures (which were never called pigs but always, by some strange euphemism, *animali negri*[1]) roam about like this, but officialdom seems to have been idle, apart from renewing its useless vetoes from time to time. The Senator's invariable preliminary notice that the straying of the *animali negri* had now reached a *grado intollerabile* served only to underline his lack of success. As for what the pigs left unconsumed and the municipal wagons failed to cart away, no householder would dream of taking a broom to it himself. 'The brooms of Rome,' says Father Labat, 'are the heavy rains.'

With no public lavatories and no domestic sanitation, parts of the town were in a dreadful condition, for people obeyed their natural needs, as a lackey informed Goethe, *da per tutto dove vuoi*.[2] Goethe was appalled at such a careless attitude. Palace courtyards, private gateways and even staircases were plastered with filth, as were the streets where the passers-by relieved themselves in broad daylight as though the beholders were non-existent. ('It is not being looked at that makes them do this, nor will they refrain when nobody is looking,' Madame de Staël was to comment.) If you

[1] Black beasts. [2] Wherever you like.

13

wished to protect your house you fixed a cross to the wall with the word *Rispetto* in large letters, and this plea for decency was usually effective. The forbidden spot was scrupulously avoided and those seeking a convenient site squatted obligingly in a space between two crosses. They were children of nature and no sense of shame restrained them and we should by no means imagine that such habits were those of the lower orders only. They were to be found throughout society—that society which so curiously mingled the lordly with the sordid. Let us conjure up for a moment some splendid reception in a noble palace, where the lackeys in their handsome liveries stand like a stately hedge up the majestic, illuminated stair, with its rich carpets and its pots of flowering shrubs. Here, at the bottom of the flight, the great princes and prelates of Rome will leave their coaches. And before going farther they will line up along the steps, each before a tub of myrtle or an orange-tree, and 'guard against emergencies', regardless alike of the presence of elaborately dressed ladies and flood damage to flowing trains.

Yet this utter lack of public hygiene, this 'ancient and venerable filth' of *Roma sporca*, did not, oddly enough, make the place unhealthy. The much advertised malaria was encountered hardly anywhere except outside its boundaries, among the stagnant rotten marsh-water of the barren and treeless country. Tales were told of the badness of Campagna air and of how anyone who spent a hot summer night in the *dintorni* beyond the walls was sure to catch a mortal fever; and as the doctors themselves believed it all, they never treated such fevers, on the grounds that God alone should cure them. A Roman going to stay at Tivoli or Frascati had either to wait for the end of the hot weather or cross the zone of 'poisonous air' in a single daytime stage. So greatly did people fear the slightest change of air that no one ever dared to move house within the city, or even change bedrooms at home, between St John's Day and All Saints'. To do so was to court the direst calamities, to avoid which landlords were forbidden to evict insolvent tenants during these months.

All this folk-lore convinced the Romans that their town possessed a noxious atmosphere whose effect they escaped only through a multitude of precautions and by the very fact of actually being Romans. They remained at the same time quite sure that no stranger could survive the climate. Should the conclave exalt any non-Roman to St Peter's throne they looked for a short reign and an early death, even if the poor man were born no farther off than Viterbo. Not that any of these myths had any foundation at all. From a health point of view it was a most satisfactory century in Rome. None even of the mild seasonal epidemics could be classed as a plague, readily as that name was bestowed in Italy, and though threats of malaria were known they were halted on the outskirts, just as in Antiquity, when writers had noted that the air of Rome was always sweet and that of Latium always bad.

The Vatican alone partly deserved its reputation as an unhealthy spot, confirmed when the eighteenth-century popes removed to the Quirinal. For here, in autumn, reigned that *aria cattiva*[1] that had struck down so many pontiffs, though they were ancient men in any case. It was probably no more than the sharp change of temperature felt in Rome at nightfall when a cool dew comes suddenly after the heat of the day, but this, though momentary, can be dangerous.

There were few large towns which had not named their streets and numbered their houses properly by the eighteenth century, but Rome was one of them until 1744. Not till that year did Benedict XIV publish a register of the streets and squares of his capital, employing in it those names which, though hallowed by a sort of unspoken, popular vote, were officially non-existent. His edict, incomplete as it was—giving only 271 streets and 185 squares —substituted a standard list for the former confused and vague designations. Of the main thoroughfares 218 were, however, still described only by the routes they followed: *del Campo dei Fiori per il Balestrari al palazzo Capo di Ferro, da S. Catarina della Rota al fiume* or *da ponte Sisto all' ospedale della Trinità*.

Benedict's reform was in fact of little practical use since it did nothing about road-signs. It was 1803 before the first *tabelle stradali*[2] were put up and then they indicated only the various *rioni*, or districts, by means of 220 white marble boundary slabs of uniform size, each with the name, number and badge of the district.[3]

There was as yet no thought of numbering the houses regularly, though something of the kind had been done as an aid to identifying

[1] Bad (unhealthy) air.　　　　　　[2] Road signs.
[3] The districts of Rome were: Monti, Trevi, Colonna, Campo Marzio, Ponte, Parione, Regola, Sant' Eustachio, Pigna, Campitelli, Sant' Angelo, Ripa, Trastevere, Borgo.

the sick during the plague of 1657. But it was soon abandoned and in eighteenth-century as in ancient Rome addresses had to be given in relation to some feature or monument supposedly familiar to all. The lawyer Domenico Sisto, for example, lived 'in the Via dei Serpenti, the house with the doorway adjoining the butcher's shop, nearly next to the Corsican guardhouse'. Sometimes the directions were even vaguer: 'in the street that goes from . . . to . . .' or 'the house to the right of the one with freshly painted shutters'.

A Roman address, one may gather, was always an approximate affair, except of course for people so well known that their mere name was direction enough. For others it was no light task to give clear instructions for discovering where they lived and the postal service, too, had its problems when it came to delivering mail.

At nightfall almost total darkness enveloped the streets of Rome. The only lighting came from the small lamps—*lampioncini* or *moccoli*—that burned before countless images of the Madonna placed at the corners by pious citizens. When at length some bold innovators did suggest an *illuminazione pubblica* of the main highways their proposals were considered sacrilegious; only the Madonnas ought to shine in Roman darkness, and the city was consequently among the last in Europe to have a public lighting system. French visitors in the eighteenth century, with their often sadly irreverent responses, did not always give the Romans credit for their godly scruple, claiming that the dim streets were preferred for other and less laudable reasons. In this, however, they failed to understand that contemporary attitude of mind which led the Romans to regard the dark as something inviolate, sacred as the privacy of their own homes. Any attempt on their nocturnal immunity savoured of police action and was abhorrent even to people who would never dream of abusing that immunity—just as the police in their turn would never dream of challenging the muffled figures in the shadow of the walls. Darkness, it was held, nightly covered the earth by law of nature and the light that would dispel it was impious and profane. All other forms of progress met with the same dogmatical resistance.

Light being thought of as a sort of meretricious snare—*l'insidia dei lumi*,[1] they used to say—carriages drove lampless in the lampless streets and nervous citizens went equipped with small lanterns to see them through the perils of an outing. These lanterns, still

[1] The snare of lamps.

to be found in Roman antique shops, were invariably cylinder-shaped with a many-faceted glass panel on one side. It was the accepted custom to turn the light away from any passer-by who, anxious to remain unseen, requested one to do so with the words, *Volti la luce*,[1] which, as Charles de Brosses remarks, was as good as saying, 'Leave me to my own devices'.

The one break in the blackout came between the death of a pope and the election of his successor, at a time *di sede vacante*.[2] Then, with so much intrigue going on, the street incident and the under-cover visit were things to be prevented, all the more so since the Holy See might well be unoccupied for months: the conclave after Benedict XIII's death ended only when driven from its quarters by an invasion of bugs. The first act of the Cardinal Camerlengo when a pontiff died was to publish an *editto delle lanterne*[3] by which all heads of households were required to light up at least one window, even if living on the top floors. It was a traditional evening walk to go and look at the pretty variety of different lamps.

For one other reason a random, compassionate light would gleam along the streets. At the sound of the little viaticum bell everyone got up and set a small lamp in his window, so that the illumination spread from house to house as the priest went by with the Host.

Since no one ventured needlessly into the darkened ways, the silence of a Roman night was broken only by a rare brawl or the sound of a lover serenading his lady. In December, however, the serenades, though not then offered to young ladies, increased in noise and number. Instead of lovers the singers would be peasants from the Abruzzi. Dressed in sheepskins, with pointed, brigand-fashion hats and armed with bagpipes, they left the mountains to play their pious tunes before the street-shrines of the Virgin. Theirs was not a free performance. Parish priest and neighbours alike would have taken a poor view of anyone who neglected to pay the *pifferari* for a novena of music for the local Madonna, and because of the novenas every piper went back to his village with enough to keep his family through the year. As for his patrons, they would certainly lose a month's sleep and could be thankful if their generosity were not repaid with questionable couplets aimed at themselves or at their wives. The virtue of citizens' wives was always a special target for the *pifferari*, who were much given to mixing their hymns with offensive pleasantry and lewd comment.

[1] Turn the light.   [2] When the seat was vacant.
[3] A lamp edict.

The quiet Roman nights followed relatively uneventful days. True, there was a frequent turmoil of festivals and any slight happening in the street was an excuse for drama and comedy; but the life of a town springs chiefly from the workaday to-and-fro of the people in it and Rome at this date was not a hive of industry. Most surprising, in a race supposed to be so volatile, was the complete absence of hurry. But if no one hurried it was probably because no one had anything to do and this, as we shall see, was largely the reason for the lack of animation in the streets.

In spite of its narrow, twisting ways, Rome of the Settecento was justifiably considered the best laid-out and organized city in Europe. 'It is the easiest thing to get a general idea of the place,' reported a visitor, 'and the hardest to disentangle the details.' For two hundred years the popes had made it their task to drive wide, straight roads through the overcrowded quarters and thus form highways between the main churches. These avenues were excellent lifelines for people emerging from the tortuous lanes, especially as the papal planners had wisely focused them—and they were often very long—on large monuments which stood as landmarks in the distance. A typical example is seen from Sixtus V's Piazza delle Quatro Fontane, with its lovely perspectives towards the Porta Pia and the three obelisks on the Quirinal, the Esquiline and the Pincio. This cunning choice of viewpoint, this stage-management, as it were, of selected objects, did more than make Rome easy to explore. It furnished grandeur and magnificence.

All the charming little squares, too, helped one to grasp the layout of the town. They are oddly asymmetrical[1] and still as picturesque as ever. The pastel-coloured houses emit that warm ochre glow that gives the newcomer his first shock of delight in Rome. The washing hangs from their windows in the time-honoured way. The same booths are there, the down-to-earth atmosphere and the feeling of the past. The stately and the simple

[1] Frenchmen often found this quality distracting and Bergeret de Grancourt, who was in Rome with Fragonard in 1773 and 1774 (a visit famous for the quarrels it produced between the painter and the man of finance) was very shocked indeed. He deplored the fact that a Roman piazza was a 'space' and not a 'symmetrical' composition. 'You will find', he wrote, 'some rare and handsome column or a beautiful fountain placed in what they call a square, though the buildings are not properly set round it.' Even the Campidoglio, its combination of grandeur and simplicity conceived by the mighty genius of Michelangelo, earned his academy-minded criticism, later to be underlined by Stendhal's, 'It certainly is, as the hidebound idiots will have it, very irregular.'

here rub shoulders as they always did, so that we still catch something of the old, cheerful relish of papal days. And where else could be found those groups of palace, church and fountain standing all together, 'like three musicians playing a Roman symphony', as Abel Bonnard puts it?

Those churches. How many were there in Rome in the eighteenth century? About the same number as now, either three or four hundred, depending on whether we count only those with their own resident regular clergy or include the private chapels of the various Orders and religious brotherhoods. Either way, they are far too many for the ordinary needs of worship; with only a step between them they make some of the streets like double rows of sanctuaries. In the last two hundred years they had multiplied as the regal luxury of the popes increased and pontifical families were garnering wealth at a great rate. The crumbs from this banquet, proffered to the public by way of consolation, took the form of the raising or restoration of churches; a church, after all, would be a house for the people as well as a house of God. In the wake of popes and papal nephews came the cardinals and Roman princes, monastic Orders and merchant guilds, building and restoring churches and chapels in the fashionable style of the day.

And this style was that set by Borromini, Bernini and their followers—the fruitful, torrential Baroque; a new style, bringing movement, brilliance and exuberance of form to the architecture of religion. Religion was to appear pleasant, lovely ladies must not be bored at Mass, and the headlong pursuit of resplendent theatrical effect produced the barley-sugar column, the vivid painted stucco decoration, the crowded, gilded figures gesticulating under the glow of paradisal ceilings. Nearly every church, built ten centuries ago or yesterday, was modishly sheathed in marble, filled with swooning angels or nice fat cherubs and decked out with an animated new façade. The Baroque danced, as it were, an exultant sarabande to the interplay of form and light and its crowning achievement was the dazzling splendour of St Peter's, capital shrine of the faith. A few churches did preserve the pure style of earliest Christian times, and their bare walls held a gospel peace. But in the eighteenth century it was the Baroque that settled what Rome was to look like and it is still a great factor in the look of Rome today, meeting us at every turn, leading effortlessly into the period of this study.

There are almost as many palazzi that will serve the same

purpose. Popes for three centuries had been establishing their families out of the public revenue and the families had lost no time in rearing huge mansions to keep before posterity their names, their magnificence and the sort of life they loved. The palaces stand on every side, in every street and square. They are occasionally isolated, like the Farnese, but are more usually in line with other houses and distinguishable only by a façade, by rows of windows and an air of dignity. There was no question of their being meant for convenience or any modest brand of luxury. Occupied by hordes of hangers-on and servants, they were built for grandeur. Nearly all the space is taken up with balconies 'big enough for proclamations', and sumptuous state apartments, while private life is relegated to a few inconvenient and surprisingly poky cabinets.

But it was a splendid existence, an affair of glittering receptions and elaborate amusements that unfolded in the great rooms of these vast palaces and was continued at the villas, ringed with their flowery gardens. Every prelate of rank had his villa, every prince of a Roman family and every banker with his fortune made. It was the necessary complement to the town establishment and similarly dedicated to ostentation. Such houses were not then viewed as mere country retreats but were used constantly, with the perfect gardens open to the public, as a rule, on certain days. The art of making gardens, like that of architecture, is a changing one and these, which seemed to a visitor from Lyons 'places of enchantment, every one a paradise on earth', bear the stamp of their own time. But they all, in the high Roman fashion, kept nature firmly within bounds. Flower-beds edged with arabesques of box resembled intricately woven carpets, squares of turf were encased in lofty walls of laurel and the whole would culminate in terraces with ornamental vases along the balustrades. Marble and water, those two great luxuries of Rome, were lavishly employed, with everywhere fountains playing, pools shimmering, statues in the shady avenues and bas-reliefs set into the walls. A garden was like a drawing-room or colonnaded gallery, 'the country as courtiers arranged it who wished to hold their court at home in the open air'.

As for its fountains, they give perpetual youth to Rome. No other city in the world has so indulged itself with water. On every side we find them, at crossroads and in public squares, under the trees at the villas, in the cloister and the farthest nook of the meanest yard. For each pontificate in turn the high jets or plumy sprays of water rose upon some lovely site. Few of the fountains are younger than the eighteenth century, when sensitive souls would complain of the noise at night, there were so many of them. They were of all shapes and sizes, modest or consequential, their waters gruff or babbling. Some were laughing and brilliant, others ran with a subdued, weeping sound. All are a delight; not as works of art only but because they are so exactly right and beautiful an adornment, and harmonize so perfectly with the architectural setting; and of them the most pleasing are Baroque. The ecstatic exaggeration and candid boldness of the Baroque artist took wings in the open air and each left his own fountain, conceived in the charming idiom of fairytale, in some corner of Rome.

Much else in the city remains largely as it was two hundred years ago. The Campidoglio, for instance, designed by Michelangelo when he was old; the Piazza di Spagna with its fanciful, stimulating mixture of the centuries. St Peter's, then newly enhanced with the lustre and ebulliance of Borromini—the list might go on for ever. There are whole districts that keep all the old atmosphere and appearance. The very heart of *Roma Vecchia* beats in the Campo Marzio; the swarming Trastevere reeks still of garlic, spices, wine. The Aventine is still an otherworldly place, with the same monasteries and the same invitation to tranquil prayer. The Piazza Navona echoes as it always did to the cackling of the market-women beneath their huge umbrellas. Even in quarters most altered by modernization enough of their former character remains for us to imagine quite easily what it was like to live there under Benedict XIV.

Take, for example, the Piazza del Popolo, later to be so superbly laid out by Valadier. In the eighteenth century the entrance gate was still as Michelangelo and Bernini had designed it and the obelisk that Sixtus V removed from the Circus Maximus was already in position. The Pincio terrace did not yet exist but the trees of that Hill of Gardens threw their shadows over the square and the newly-built twin churches of Santa Maria dei Miracoli and Santa Maria in Montesanto—one for worship, one for balance—framed in their 'truly theatrical' fashion the convergence of the three great avenues leading to the heart of Rome. Each of the three had, and has, its special nature and every traveller was said to choose the way best suited to the object of his journey. Poets went by the Via del Babuino, merchants by the Corso and churchmen passed along the Via Ripetta. Artists lived in the Via del Babuino even then and the Via Ripetta leading to the Vatican was lined as now with churches and palaces. The shops in the Corso alternated with handsome patrician houses; one of them, the Palazzo dei Caroli, was the embassy of France and another, the Salviati, her Academy of Art. Yet all these noble buildings lay cheek by jowl with the pungent booths of the fishmongers and their great pans for open-air frying, while the odour of rotten cabbage from the vegetable market in the Piazza Colonna was to upset Stendhal at a later date. By way of compensation, however, delicious whiffs came wafting from the stoves round the column of Marcus Aurelius, where both merchants and householders came to roast their coffee.

Absurd as it sounds, the truth is that nothing in Rome has changed so much since those days as the classical remains. The widespread interest that led to the great excavations and gave new life to the ruins came a hundred years later. Before this, all about them was disorder and decay. Maltreated by man and exposed to the elements, the old monuments had crumbled over the centuries. Temples, palaces, baths and amphitheatres were stripped of their gorgeous decorations by Emperors from Byzantium, pillaged by barbarians, turned into medieval fortresses and finally ransacked by the artists of the Renaissance.[1] Everything that could be torn out was re-used in churches and palaces in the city and elsewhere. Together with the inevitable damage by flood and earthquake, this spoliation meant progressive ruin for the once unmatched glory of ancient Rome.

The Forum had reverted to its beginnings and was again a cattle market, rife with weeds, surrounded by buildings buried more than half their height in earth. Skeletal fragments of wall and broken arches were hardly visible above the ground. 'The soil had risen to the necks of columns and shrunk them into boundary-stones.' The classical world was lost under thirty feet of rubbish. At the Basilica of Constantine (wrongly thought to have been the Temple of Peace) this rubble was heaped to the springs of the three great arches and the spaces between them were walled in and used as stables. The arch of Septimius Severus, filled with earth so high that one could reach up and touch the cornice, was a barber's shop. The Tabularium lay beneath a vast mound, showing the capitals

[1] Raphael made an inventory of destruction he had witnessed for himself. The list is long and includes the Temple of Ceres, and large parts of Nero's Forum and the Baths of Caracalla. Seven thousand ancient columns, whole or broken, were at this time incorporated in new buildings and many more must have gone to the limekilns, together with priceless statues and heaps of marble tablets whose inscriptions would have been of immeasurable interest today.

of three entombed columns. From Poussin, Claude Lorrain and Piranesi we can see what the desolate wilderness looked like, engendering a poetic melancholy that caused the excavations of the nineteenth century to be denounced as a threat to the romantic beauty of the Campo Vaccino.

The Forum apart, the ancient ruins suggested not even the bare bones of ancient splendour. The plan of the Palatine was untraceable among the chaos of broken walls and everything movable had long ago been carried away from such parts of it as were accessible.[1] The Coelian Hill was a mere confused tangle of heaped-up ruins. One could no longer recognize the magnificent mausoleum of Augustus, and his great Egyptian obelisk, that had been Rome's sundial, lay dead and discarded in a corner. The Theatre of Marcellus, a masterpiece of the best period, had lost forty of its fifty-two external arcades. At street-level anvils rang in the dim workshops that were once archways and rags fluttered from windows in the dilapidated walls above.

Huge trees grew in the arches of the Baths of Caracalla, jasmine and acanthus in the crevices of its walls. Nothing now suggested that baths had ever existed there.[2] The same fate had overtaken the Colosseum, once the largest fabric in Rome and most typical of the spirit that was here, a building like a grand epilogue, the harsh, tough fruiting of Antiquity. Only half the outer wall was left and that threatened to crumble away; the interior was damaged, the arena choked with the accumulated debris of centuries. Not one marble seat remained and ivy and black-berries rooted over the stonework.[3] All that endured were those ancient monuments which the popes rescued by diverting them to Christian purpose. Among these were the Pantheon when it became the church of Santa Maria ad Martyres and two great halls in the Baths of Diocletian, refashioned by Michelangelo into the churches

[1] A visitor leaves us this description of the Palatine: 'The masters of the world lived here, from here their decrees controlled the universe. It is utterly deserted now. An old gardener protecting his hens from the foxes which, he told us, caught them all in the end, and a few tattered ropemakers working in the shade of a foot or two of ancient wall, these were the only live creatures we encountered in a walk of several hours in the middle of the day.'

[2] Even an archaeologist could write, 'There may well have been some baths here; many authorities mention them.'

[3] The surface of arena and auditorium were covered at this period with plants and flowers unknown elsewhere in Rome. The botanists compiled a Colosseum herbal demonstrating the existence of a primitive flora resembling that of Hymettus.

of San Bernardo and Santa Maria degli Angeli. Hadrian's tomb in its guise of state prison and papal stronghold also escaped destruction, as did the columns of Trajan and Marcus Aurelius when crowned by statues of Peter and Paul. And in this very century Benedict XIV put a stop to the vandalism that was pulling the Colosseum by inches to the ground when he consecrated it to the Passion in memory of the Christian martyrs.

These enormous vestiges, tawny and bare, were no more than a stony skeleton of the ancient city, but at every step in the street one came upon its traces. Rome of the eighteenth century was constructed almost entirely out of classical Rome. The houses often consisted of blocks of travertine stolen from the Colosseum or the Theatre of Marcellus; they might embody fragments of Pliny's 'everlasting walls'. The 'great army of conquered columns' not only filled the churches and palaces but could be seen in lowly station on every side, holding up the roof of shop or trattoria, 'lending their stately framework to the simplest avocations'. Antique statues might have their honoured places in the salons and lobbies of the rich, but they stood as well in nameless backyards, most probably with somebody's washing drying over their arms. The image of St Helena in the Church of the Holy Cross was an antique Juno, a dead pope lay in Agrippa's porphyry coffin. The cross of Christ gleamed on obelisks from Egypt. The debris of Antiquity was everywhere apparent; walls of clay held scraps of colonnades. In the prevailing lavishness old bas-reliefs were embedded in steps for St Agnes' Church without any interest being raised in what they represented.

But the ages tangled and overlapped without incongruity. It has been Rome's constant prerogative to weave from the wreckage of the ancient world and the splendours of her present day a fabric of her own. When she became a modern capital and had to bring herself up to date she did not shrink from the sacrifices involved. Many houses were demolished to make room for central arterial roads, discordant buildings went up, many gardens were destroyed. The majesty and charm of Rome were bound to suffer, despite the efforts made to save them.

It does not really matter. By some slight selection of itineraries, some mental resolution of discords and blotting out of untoward additions, the modern traveller will easily find the old easygoing Rome of the Settecento, with all its state and all its misery, the surface disorder and the grateful concord of existence.

This then, is the framework within which to study a people as full of contrast as their own city or history; a people, moreover, in their golden age. The spell of Rome takes many forms and perhaps the old ways, as well as the old stones, may capture the imagination.

GOVERNMENT

The temporal domain of the Holy See in the eighteenth century was the largest in Italy after that of the Two Sicilies; the banner of St Peter flew from the Tiber valley to the boundary of the Venetian Republic. It might not be obviously strong, lacking as it did natural frontiers with either Tuscany or Naples, and of all the western capitals Rome was certainly the most open to surprise attack. And yet, when every other realm had been overthrown, transformed or fragmented, that of the popes had remained stable through the ups and downs of ten centuries since the time of Charlemagne. Stability was inherent in its structure. Ambitious neighbours were checked by religious awe and its maintenance was a matter of advantage to every ruler in Europe. On the despotism of the Pope all despotisms depended, receiving from him the great justification, 'Authority is of God'—a word worth many armies.

There was no more absolute sovereign than the Pope. His authority was limitless. In his person he united temporal power over the States of the Church and spiritual power throughout the Catholic world, and so his wish was law, both secular and religious. When he spoke his words were backed by devil and executioner. He was the most marvellous, the most awful of sovereigns but his temporal power rested on feeble props and he was by no means the most redoubtable. His army was a caricature, his Treasury served as a general lucky dip and in his states the penal system was a mockery and justice very chancy. Steeped in corruption, his police were useless and discredited. The Holy See had no sort of economic strength and its subjects lived in idleness. All these grave defects we shall examine later; for the moment we may note them as productive of extreme confusion and observe a degree of anarchy as the most striking result of pontifical despotism.

Anarchy existed because that despotism, in theory absolute, was hampered in practice by the benevolent role its ruler had to play. Meekness was a bounden duty for the Vicar of Christ and the road from meekness to weakness is notoriously short. The Pope might speak with firmness, even with severity, but concern to remain a father to his people inclined him to temper his own edicts. As a

result he was listened to 'with more apparent reverence than submission' and treated by his subjects as a ruler to be suitably adored
and safely disobeyed. The people did more or less as they pleased
in consequence, taking liberties that soon hardened into custom
and the Pope, instead of imposing his law, made the fatal mistake
of yielding to theirs. The government developed into what at first
sight seemed to be actual democracy, commanding unanimous
popular support; and closer inspection would indeed reveal this
autocracy as the most democratic of organization: especially since
the Papacy was open to men of mean beginnings. Had not the
lowliest Franciscan friars risen to Peter's throne?

There were contradictory elements to be found, such as the
presence within the Roman state of all the paraphernalia of an
aristocratic republic. Here we have a sovereign pontiff, elected by
the cardinals of the Sacred College, who then surrender their every
right of counsel and control into the hands of the leader they
have chosen from among themselves. More, their sole desire is to
reinforce his authority, his intimates because they will probably
profit by his position, others because they hope to take his place
and are naturally against restricting power that may one day be
their own. Out of all these contrarieties, and all the practices they
led to, the Holy See, in wisdom and in continuity, had managed to
forge that complicated instrument of rule, the papal administration; a system not without its slight and decorous absurdities, but
meticulous and perceptive.

In addition to the Congregations dealing with the affairs of
Church and State, it included ministers. They were only two in
number and they were in theory spokesmen for the cardinals and
nothing more. But one, the Secretary of State, the Pope chose himself and made his close confidant. If not in fact prime minister he
was certainly the minister who mattered, directing home and
foreign policy and chief of police and of the army. The other, the
Cardinal Camerlengo, was not appointed by the Pope but held for
life an office of supreme importance during times of interregnum.
From the moment when he announced, with all the prescribed
ritual, the death of a reigning pope and took the fisherman's ring
from his finger, the Camerlengo held complete sovereignty until
a successor was elected. He coined money and stamped it with
his own image, was attended in public by the Papal Guard and
organized the conclave. Law and finance came permanently under
his control and he was, traditionally, at odds with the Secretary of

State. Under some pontificates there was also a Cardinal *Padrone*, a functionary more powerful even than the ministers, whose duties were undefined; he helped the Pope. Often he might be one of the Pope's nephews. Notably this position was filled in the eighteenth century by the Cardinals Albani, Corsini and Braschi, nephews respectively of Clement XI, Clement XII and Pius VI.

The Congregations were the great councils responsible for all affairs of State. The chief dignitaries of the Church were distributed among them for the Sacred College was in some sense the Pope's Privy Council and each member must exercise a share of government. Not all the many Congregations were of equal importance, but a cardinal presided over each. In the spiritual province alone, and to name only the most considerable, there were the Propaganda Fide, the Inquisition, the Index and the Congregation of Rites, the Congregations of the Consistory and of the Council of Trent and others to deal with episcopal residence and ecclesiastical immunity. Though the functions of each were clearly defined in its title, running fights went on as to which was responsible for what. Domestic relations, for instance, came under three Congregations and several large departments, the struggle regulated only by an extraordinary tangle of precedent and privilege. To add to the confusion, the city of Rome enjoyed a special régime under its own Governor and this prelate, though not a cardinal, dealt directly with the Pope and served almost as a third minister, the minister for Rome. In his hands lay the powers of governor-general, head of police and supreme judge, though he had to work in conference and accord with the Conservatori, or city magistrates, and especially with the Senator. He was also answerable to the three domestic Congregations, to say nothing of any others which could find the slightest excuse to interfere on particular points. All this complexity meant constant friction between Governor and Congregations, further aggravated by strife within the Congregations themselves and rivalry among the various bodies they were supposed to be looking after.

Nor did such rivalry turn only on the meaning of rules and regulations, but spread to their application within what may be fairly called a chaotic system lacking any central legislative authority. The Pope had plenary power to make, revoke and alter laws. He promulgated his will in various forms (*motu proprio, chirografo sovrano*[1] or by papal Rescript) all with the force of

[1] Of his own volition and in his own hand.

law, present and future. The Sacred College was not actually a legislative body but each Congregation legislated in its own sphere, as did certain individuals who were not even cardinals. Thus fiscal laws emanated from the Treasurer and criminal laws from the Governor of Rome. All these edicts from so many different directions were inevitably somewhat non-coincidental but authority was happily so weak that the problem solved itself automatically. An ambassador once accurately described the situation when he told his government, 'In Rome everyone gives orders and nobody obeys them and really things work well enough.'

Everyone did indeed give orders at Rome in the eighteenth century, making laws and issuing regulations. This would have mattered less had the laws not been interpreted and applied by an army of petty officials profiting by the disputes of their superiors to impose arbitrary decisions of their own. The town in fact was overrun by officials, as it had always been. Always the crowds of placemen and servants had swarmed about the Holy See, for every pope placed his personal entourage in newly created niches and what began as a facet of worldly pomp had ended as a tool of government. There were something like a hundred ministries in Rome, each with a large regular staff and a mob of lesser functionaries. Had these all turned up together it would have been a puzzle to find room for them—the Dataria alone employed four thousand. Partly, the difficulty was met by lengthy recess and frequent leave, and individual slackness did the rest.

To the huge multitude of clerks to the Congregations—thirty thousand or so, it was believed—must be added the staffs of the papal palaces. The Lateran, Vatican and Quirinal employed whole populations of their own, ranging from masters of ceremonies to the Sistine Chapel choristers and the bearers of the *sedia gestatoria*.[1] To possess a job there made anyone an official, and this included the turnspits and stableboys. True, it was no highly-paid host of clerks and underlings, but whether they lived well or poorly they were all living at the state's expense and deriving each his share of consequence. The historian Louis Madelin estimated that officials made up one quarter of the residents of Rome and three quarters of those 'who did not beg', and his reckoning may be on the low side. With their families this privileged class probably amounted to seventy or eighty thousand persons. So much was proved when Napoleon, planning to replace the whole muddle by

[1] The Pope's (sedan) chair.

his own imperial régime, found he would have to dispossess, not only a sovereign and a government, but an entire population.

We may gather from this description that the Roman State was anything but a shining exemplar to the abounding political theorists of the eighteenth century. Its every rule, in fact, ran counter to what the best authors would advise. To Frenchmen who had absorbed the sage principles of Montesquieu its government was, flatly, 'the worst imaginable'. And indeed one might with reason expect that under so unreasonable a system all authority would disappear and all power disintegrate. Yet nothing of the kind occurred. Nor is it enough merely to acknowledge, with the diplomatic observer quoted above, that things worked well enough. Rome in this century was politically the most secure of European states and socially the most stable.

The reason is found in the very special underlying spirit of pontifical rule. It possessed a hidden strength arising from humanity and broadmindedness and from the fact that basically it left people alone to do what they liked. Power, it should be remembered, was in the hands of churchmen, inclined by Gospel influence and by habit of life to goodness, charity, understanding and all forms of gentleness. The Holy Father at the top of the pyramid set them the example and any of his cardinals might succeed him there. All were hoping to do so and all were making preparations, sometimes by means of intrigue, it is true, but always by the show, if not the exercise, of Christian virtue. Behind them pressed the crowd of prelates, all candidates for the purple in their turn and all practising the correct behaviour in advance. Behind them again were the rest of the clergy, each in his own place shedding his own light. The lowliest ecclesiastic stood above the greatest of the laity. The temporal world was dominated by the disposition and hierarchy of the Catholic Church and impregnated with its spirit.

Laymen indeed held a mass of small government posts but, as we shall see, they nearly all wore canonical dress and their dearest wish was to resemble their masters and paymasters as closely as possible. This exact conformity to the model, this complete acceptance of its standards, was for the non-cleric the required condition for promotion and even for keeping his employment. Very naturally, therefore, he melted into an organization with whose attitudes and aspirations he was in tune.

The leading feature of this society—uniform in spite of its

29

divisions in rank—was a constant and general desire to please. 'Those who count for anything are intimately linked by the exchange of good turns and mutual obligation.' Exalted prelates might squabble among themselves for prestige and prerogative, but at the lower levels, where everything was settled in the end, allotment of power was amicable and unruffled.

The old, enduring relationship of patron and client meant that the lower classes depended on officials of every kind, and so the special way in which things were done at these lower levels was in fact the loom that wove the fabric of social life and gave its colour and character to Rome. If the protection of a cardinal were out of the question, then that of some humble *fratone* or penpusher was sought and found. The great thing was, always, to be protected, and to defer to one's protector in all things. This was a fundamental rule and universally accepted. It was dictated, moreover, by a sort of public morality and furnished a basis upon which things certainly went 'well enough'.

The people of Rome disliked work and welcomed anything that might relieve them of it. They were delighted at having to pay no taxes, and to have food and amusement provided, all through the contributions of Christendom. The thought of their uncultivated countryside hardly intruded so long as a paternal dispensation was keeping them in bread and wine and even buying them water-ices. Justice might be tardy, but it did not worry them. 'You lose your case in the end, so better in twenty years than twenty days.' The police were no bother and one could manage any small difficulties alone. Poverty was no great hardship, it would not last for ever. Somebody might become a cardinal, somebody might win the lottery and the most disgraceful ragamuffin be rich as a Jewish banker. Today was pleasant under this régime, tomorrow full of promise and if foreigners chose to criticize, the Pope's contented subjects took very little notice.

Their normal loyalty to their paternal and fostering, if despotic, government did not in any way prevent their abusing it on every possible occasion, all the more so since the Papacy never checked their gossip and they could indulge the traditional Roman love of carping to their hearts' content.

The only daily paper, *Crakas*, was strictly controlled, a mere gazette of facts presented without commentary, but the public had a throng of kindly informants to keep it abreast of current happenings. Some cobbler or barber at every corner had the talk of street and palace at his fingertips and would expound to all comers the affairs of Church and State, the intrigues and the stratagems and who was in love with whom. There was always lively interest in the goings-on of priests and monks and churchmen, natural in a city that contained so many of them, and the interest was not all unfriendly. Complete submission to the established order and sincere devotion to the Pope from whom it stemmed might co-exist in the Roman mind with rooted opposition to authority of any sort; but it was an opposition strong enough only to deride the organs and agents of government. It was, as Madame de Staël said, the tactics of children who obey their teachers so long as they may laugh at them.

Lampoons and epigrams showered from all sides. Casanova on the very evening of his arrival fell in with a large gathering of priests (or what looked like priests), and was astonished to find that their talk was a sort of jeering-competition against the Pope, his administration and officials. One had composed an inflammatory sonnet on some ecclesiastical dignitary and read it out to guffaws of approval. Another declaimed verses tearing one of the great families to shreds and a third was telling how he left the household of a certain cardinal when His Eminence refused special payment for 'special services'.

Yet conversation like this, heard in company relatively restrained, was as nothing compared with the libellous statements deposited on the 'talking statues' and read by every citizen. These satires were called *pasquinate,* or pasquinades, after a frolicsome tailor who lived in the Piazza Navona in Julius II's reign; such vehicles for the vinegar wit of Rome originated with him and they were still modelled on his efforts. He became famous for the gusto of his jests against government, cardinals and Pope and after his death was credited with more wit than he ever really had. When a much mutilated classical torso came to light not far from his shop and the experts could not agree as to whether it were Menelaus or Patroclus, the people stepped in and christened it Pasquino. The city fathers sanctioned this stolen identity and the pseudo-Pasquino stands beside the Palazzo Braschi in a square that bears his name. After dark, unseen hands would stick satires and rude commentaries on his pedestal, which entertained the whole town in the morning and frequently moulded its opinions. Pasquino indeed became the public voice. The mischief-loving Romans found an equally caustic partner for him in the huge antique statue of a water-god, originally from the Forum of Caesar.

He was renamed Marforio and today languishes, as though 'to expiate his many shocking speeches', outside the Capitoline Museum, looking rather as though he were the concierge. Pasquino and Marforio were joined by other talking statues, the Facchino, the Abate Luigi and Madame Lucrezia, and together they formed a *consiglio degli arguti* that supplied the place of a free press in papal Rome and was indeed, as has been said, the press itself.

The pasquinades were hawked round the cafés and thence invaded the markets and government offices. They even reached the pontifical antechambers, yet no one took offence or tried to unmask the authors, however far—or frequently—they went in the direction of out and out defamation. They have in fact served largely as the tainted source of much evil report upon the men, manners and institutions of the Roman State. Rigorous laws existed to enforce severe punishment for seditious libel, but a soft-hearted seigniory had let them lapse and popes in the eighteenth century were not easily upset. A single exception, and not a very harsh one, may be noted to their self-imposed forbearance. When the cardinals in conclave were under heavy fire from Pasquino during the interregnum of 1774 a Florentine abbé named Gaetano Sertore was found guilty of having concocted a playbill for an imaginary but highly disrespectful drama to be acted by prelates of the Church. For form's sake he was condemned to death, but immediately pardoned and even received a hundred crowns from his chief victim, Cardinal Zelada.

The puppet-shows, too, so beloved of the Romans, blatantly mocked authority and the papal censorship left them alone. The popes were evidently aware that outlets of this kind were necessary —grievances were aired in safety and more painful demonstrations avoided. A government, as Louis Madelin observed, is always pleased if Gracchus will play Harlequin.

THE POPE

The Pope, in a time-proof fabric, was the keystone of the arch. Absolute master of men and their possessions, he exercised a searching, yet mild and gentle, despotism over his worldly realm. His rule in Rome had been unchallenged since the days of Charlemagne but in the eighteenth century many covetous glances were being cast towards the Papal States and the germ of the Roman Question already existed in the council chambers of

Europe. We shall consider later the dwindling international importance of the Papacy and here confine ourselves to studying the Pope among his own subjects, in a purely Roman context. And his own subjects brooded not at all upon the world's affairs. They merely looked to their ruler, as confidingly as sons to a father, for their every requirement, eternal welfare included, while of course expecting him to provide protection and a livelihood here below to begin with.

The daily existence of the popes changed a great deal during the century. Their traditional home had been the Vatican, that great complex, born so magnificently of the whims of twenty pontiffs, with nothing of its size and kind to match it in the world. But gradually less and less time had been spent there and the Holy See was now established in the Quirinal, built originally as a summer palace by Sixtus V. Here, though there was certainly less space, what there was belonged exclusively to the Pope and his court, whereas most of the Vatican had been taken up with galleries, art collections and chapels; they even had a cannon foundry there. Dark corridors, tiny tunnels and 216 staircases formed an impossible labyrinth and further impeded inter-communication. At the Quirinal there was altogether more elbow-room for the host of cardinals, bishops, *monsignori, auditori* and protonotaries, and the pontifical court hardly ever returned to the Vatican save in obedience to the established usages of Holy Week. The pomp of the Church unrolled in the glittering, golden apartments of the Quirinal, following there its rhythm of strict protocol. For the contemporary papal court was quite as formal as that of Versailles, precedence was as finely graded here as there and the undeviating ceremonial code was like a Chinese puzzle.

This formality was all the less to be expected since the Pope encountered so many informal characters in the course of his daily life. Around him a whole world of minor attendants, from the chef in his white hat to the postillion pluming himself in his best uniform, went about their business practically ignoring him and the palace was full of lower as well as upper servants, some better trained than others. The number of jobs, and of people to do them, had swollen enormously. Besides the *bussolanti*, or domestic retainers, there was a motley assemblage of victuallers, mace-bearers, ushers, porters and grooms by the hundred. They were reinforced by a further contingent who took up their quarters merely on the strength of being compatriots of the Pope or cousins

33

of one of the footmen. They lived in the antechambers, often whole families together, quite as though they were at home and behaving accordingly, so that the magnificent sovereign shared his roof in unanticipated intimacy with an outer fringe of lackeys and dependants. His doors, too, stood open to all comers and his callers were often strangely matched. Here the princes of the Church rubbed shoulders with plain peasants up from the country visiting some relation, a deacon perhaps, or stable-hand; a pretty girl crossed a gilded salon with a tray of cucumbers on her head and down the state staircase came the unwashed Capuchin with his red umbrella and his basket of scraps. 'The simplest life, spent in the humblest labour, merged with the show of a royal court.' And in that climate of general compliance nobody marvelled at it all. It was neither resignation, canny self-interest nor any particular in-born characteristics that made people take it so much for granted. It was just that they were used to it. Distinctions of rank made as a rule no difference in Rome and it was rare, as we shall see, for any-one to put on airs.

Such an agreeable way of looking at things made domestic life at the papal court a friendly business, in contrast with the solemn dignity of its official occasions. The eight popes who reigned in this century differed widely in make-up and disposition—the austerity of Benedict XIII eating his frugal dinner with his fellow monks is a far cry from the elegant poise of Pius VI, the scholarly *grand seigneur* with his dream of restoring Rome to her glory of Renaissance days. But each in his own way shared that reassuringly free temper of the times, their sociable good fellowship. Proof is no farther away than the Quirinal gardens. We have only to consider all those water-jokes, all those jets spurting without warning at people's feet from little underground pipes and drenching women's skirts and prelates' robes, and to recall that all the popes are said to have relished this sort of thing tremendously. Clement XI may have been the one exception, for according to Pasquino he was 'perpetually in tears' and less roguish than a later pontiff who tripped his cardinals up to make them fall into the fountains. But most of them, without going quite so far, enjoyed a joke. Benedict XIV loved to tease his friends and would gladly leave a processional route to linger outside some tavern where he knew the wine was good. Clement XIV would sit happily with a looking-glass in his window in the Quirinal and dazzle passers-by with reflected rays of sunshine.

But for all its relaxed atmosphere we should not imagine the papal court as free of scheming and intrigue. The plots went on, only conducted in a greater cloud of suavity than at any other period of history, with every step carefully tested first and double-dealing masked as courtesy.

If no pope of this century were remarkably clever, all the popes were at least good men.[1] Almost all were of Roman origin, educated in the seminaries of their native province, men whose experience lay entirely within the Church. Ascending the throne late in life, skilled in the arts of government, their last intention was to make changes of any kind. Nor, for that matter, did anyone expect them to do so; the sponsoring of innovation would mean the certain loss of good report. They agreed completely with the ecclesiastical thought of their time in viewing themselves simply as trustees bound to pass on the crown of Peter as they received it to the next possessor.

Unfortunately this passive attitude, perpetuating all that was archaic and precluding any sort of forward policy, was not the weapon to defend a Papacy that reached its zenith in the sixteenth century and had sensibly declined since. Three of the five great European powers were now in schism and the princes of the Catholic world had taken to signing treaties without reference to the Pope—not, perhaps, surprisingly as it was against him that the treaties were usually directed. The disaffection of their kings set a poor example to subjects distracted from their age-long veneration for the Holy Father by the rise of 'philosophic' doctrines, and one result was an alarming fall in the cash tribute that fed the Vatican coffers.

Courage and dynamism, in such threatening circumstances, were the prime necessities. But the popes of the eighteenth century faced the storm armed with nothing but their unavailing goodwill. They could not ward the danger off yet should be given credit—if credit it can be called—for hiding it from their people behind the soothing administerial façade. And indeed the Romans never realized how great nor how near the peril was. Never had the ship of Peter's state seemed to them to sail in calmer water and of all their pilots of this period the most beguiling was unquestionably the incom-

[1] The eighteenth-century popes were: Clement XI (Albani) 1700–1721; Innocent XIII (Conti) 1721–1724; Benedict XIII (Orsini) 1724–1730; Clement XII (Corsini) 1730–1740; Benedict XIV (Lambertini) 1740–1758; Clement XIII (Rezzonico) 1758–1769; Clement XIV (Ganganelli) 1769–1774; Pius VI (Braschi) 1775–1799.

parable Benedict XIV (1740–1758). Scholar, *littérateur,* patron of art and artists, lively of speech, exemplary in conduct, his tolerant outlook won him the friendship of every prince in Europe and that of the Sultan Mahmoud besides. He had the first reputation of his day for wit and repartee, though the sad fact was, as we may read in Lalande, that he preferred swapping stories with his cronies to the fatigues of policy-making. His easygoing ways are clear from the anecdote of the fanatical monk who appeared before him, convinced that unheard-of disasters were about to fall upon the Church, since Anti-Christ was born on earth. 'And how old is he?' the Pope inquired. The monk, still lamenting, replied that he was three. Benedict sighed with relief. 'In that case,' he said, 'my successor can see to him.' Here we have an indubitable sidelight on that decline of the Papacy that was soon to become so obvious; and the tale sums up very neatly the contemporary Roman attitude to life.

It is hardly necessary to emphasize in what general venera- tion the Pope was held, showing himself to the faithful on great occasions with a gorgeous ceremony that is practically unchanged today. We may however note that after a casualty in 1769 the ancient tradition of the papal *cavalcata* was abandoned. A newly elected pope used to ride on a white palfrey to take possession, as bishop of Rome, of St John Lateran, *caput et mater* of all the churches in the world. Clement XIV's mount stumbled and threw him.[1] Since that day the palfrey has been replaced by a coach up- holstered in embroidered crimson velvet and gold braiding and drawn by eight horses of purest white.

Another and unlooked-for change took place when the solemn papal benediction developed into something very like a military parade. An impressive body of troops in glittering accoutrements would be drawn up in the Piazza del Quirinale well in advance and as the pontiff from his balcony blessed the crowd below helmeted heads were bent, the cavalry lowered their sabre-points and the infantry on their knees presented arms. The air rang with a clangour of cannon and bells.

When we remember how painfully weak the armed forces were, if indeed they could be said to exist at all, there is something comic in the spectacle of the popes making room for them in religious

[1] The Pope finished the journey by coach, with the remark, 'This is taking possession more like Paul than Peter.'

ceremonial. Romans had ceased to be military-minded four hundred years ago. The more they admired the bandit the more they despised the soldier, considering him almost as bad as a *sbirro*[1] and the pontifical army, which relied on volunteers, was hard put to to find them. It numbered fifty thousand in the preceding century and less than three thousand on the eve of the French Revolution, with an undiminished complement of officers standing at one to every ten men. It was not a force remarkable for discipline or martial spirit and came under a Congregation, like all other instruments of the Roman government, with a cardinal for commander-in-chief. Most of it was stationed about the papal territory with the aim of suppressing banditry, and the French writer Dupaty tells us how it accomplished this mission: the troops, he says, 'are legalized brigands making war on other, unlegalized brigands'. Very few—three hundred grenadiers—were garrisoned in Rome, 'more like gentlemen's gentlemen than soldiers [another French opinion] and their general has a rupture'. They were charged with the security of Castel Sant' Angelo and its laughable defences.

A few troops with ancient muskets and most resplendent uniforms undertook the ceremonial duties we have seen on the Piazza del Quirinale; and to complete our picture of the fighting strength of the Holy See we may add that by water it was even weaker than by land, with three old and poorly armed vessels comprising the whole navy. On all the considerable coastline there was not one port fit to use.

The Swiss mercenary corps which since the reign of Julius II had guarded, and still guards, the papal palace did not count as a military arm. Its equipment was unchanged since the Renaissance, as was the costume, designed, they said, by Michelangelo, which still gives the Papal Guard something of the look of jacks in a deck of playing cards. The Guard, so well-dressed and hearty, had to stand a lot of ridicule: it never came under fire except from the rockets on St John's Eve, it fled before the only foes it ever saw, the sun and rain. And indeed throughout the century the Swiss gave no special proof of soldierly valour. Apart from palace duty they had nothing to do but act as monitors or merely stand about, but still they grumbled at the trials of their calling. Montesquieu repeats what his valet heard from one of them—'how he had to carry on, hot weather or cold, and get through three loaves and a

[1] Spy—assassin.

flask of wine every day; and how he had caught pleurisy, he claimed, just waving carriages out of the way'.

When the Romans met their sovereign walking in the city with a small escort they would press about him, unabashed by his awesome rank. He would stand there listening to heart-to-heart complaints from housewives at the rising price of oil and candles, and bestow words and blessings all round before passing on to the sound of enthusiastic acclaim.

Oddly enough, not even the most popular of popes ever received, among the universal good wishes of the people, the wish for length of days. A long occupation of the throne was something not readily forgiven. By common consent seven or eight years were quite enough and anyone who overstayed them ought to be ashamed of himself. The conclaves did their best in this respect with their heavy leaning towards age and infirmity, and had good and sufficient reason for preferring the ancient and the feeble. For there existed a venerable, worrying superstition to the effect that, no pope since Peter having reigned for twenty-five years, Rome would fall should one ever do so. The dictum, *Non videbis annos Petri*, embodied the belief.

There were sternly practical reasons for this wish for a frequently vacant throne. A lingering pope postponed the drawing of that great lottery in which all had tickets and anyone might win a prize. As Dupaty explains:

'Cardinals have tickets marked "Pope", prelates tickets marked "cardinal", priests have prelate tickets, the nobility tickets for extended credit. Some have tickets for jobs, merchants may draw good markets, beggars alms and all are sure to get the celebrations and something new to look at.'

And each pontifical election certainly brought its redistribution of offices, benefices and employments. The cardinal ascending the throne was no isolated individual; he possessed family, household, hangers-on for whom his career was as their own. His winning ticket meant a win for the whole concern, each member of which had, in turn, protégés who must not be left out. The new pope's bounty, spreading from one to another, embraced multitudes. Charles de Brosses gives his concise explanation of how this transference of public property—for it was naturally understood that Church and State defrayed these continual monetary adjustments —worked.

'The sovereign is always an old man, his days are short. Often he is incapable of doing things himself and surrounded by relatives whose one idea is to play their hand quickly while it is yet day. And every change brings on a fresh set of robbers to replace those who have gorged themselves already.'

Such, then, were the most common results of that nepotism for which the popes have been so bitterly blamed, often with no account taken of the plots and intrigues shadowing them. Against such menace they had no protection but their families. Their families must therefore be strong. Nepotism, by no means dead in the eighteenth century, scandalized no one. Clearly the sovereign pontiff had every right to administer the revenue as he chose for the benefit of kith and kin. Had he scorned the tradition there would have been quibblers ready enough to criticize him. With a custom so universally approved, the Settecento popes took heart of grace from the shining examples of their predecessors and scrupulously they avoided any break. Clement XII reared the Corsini fortunes, the Lambertini owed to Benedict XIV their place among the wealthiest clans in Rome, and the Braschi palace stands in evidence of the avuncular care of Pius VI.

Others, besides the direct beneficiaries of his generosity, might look to gain from a new pope's election. Only one cardinal emerged victorious, but those who voted for him would see their efforts amply rewarded. It was customary on election to give up all livings and offices to one's chief supporters, by no means an inconsiderable bonus for them. The people, too, had their share. As soon as the pontiff was proclaimed they fell upon the rich palace he had lived in as a cardinal and stripped it of furnishings, jewels and plate until only the bare walls were left. There was in this no question of vandalism. The new pope at his coronation threw to the crowd beneath the Lateran windows three handfuls of coin, gold, silver and bronze, with the words, 'Silver and gold are nothing to me; what I have, I give you.' This pronouncement, taken literally, gave meaning and justification to the sack of his palace.

The coming to power of another family and another faction brought many more good things to the commons. There were stately ceremonies with accompanying doles of money, new cardinals were created, the personnel of the court was changed. For weeks life in Rome was one long joy and festival, with fireworks and illuminations on all sides, dancing in the streets and water-ices free—this last always a highly appreciated treat in Italy. Dupaty, observing the excitement, cried, 'Why all the triumph and intoxication, this delirium from one end of Rome to another? Has she won some victory? She has indeed—a pope is dead.'

And, for all the moral and religious motives there were for venerating the pope, his death was hailed with general gaiety. Your true Roman always has his eye on tomorrow, 'his pope is a king who is dying all the time'. If the Pope fell ill, therefore, the news went through the town like wildfire, lighting flames of exhilaration everywhere. Reports became immediately as grave as possible, to be immediately contradicted from the Quirinal, whose inmates stood alone in hoping for a happy outcome and who maintained their assumed optimism up to the final bulletin. Their successive reactions are summed up in the old Roman saw, *Malato, meglio, morto*—Ill, better, dead.

The superstitious knew how to tell for certain when the Holy Father was about to die: the bones of Sylvester II (who had been a Frenchman from Aurillac in Auvergne) would be heard rattling in his tomb in the Lateran and then the end, they said, could not be long.[1]

[1] Sylvester II was pope in AD 1000, the first Frenchman to occupy the throne and the first pope to conceive the idea of a crusade to free the Holy Places. Being a very learned man he was mistrusted by his contemporaries who suspected sorcery when he set up an observatory, a quite modest and primitive affair, in the Lateran palace. He was accused of selling his soul to the devil in return for election and one of the clauses of their agreement was supposed to forbid his going to Palestine under pain of instant death. It so happened that as he went to celebrate Mass in Santa Croce in Gerusalemme he collapsed suddenly as he set foot in that church where St Helena had deposited sacred earth from Golgotha. Recognizing what a trap the Prince of Darkness had set for him Sylvester, legend said, confessed before he died. It was ten years before his body was admitted to burial in St John Lateran nor can it properly be said to rest there, for, according to the popular belief, the accursed pope's bones rattle noisily when the reigning pope is near to death. For centuries this was taken as a sign by which to judge how seriously ill the pontiff really was.

CHAPTER TWO

SOCIETY

The undisputed élite of the Roman aristocracy consisted of some thirty families, all involved in political struggle since the high Middle Ages. Among them in the first rank stood the Colonna and Orsini, who had maintained veritable armies out of their enormous wealth in the fifteenth and sixteenth centuries and allied themselves like so many sovereign states with the princes of Italy. After them came the houses of Savelli and Conti and many more, none in their own opinion inferior to the greatest of the land. All in fact took pride in descent from some ancient Roman hero, the Mattei from Mucius Scaevola, the Santa Croce family from Valerius Publicola, the Cenci from Crescentius Centius. Not that there was ever any proper proof; these things rested on traditions valuable only for sheer ancientry. When Napoleon once asked one of the Massimo clan whether he were truly descended from Fabius Maximus he received the reply, 'I could not prove it, but the rumour has been current in our family for a thousand years.'

Others of noble but less venerable origin went back to feudal times, the Gaetani to an eighth-century tribune of Rome, the Altieri to a mayor of the palace under Otho II, the Orsini to a senator of A.D. 1200. The Colonna were rich enough in the twelfth century for Paschal II to strip them of all they possessed. The families of Corsini and Doria were powers in Florence and Genoa respectively before settling in Rome in the fourteenth century. And these long-established houses had bred many popes, for, in those days when popes were made by princes, their influence was always brought to bear upon the conclave.

Later the tables were turned and popes made princes of their nephews. None, since the days of Sixtus V, had ever neglected to do so and it was by this road that the families of Aldobrandini, Borghese, Ludovisi, Barberini, Chigi, Rospigliosi and Odescalchi entered one by one upon Roman nobility. Their uncles having thoughtfully provided money and benefices to match the honours, they were, as princes, well endowed. The newly ennobled hastened to intermarry with the old feudal families, themselves often less rich than they had been; and for this reason so many of the great Roman houses carry linked names, one from a papal and one from an ancient aristocratic line: Doria-Pamphili, Barberini-Colonna, Borghese-Aldobrandini, are among them. From the mixture of good blood and wealth there sprang a brilliant ruling class into which the popes from time to time saw fit to recruit an occasional parvenu. Some opulent banker might be included in the patrician lists at the sovereign pontiff's order and could then buy himself a barony, or even a duchy. Purchasing-power and the valuable alliances at its command sent the financiers rocketing into the highest strata. So the house of Torlonia rose, whose first-known forbear was in domestic service before turning speculator and banker.

All these nobles, whether of papal or feudal origin, were immensely rich at the opening of the eighteenth century and almost always a pope had made them so. But for many of them it was to be a fatal period. Luck like theirs could only happen once. It was for one thing very rare for popes to be elected repeatedly from the same family; for another, the nobility, immersed in piety or pleasure, neglected the management of their estates and never thought about investing money profitably. Again and again the rate of interest was to drop and nibble away their revenue and final ruin came with the revolutionary troubles that despoiled them at the century's end.

In Rome the nobility was less powerful than elsewhere. It did not form a privileged body and, having had no part, as in other countries, in the foundation of the State, possessed neither inordinate rights over the commons nor any monopoly of employment. Since the laity were debarred from a career in government the nobles, apart from a few with charitable and unpaid positions, were not numbered among the holders of high office. Their part was purely honorary. To a Roman prince was reserved the wholly decorative title of Roman Senator, while others gave public attendance on the Pope as lay privy chamberlains. Those who served in the Noble Guard were only there for show. By a single, unexplained exception a noble presided over the post, but his was a ludicrously small department. For the rest, there was no advantage in aristocracy beyond that of seeing one's sons, if they happened to enter the Church, rise more rapidly than other people.

Those sons, moreover, received an education perfectly calculated to continue their subjection—voluntary as it was, and with its touch of grandeur—to that superior dispensation. The princely Roman did not have his mind broadened in youth by study in great colleges. He stayed at home with parents and Jesuit tutor to absorb Latin, Church history and heraldry, acquiring in this way little intellectual furniture but a good bottom of morality, being thoroughly imbued with ideas traditional to his class. That is to say, he was acquainted with the glorious tale of his ancestors and boundlessly admired them; he acknowledged strict obedience to the will of the Church as the only basis of moral law; and loathed revolution, considering as devil's work the novel notions of the Age of Reason.

By the time he grew up the young prince had settled to a life of visits, of strolling in the Corso, of concern with carriages and horse-flesh. He would also join one of the religious societies, attend its meetings faithfully and obey the rules, unattractive as they might be. He did not travel. Resolutely he ignored anything that took place beyond the frontiers of the Roman State; often indeed the city gates marked for him the limits of the known world. He would be married at twenty-five to a young girl as simple as himself, fetched from a convent to her wedding, and his children's up-bringing would be the copy of his own. But before we dismiss him as a nonentity let us be clear as to the true nobility of his nature. He would never disobey the code of honour. The guiding light of his life was charity, a little ostentatious sometimes but always broad, active and sincere. 'He did not know the pictures in his gallery but, like his park and his villas, anyone could visit it.' He included his humbler neighbours in all his great family occasions. He was a simple man, speaking to his servants easily and as an equal. Not for him the superior smile seen on high-born faces in other parts of the world; in Rome it would have been laughed at. One striking aspect of the general moral climate was the similarity of manners and interests at all levels, however incomes varied. The nobleman discusses music with his valet and the duchess talks of love to her hairdresser's wife, each with her own point of view. This unforced mingling of ranks sprang from more than mere natural Roman good humour, for they shared equality, here as nowhere else, in another very important thing: there were no obvious dis-tinctions in those factors—education, appreciation, taste—from which class barriers may usually arise. 'The gifts and vivacity inborn and common to all were, in the upper classes, more notice-able than culture'; and the culture of the upper classes, we have seen, was scarcely of the upper reaches. There was a saying in Florence, which prided itself on having remained an intellectual centre, that knowledge never kept anyone awake at Rome.

But the unarrogant Roman aristocrat still considered his first obligation that of making a good appearance. He must have lackeys by the dozen, festooned with gold braid, well-fed horses and freshly painted equipages. He must support his dependants, give brilliant entertainments. Fail in any of this and he sank to the level of the *caduti*, those of his peers who had gone down in the world, whose names were never mentioned. His fortune, in fact, so long as he could keep it, was his only glory.

Noble tradition decreed that all such fortune be expended on display. The princely palaces stood in every part of Rome, built by the greatest architects in preceding centuries, their majestic staircases and huge galleries frescoed by the greatest painters. In the salons hung the most wonderful pictures, masterpieces of sculpture ornamented the courtyards, their stables were full of valuable horses and costly harness. Withindoors, luxury was the accepted rule and the nobles lived like feudal lords, dispensing justice in the quarter round, whose highways and police were their affair. Their households were nothing less than royal, with major-domos, stewards and underlings and a whole band of gilded courtiers to follow the master round. He of course, was robbed out-rageously by them all and quite aware of it. But what could he do to stop abuses unless he spent his days unthinkably checking account books?

The show of luxury, however, was for external consumption only. For daily life the great families deserted their state apart-ments and in doing so exactly mirrored the society they lived in. That society paid tribute to patriarchal heritage in its tremendous outward display and dazzling assemblages, while pursuing a domestic pattern of the simplest kind.

Scorning any effort to be merely impressive, the aristocracy left nothing undone, nevertheless, to take the lead in public, com-peting with each other fiercely. We need only consider the Carriage Competition. Carriages were the great obsession of Rome, her surest status symbol. They were of all shapes and sizes—nothing plain, of course—and even the livery coaches on inexpensive hire to foreigners were included in the show. They might be old, but they were bedizened; the horses might come out of the Apocalypse, but the drivers wore square wigs and gold braid. The luxury of a cardinal's carriage we shall describe later, the bronze-work, the plumes and fringes of the roof; and the princes drove about more magnificently still. Only the noble families, registered in the Golden Book of the patriciate, might have gilding and painted panels on the outside of their coaches, or upholster them in velvet. Some were entitled to the special privilege of a glass coach, or *carrozza a cristalli* and went by in view of all beholders. These aristocratic equipages were surpassed only by those of pope and ambassadors. When Prince Borghese once claimed that his carriages were finer than the English ambassador's, Cardinal de Bernis' coachman was called in to arbitrate on the interesting point. He was a very suitable choice, for his master was supposed to keep the most elaborate vehicles in Rome at the French Embassy. Three of them, sent by Louis XV, had caused a sensation when displayed in the Place du Carrousel in Paris. They were more sumptuous than anything seen before and so heavy that buffalo were needed to drag them from Civita Vecchia.

If occasionally outclassed, then, by foreign envoys, the Roman nobles got their own back in the Carriage Competition when it came to numbers. The Prince of Gallicano had sixty, the Constable Colonna eighty. Young Luigi Braschi, with the wealth showered on him by Pius VI, his uncle, owned twenty and still did his best to give the impression that they were not all. 'And what did you think of my hundred carriages?' he inquired, conducting the Marquis de Breteuil round his stables. 'These twenty are absolutely splendid,' that ready diplomat rejoined, 'and we can see the rest another time.' The old Marchesa Altieri had only one, but in that one was drawn behind six horses to attend Mass in the Gesù, just across the street from where she lived.

Bewigged coachmen, in brilliant coloured liveries thick with gold braid, drove the nobility of Rome. They were elevated persons in the hierarchy of servants and their haughtiness was proverbial. The masters whose glory they shared would always get them out of trouble and the uniform they wore ensured deference and conferred a kind of immunity upon them. On one occasion, when a coachman of the Prince of Conti earned a flogging, the Governor of Rome insisted that he remove his beautiful laced coat first and was thus able to assure the Prince that his livery had not suffered insult.

Couriers went before and beside the princely carriages and lit the way at night. Being a courier was badly paid but had marked sporting appeal, for the drivers liked speed and sometimes ran real races. There was the dastardly conduct of Cardinal York's courier towards the horses of Princess Rezzonico, wife of the Senator of Rome: he threw his lighted torch at their noses in an effort to stop them beating his master's coach to the French Embassy, and a diplomatic incident ensued.

Not all nobles maintained these lavish households. There were many besides the leading families who shared the same traditions without the money to keep them up. Such lesser nobility formed a numerous class, no longer opulent though passably rich, tending to identify itself with the princely aristocracy in habit, opinion and, with due allowance for the difference in fortune, in its way of life.

THE CLERGY

The great power in Rome, after that of the Pope, lay with the cardinals, varying in number between sixty and seventy in the eighteenth century, men whom the Pope himself chose for their virtue, extensive learning, wisdom and apostolic zeal. Some possibly owed their success to intrigue or to friends in high places, but such were the exception, part already of a disappearing order. It was not yet necessary to be a priest before one was a cardinal (that came at a much later date), but deep piety in prelates and exemplary life were by now essential for advancement. The merits of Cardinal Dubois and of Cardinal Tencin, certainly, are open to question and one cannot but approve the sentence that consigned Cardinal Coscia, Benedict XIII's chief minister, for nine years to Castel Sant' Angelo. But the entire flock—undoubtedly virtuous as a whole and a stranger to the dissolute ways it is accused of—cannot be condemned for three black sheep in a century. Unhallowed Roman gossip about the private lives of a few cardinals was fed from partial sources and does not merit serious consideration. It was mischievous tattle of the kind that furnished ammunition in plenty for enemies of the Church, who would attack her ministers with anything that came to hand.

In theory, as we have seen, the Sacred College were invested with all the powers of government. They had in reality delegated their every right to one of their number when they made him Pope. It had long been the custom for him alone to speak in the Consistory, where the cardinals confined themselves to nods of agreement, and their role was little more active in their own Congregations. They held so many and such different public offices in turn, passing perhaps from legal affairs to war and finance, that they never had any one long enough to master its technique and traditions. It was at times alarming to see how out of touch they were, as when the Hospital of the Holy Ghost was confided to a cardinal who abolished its mental department with a stroke of the pen on the curious ground that, since Our Lord cured sickness but never lunacy, 'we should not meddle with it'. Generally, however, they were saved from making ludicrous or awkward rulings by reliance on *auditori* and secretaries, the permanent officials who really ran public affairs.

The cardinals came fully into their own again at one all-important juncture. When a pope died it was their task to choose a successor and because of this unparalleled authority they ranked as royal princes and were addressed by kings as 'cousin'. The papal election had for each individual cardinal an importance all its own, since he might hope to win it. A conclave always resembled a lottery. Rumour and politics were woven into it, as well as luck, and bets were laid on the Holy Spirit's chosen ones as though they had been racehorses. Stendhal records the saying of a cardinal's servant that 'his master was like a man who every eight years put his hand into a hat full of white tickets and tried to draw the black one that conferred a throne'. All depended on being able to manage things when the unprecedented chance came round.

Created by him, established by him, the cardinals were like a spiritual family to the Pope and his court was naturally the pattern for them. Their mode of life was guided by his, they tried to transplant to their own palaces the pomp and customs of the Quirinal. For they were princes not only of, but in, the Church, having each his court, elaborate or simple according to his taste and means. The least an eighteenth-century cardinal could do 'to keep up the state and standing of the body he belonged to' would seem absurd and challenging pretension today. Official parade was no more avoidable than that of the services in church, even by those who might prefer a studious, simple life. Luxury was the necessary accompaniment of their position and that position would suffer should they employ fewer than fifty waiting-gentlemen and men-servants. There was a Jesuit cardinal so humble that he wore the same habit, which the Pope had given him, for twenty years, and yet his household numbered fifty.

Obviously those cardinals who were the nephews of popes, past or present, or who came themselves of princely blood, lived all the more splendidly for having to maintain a family reputation for openhandedness. Such had their chamberlains like those of the Pope, their chaplains and masters of ceremonies, doctors and legal officers. A troop of gentlemen attended them, a cloud of pages hung about their palaces. There were lackeys and porters, cooks, coachmen and the rest by dozens, with all female labour strictly excluded.

In all these courts, great or small, there reigned a common ceremonial, founded on that of the papal court and equally stringent. Rules of etiquette were unbelievably involved. If a Roman cardinal were to receive foreign cardinals, for instance, the precedence of everybody in the room was complicated by the fact that each Eminence must be placed, not only in relation to his host, but in relation to the door as well. These considerations could never be ignored, for giving a guest the wrong position was easily construed as mortal insult. And, as at the Vatican, all the rigorous formalism went hand in hand with an astonishing laxity. Strangers came and went on private errands of their own and the cardinals put up with it, as did the Pope and the great nobles; trespassers were, by custom, never prosecuted. In the absence of the master of the house his staff and servants would entertain their friends with anything from light refreshments to a copious spread. Barriers of rank were non-existent. The cardinal's valet offered his snuff-box and his cardinal cheerfully took a pinch. Domestics joined in the conversation. Prelates in groups would gather round some oratorical menial making a speech in the courtyard.

But when the cardinals 'appeared in public', as it was called, all their dignity settled again about them. A cardinal on one of these official drives from place to place in Rome took his entire complement of carriages and every member of his household with him, and the mode produced some gigantic cavalcades. How gigantic may be envisaged when we learn that the usual retinue of Cardinal de Bernis comprised thirty-eight footmen, eight couriers, ten Swiss, four gentlemen, two chaplains and eight *valets-de-chambre*, apart from his coachmen, grooms and equerries on horseback; but then, he was the French ambassador. The shabbiest cardinal had at least three coaches to his name, black, and decorated outside with gilded bronze mountings. The huge plumes on the top, and the dark clothes of the passengers, who were always priests or monks, gave them a funereal air, with no touch of colour but the knots of red silk at the horses' heads. When the combined Sacred College joined the Holy Father for some ceremony their mere presence created insurmountable traffic jams, especially if they went to the Quirinal with its narrow courtyard and difficult approach.

A cardinal's retinue, as his stately horses trotted through the streets of Rome, had precedence over everyone. Should it pass near a guardhouse the guard was turned out, in the somewhat casual fashion of the local military. 'The carriage draws near, the sentry gives a loud warning; the soldiers sitting at the doorway get slowly to their feet and go in search of their equipment. By the time they are fallen in the carriage is well on its way and they all sit down again.' Giving a similar performance the drummers, too, were never quite quick enough to beat the prescribed salute as His Eminence drove by.

A cardinal, for health or pleasure, might sometimes take a walk.[1] Even then, however, he was bound by rules of behaviour towards other cardinals, some of which are laughable now. Thus an Eminence in a carriage who met another on foot had to get out to greet him properly. We read in a contemporary letter:

'After many bows, gracious smiles and protestations of attachment, the cardinals took leave of one another, but the one in the coach had to walk on some way instead of driving, and keep turning back and bowing to the one who really was walking. He on his side did the same and so they continued until each was out of sight.'

The people, as we have seen, took a lively interest in the ecclesiastics and the cardinals would pass by to the murmur of their own names, uttered sometimes in respect, sometimes in mockery. There were nicknames too, affectionate or otherwise. Each had his reputation, good or bad, and the fact that all the evidence was usually hearsay only made it more like gospel truth. Some cardinals became fashionable favourites, with crowds waiting for them to emerge to demonstrations of approval and devotion. Admirers would acclaim one of these heroes in the street, then rush to a farther point along

---

[1] The generally popular stroll, taken in the mornings, led from the Porta Pia to the Quirinal and this was also the favourite walk of the popes. The road was well paved, frequented by many prelates and elegant women and it was permissible to greet strangers there.

the route and so escort him all the way from his palace to his church. In this manner they followed him about for hours, their own affairs forgotten.

It was from among the prelates that the Pope selected cardinals. In other countries the term meant only bishops and archbishops but this was not so in Rome. The Roman prelacy in the eighteenth century was a spiritual and temporal aristocracy created by the Holy Father who was its fount of honour. Membership was open to those who had not necessarily risen through the hierarchy of the Church. It was never too late to join and one might leave at any moment—many a *monsignore* had forgone his great prerogatives to take a rich patrician bride.

The prelacy was a convenient institution, a school where one might rise to be a cardinal. Naturally, every prelate lived in hopes of a hat and his worldly standing rather depended on how likely he appeared to get one. The gifted youth—one could enlist quite young among the prelates—put on violet stockings as soon as he became a *monsignore* and embarked upon the road to advancement, a road that went by way of administration, diplomacy, the higher reaches of the law, and office in the Sacred Congregations or in their subsidiaries. But there were far too many prelates. All those apostolic protonotaries, those *auditori* of the Rota, those clerks and *rotanti della segnatura* meant a large entry of candidates for a limited number of red hats and even then did not include a throng of singularly well-placed aspirants with nothing to do but loiter ornamentally about the throne.

The whole body of the Roman clergy thus converged irresistibly upon the highest rewards the Church could offer, up to and including the tiara, though the really arduous stage must have been the long-drawn-out approach march of the *monsignori* to the purple. Each went about this in his own fashion, but best of all was to stick to the rules while making skilful use of the slightest incident that came along. As one contemporary cardinal declared, 'I know neither theology nor church history, but I know how to live in a court.' The clever man was the man with art to make his way—*camminare*—and patience, luck and flair were necessary cards in the game. When a pope died all the prelates who shared his influence or were his confidants or protégés were cast at once into the shade. Honoured and flattered until their master's disappearance, their toadies vanished immediately and future prospects grew ominously dark. In these circumstances some would retire to enjoy their collected livings and pensions in peace, but the majority, rather than abandon the pursuit, addressed themselves to those cardinals whom they thought most likely to succeed and worked to gain their favour and good graces. This led to sophisticated play with gifts and adulation, with recommendations and petitions, and it is hardly surprising that Roman politics, in such an atmosphere of unrelenting contest, turned upon intrigue, deceit and folly. Benedict XIV, the kindly Lambertini pope, called Rome a hell for pontiffs but considered it a prelate's purgatory. One can quite see what he meant.

He also pronounced the Eternal City a paradise for *abati* and nothing could be truer. Here was pleasant living for more than 6000 priests and monks of all kinds. The census of 1709, to be exact, showed 2,646 priests and 3,556 monks and other religious, excluding 1,814 nuns. Rome contained 85 parish churches and over 300 others served by monks or chaplains. There were 23 seminaries, 240 monasteries and 73 convents.

The Roman clergy, then, taken as a whole, were rich. Of the 36,000 dwellings in Rome they held 20,000 on the unbreakable tenure of mortmain. But, contrary to what historians have too readily believed, the revenues of the religious houses were small and estimated at about 930,000 francs by the French authorities at the end of the century. Nevertheless, by strict management and by the frugality that was both in accordance with their rule and natural to them as Italians, the monks still had enough to be large-scale employers of labour and very generous almsgivers. To this fact they owed their influence, as to the way in which their many orders penetrated to all levels, until there was no section of society where their voices were not heard. Between the Dominican with his well-bred penitents and the humble mendicant friar, the common man of the Church, there were ranged thirty Orders, each with its own particular approach. Of them all the Capuchin friars were dearest to the people, going barefoot in the streets, their wallets on their backs. They were loved, and talked to, and treated in the taverns. They were given little offerings of bread and wine, which were shared at once with those in greater need. To earn a pittance for their order the Capuchins would perform small, badly paid jobs like pulling teeth or carrying candles at funerals or even, 'if they had the head for it', modelling for painters.

As for those who served the parish and other churches, they all started out in such a way that intellectual worth, at least, was guaranteed. Any promising child was at this period directed towards the Church by relations fondly hoping to see him in due course the family provider. Who could tell? He might be pope some day. This prospect, doubtful as it was, fired many an imagination, understandably enough when we recall how strong a gambler's streak the Italian imagination contained. In any case, no other career was open to a young man of talent and decent schooling. It offered him an easy and perhaps an opulent existence and placed him, however obscure a ministrant he might remain, in that class which engrossed all the power and all the honours. In a land where everyone dreamed of acquiring some privileged shelter from the rules and regulations, there was no more potent advocate than a priest, whatever his rank and function. It was this, rather than his sacred character, that gave him power; power and, consequently, social importance.

Such was the prestige of a churchman that it was fashionable to wear ecclesiastical dress without necessarily having taken religious orders, or even intending to do so. Rome was full of these pseudo-clerics and the breed was not easy to identify. Young men might dress as *abati* as an introductory announcement of their having chosen a church career—some so extremely young that you might see wet-nurses suckling Franciscans and Carmelites of six months old. Others did so because it was usual in their professions. The apothecary neglecting to look like a priest might find that he had lost the custom of the cardinal his neighbour; lawyers and doctors by wearing bands seemed to improve their lowly situation. All the civil employees of the papal government, although often married with large families, did likewise and so became indistinguishable from their truly ecclesiastical fellow-clerks. It was most difficult to know one from the other, for here the proverb was reversed and the cowl did make the monk. This costume, which made a man to all appearances a member of a venerable calling, gave him its advantages and some of its opportunities as well. Nor, indeed, the least of those opportunities, since the beginner going on the recommendation of some obscure *fratone* as a minor clerk to one of the Congregations might well find himself, a few years later, clothed in violet silk among the glorious band of *monsignori*. It was a matter of dexterity, of gifts and patronage; and always there was the saving qualification that true piety could be its own sure means of success.

But the wearing of clerical attire was essential from the start. When the young Casanova, dressed to kill, arrived in Rome to pursue his career as seducer and adventurer, he was given this advice by the worthy priest who acted as his mentor: 'I trust you will change your attire and appear as a simple *Abate* when you take your letter to Cardinal Aquaviva; fortune does not smile on people dressed as you are.' That same evening he found himself apparently the only non-ecclesiastical guest at the table-d'hôte at his inn. In Rome, he says, 'everybody either is a priest or trying to look like one'. There being no law against adopting the habit, all who wished to command respect could put it on. Bergeret, staying here in 1773, remarks, 'everyone above the common level seems to be a priest of some sort', and Dupaty echoes him: 'rags or a soutane are the only wear'.

All these *abati*, all these ostensible ecclesiastics bent upon place and preferment, were frantic careerists. They competed against each other ruthlessly and success might well demand qualities that men of goodwill could not honestly admire. Finding himself among these youthful schemers, Casanova soon saw what their incentives were.

'Here in this ancient capital of the world [he writes] the man with his way to make has to be a chameleon, reflecting every shade of the atmosphere around him, a Proteus to assume any form. He must be supple, insinuating, false and deep, stooping often, full of treachery and candid in appearance. He should always seem to know less than he does, and be patient, and never raise his voice. He must control his expression and be icy cold when anybody else would be on fire; and if, as is usual with people in this state, his heart is empty of religion, he needs religion in his head. He will know himself a hypocrite but, if he is honest, bear the mortification in silence. He were better to quit Rome, if such conduct disgusts him, and seek his fortune somewhere else.'

Our *abati*, it may be added, gladly adopted as part of their armoury what Montesquieu calls *la recommendation corporelle*, or making the best of themselves, and few of them kept to the traditional severity of clerical garb. They wore the black habit, long *justaucorps* and short breeches, but they wore them with considerable dash. Stockings rose immaculate from silver-buckled shoes, the silken cloak floated about the shoulders caught with ribbon at the elbow, and on the powdered wig reposed the tricorne hat, 'ever ready for the deep obeisance or the well-directed bow'. They embellished every fashionable function with a polished gaiety in which, according to the Comte d'Espinchal, not even a captain of dragoons outshone them. Many of them, too, acted as general factotums, gatherers of information, preparers of the ground in delicate negotiations, inquirers after favour, marriage-brokers, procurers of women for wealthy foreigners; spaniels for all who wished to avail themselves of such gifts and such compliancy.

It was not exactly the sort of thing to give the clergy a good name and contemporary gossip pauses for no tiresome distinctions between true churchmen and those who merely wore the clothes. And yet the clerical class was indeed very numerous, with manners as varied as its various ways of life. It included amorous *abati* undismayed by bedroom epic, as it included real saints, unlettered priests and enormously learned prelates. Inevitably, with such numbers, the tares got in among the wheat. But whatever its character, it was still the governing class. In papal Rome everything depended, more or less, upon the Church and what was outside the Church derived consideration from her alone.

THE MIDDLE CLASS

The middle class, which was becoming of first importance in most countries of Europe, remained here a weak link. The bourgeoisie lacked money and independence and no prestige attached to the liberal professions. There were many reasons for this, many of them to be found in the structure of society itself, and faulty education was not the least among them.

The Church, the shepherd of souls, held a monopoly of teaching. It was nowhere laid down in law but was nevertheless a fact, since outside the Church no schooling was available. Fifty-two schools for primary instruction existed in Rome, free and open to all; and if we remember that every village in the Papal States, too, had a school of its own, we may fairly say that opportunities for learning were better than anywhere else in Europe—much as this would have surprised the French *philosophes*, who always claimed that the popes carefully kept their subjects in benighted ignorance. In practice, however, the schools were open to few but middle-class boys; lower-born children rarely reached them. It was not that these children were deliberately excluded; but work, for the working classes, had never been the rule of life, and their offspring would have been remarkable had they rejected the vegetative example of parents and relations. The schoolmasters, far from combating the non-attendance, actually encouraged it by their sporadic and unattractive teaching, for the basic principles of their craft escaped them. In addition to all this everybody, at school or at home, had in his mind's eye the formation of pious people, thinking an uninstructed child as likely to become Pope as a highly educated one, if God so willed. Sixtus V, an almost unique example who started life as a swineherd, was usually brought forward in support of this peculiar theory.

For pupils of the noble and middle classes secondary education was provided at many colleges—the Clementino, the Nazareno, the Bandinelli, San Pantaleone and others. These seem to have been well staffed, since eighteen professors taught at the Nazareno alone. The two centres of further education were the Collegio Romano, the Jesuit establishment founded by Gregory XIII, and the Sapienza, which was nearly as old as the Sorbonne. Both these great colleges offered many disciplines besides theology and ecclesiastical history, including literature, law, medicine, surgery and even oriental languages, but these subjects received such a weighty religious imprint in the teaching as to become distorted and lose much of their appeal. Physics, chemistry and the exact sciences as a whole were poorly thought of and a certain taint of impiety clung to those who studied them. Astronomy was considered subversive and botany ignored.

Despite so considerable an educational apparatus, then, the practical outcome was a disappointment. The common people knew nothing; the aristocracy, walled in by tradition, never grew up and the half-awakened middle class produced no sound authors, no scholars, great jurists or clever doctors.

The gifted man turned perforce to Church or government for a career, with the result that the liberal professions were cluttered with also-rans and their members regarded as discreditable persons. Lawyers, it was said, were by definition dissipated, and most unpopular, yet their numbers increased. As many as 1,200 operated in fierce rivalry with the *curiali*, who were officially licensed to represent and assist defendants in the pontifical courts. Such a multitude could hardly simplify procedure under a judicial system which was itself calculated to prolong them interminably. The

55

lawyers lived on the length of cases, the repeated re-hearings and the eternal transfers from one court to another, but they did not live well. None of them, were he eloquent as Cicero, could possibly grow famous for the simple reason that everything was done in writing. If they did have to speak before a judge they adopted a dramatic tone and stance as though by instinct. So much was the tradition of oratory a part of their profession that they went in for impromptu speechifying in the wineshops, thus earning the reputation of freethinkers and undermining themselves further. A lawyer had to be content with minute fees and eke out a living as private adviser to some rich family. If this failed he might act as bookkeeper for a merchant in the ghetto, but whatever he did he never rose to any very impressive position.

The doctors fared no better. For most of them the only alternative to starvation was some post not much above a servant's in one of the great houses. They would gather in groups outside the chemists' shops to waylay customers and offer them cut-price treatment. Their strictly controlled official fees were scarcely exorbitant[1] but, meagre as they were, the patients invariably complained. Medical men were suspect to begin with, because the whole profession was thought to consist of dedicated materialists; further, and chiefly, because nobody believed they knew their business. The legend of their incompetence was so firmly established that a sick man's ignorant doctor was automatically blamed in case of death; in case of recovery thanks, of course, went to the Madonna. The doctor himself could use the same technique. 'Our Lady was with me,' he declared if he did effect a cure. The most reputable practitioner could not escape calumny and when a pope died his doctor's house was painted all over with vengeful slogans. Had the pontiff been in good health before his illness, then Pasquino would have a word to say, as when he once announced the odd thing that had happened on February 10th—'a fierce lion had been slaughtered by an ass'.

One cannot but agree that current medical methods justified this wary attitude, for they were exactly those of Molière's M. Purgon; almost any ailment warranted 'a purge for luncheon and a bloodletting for dinner'. It was, of course, the fashion of the day, but where the French doctors supplemented these basic manœuvres with weird mixtures that make one feel sick even to read

---

[1] They even had to treat the destitute for nothing, which neatly solved one problem of social security.

about, their Roman colleagues leaned rather towards a savour of pastry and sweetmeats. Laurel water and salted pistachio nuts were prescribed against the plague, that is, any sizable epidemic. Fever called for chicken broth with gum syrup, carbuncles for a flour paste mixed with pepper and sulphur. These confections were made up either by the pharmacists, who were practically indistinguishable from druggists and spice merchants, or by the barbers, who were also handy at small services like cupping and leeching. The surgeons themselves were not allowed to give any sort of medicine by mouth. In the medical world, divided as it was into the holders of various kinds of diploma, they only just beat the bone-setters for the lowest rank of all.

There was, then, no sphere in which an important middle class might have developed, for Rome, with her liberal professions in this parlous condition, had neither large-scale industry, commerce, nor any prosperous agriculture.

At the end of the century Pope Pius VI was to drain the Pontine marshes and so bring into cultivation land hitherto left to the blight of malaria. This led to the emergence of a rich landowning bourgeoisie drawn from the country peasants, a class which, by the time it decided to look for its ancestry among 'Livy's heroes rather than Cato's slaves', was to claim membership of the nobility. Similarly, a middle class would arise among the lawyers as the power of the laity increased, but these changes lie beyond the limits of our period and were not then even thought of. All through the eighteenth century the middle ranks of Roman society lacked scope and opportunity. The most gifted among them could rise from the slough only along those administrative and ecclesiastical paths that took them into the governing class with its monopoly of power, influence and reward.

But the Roman burghers in their unelevated station never sinned through false modesty. They had their own exclusive pride and cherished a collection of inane shibboleths, such as refusing to carry the smallest parcel in case anyone assumed they had no servants. What they liked was to be seen, wear jewellery and go flaunting round the taverns in satisfactory demonstration that they had money and could spend it.

THE WORKING CLASS

Eighteenth-century Rome forms an unsuitable subject for those wishing to study a people groaning under some inhuman load of labour. Visiting foreigners dwell again and again upon the national inactivity. 'Imagine a populace,' writes Charles de Brosses, 'one third of whom are priests, one third doing very little and the other third nothing at all.' Sismondi says any Romans not in rags were either in the Church or in service, while according to Montesquieu they all lived, without a stroke of work, on the combined contributions of the Christian world. Montaigne too had marvelled at a city made rich and beautiful by no effort of the inhabitants. It was true that an ecclesiastical sloth seemed to affect everyone, but those who dismissed the people as entirely lazy were somewhat misled by appearances. The churches and palaces alone that were built, restored or decorated during this period suggest a very different picture. Skilled masons, painters, stuccoists and ironworkers everywhere toiled at their demanding crafts. All over the city were the artisans in their shops, not, perhaps, over-exerting themselves but able men, industrious and inventive. The great drawback was that these shops were too often shut. Every day of the year, as a contemporary noted, the whole town, or some entire district or section of the population, was busy doing nothing in celebration or in memory of somebody or something.

There was also the siesta which cut into the working day and lasted well into the afternoon; and after the siesta it was quickly dark, and closing time. But the main difficulty was always the irregularity with which a business opened at all. Excellent as he was when penniless, the Roman worker of the period relapsed into happy indolence with a crown piece in his pocket. He retained a classical appreciation of the dignity of leisure. 'Working,' remarked a visitor, 'is so much against his nature that he needs very good reasons before deigning to exert himself every day.' And the simplicity of his wants effectively minimized any such reasons; he came of a sober race and the weather disinclined him to indulgence.

And yet the reluctant artisan and the rather occasional worker were only a small minority of the commons. An enormous number of Romans led a poor existence without regular employment, and this *farniente*[1] they greatly preferred to any comfort that might have come with toil. It was not sloth on their part, nor any lack

[1] Idleness.

of ability, but the deliberate choice of a given way of life. Their only ambition was to abstain from action, their best pleasure simply to live, and enjoy that process for its own sake, 'with no delight besides'. They understood how to stroll and gossip and pass the time agreeably. The old Roman proverb, *chi si contenta gode*, 'the contented man enjoys himself', summed up their philosophy. And they were contented with the little they had, needing no more than a cool salad and a glass of water to remain their normal cheerful selves. 'Their temperament,' it was said, 'inclines towards joy as a plant towards the sun.' Having learned by experience that their daily bread would somehow be forthcoming, they came singing from their houses every morning when other people would have been going mad with worry. Never in human history can the tragic element have been so completely missing.

In the matter of supplying bare needs anything was allowable, short of actual labour. The clever ones imposed on the credulity of others and lived at their expense. Parasites and near-swindlers, they would attach themselves to some patron, offer him advice and produce sonnets in his honour. From him they extracted money and—the main point—ate at his table, paying their way with flattery. They were known as *cavalieri dei denti*,[1] colourful characters, to be met with in Goldoni's comedies. Others got a living from shifts and shady dealings, on or near the verge of starvation according as to how well their wits were working.[2] They rented apartments, hunted for relics, dealt in cameos, organized concerts. The French novelist Henri Régnier thus describes one of them: 'As long as anybody wanted to get rid of money, he had the very thing—music, food or simply women.' Many such freelancers kept establishments of the sort that might be politely termed 'beauty parlours', while others knew all there was to know about cards and 'every trick to lighten the unwary gambler's pocket'.

Only the more talented could aim as high as this, but it was never difficult to find some unburdensome method of turning a coin or two. Tipping—the *buona mancia* as it was called—was universal

[1] Literally, Knights of the Teeth, men who found a living by flattering rich people.
[2] The lowest rung of the ladder was occupied by the vagabonds who haunted the outskirts of the *erbaria* in the Piazza Navona, making their home there and sleeping on the steps of Sant' Agnese or in the house-doors. They were akin to the *clochards* of Paris, but no doubt less deserving, for some of their activities were very dubious. They were called *sbirri* and hucksters, but were tolerated and even protected, like mascots.

and any excuse served to demand money. With no street-lighting save the little shrine-lamps before the Madonnas, anyone could make a small income who obtained a lantern and acted as guide to the stumbling pedestrian. Opening a door, announcing a visitor, giving up one's place at some ceremony and looking pleasant about it, were all so many pretexts for inducing a tip. Those with the gift of the gab could preach in the porches or in the more retired nooks of churches and take the hat round after the impromptu sermon.

In this land, with its acknowledged object of minimal activity, starvation could always be warded off by begging, for the hand of charity was proferred everywhere.[1] Mendicants as a result flourished amazingly in eighteenth-century Rome. A few rags and a sore of some kind to exploit, and they were sure of a meal. Roman piety knew no hesitation. Beggary was encouraged as a God-given institution, protected by the police on the grounds that it constituted an appeal to one of the three great theological virtues, and the papal government could scarcely forbid or control it. Had not the Church from its earliest days admitted calls on Christian charity?

Beggary was a paying proposition, for everyone, even the poorest, gave as much as, and often more than, he could, from ingrained good nature as well as the occasional wish to shine. Any cripple, or anyone who could manage to look at all pitiable, adopted this sure and, what was more, respectable, means of livelihood. The beggars in Rome wore rags, like beggars everywhere, but they had the secret of appearing most dignified and even rather noble in them. As they leaned against the temple columns they might have been philosophers from the Antique world, preserving their pride intact by the oratory with which they charmed contributions out of passers-by. Mendicity and thieving often go together, but this was not so in Rome. Here there was nothing petty, nothing dubious, about the suppliant lying in the sun with an old coat draped majestically round him.

His companions were legion. Knots of them chatted or played cards at every palace gate, on the steps of every church, always ready to break off politely if a visitor should pass. When the great

[1] No further than the church door, however. Elsewhere reward must be given for the smallest services, but worship was free of all expense. Seats were not for hire, no collections were taken and there was no question of tipping the sacristan when he produced the relics on request.

stairway from the Piazza di Spagna to the Trinità dei Monti was built in 1724, the steps became their best pitch on account of the many reputedly open-handed foreigners who stayed nearby. The Piazza itself was the haunt of somewhat superior beggars who could ask for alms in any European language and tell anyone's nationality at a glance.

The man of the Roman people who was neither lackey nor craftsman, parasite of some kind nor beggar, simply did nothing. He belonged to that final third distinguished, not entirely flippantly, by Charles de Brosses. It was, if we may so put it, a large third, for the French authorities at the end of the century were to find close on 70,000 adult Romans all perfectly healthy and unoccupied. This idle host lived as best they could on the inexhaustible charity of Rome. It was a relief-town, where the clerical régime justified its existence by the broad exercise of charity, where the most wretched citizen could never die of hunger and help was provided in every misfortune. There was a cardinal's Board of Subsidies from which the poor received incredibly generous rations; in time of famine the Treasury paid for the grinding of imported wheat and gave a free bread allowance. Papal workshops were maintained for the employment of the poor and sick, who 'sat there with their arms folded, and a cardinal superintending'.

The wide network of official charity was supplemented by the large charitable enterprise of the confraternities and the religious houses. The great families, too, were very bountiful, disdaining parsimony on the score of rank and tradition. Apart from what they gave to regular good works they answered every one of the countless calls for assistance made upon them. Begging letters were written at every street corner by the public scriveners who sat out of doors, 'hats on their heads, umbrellas beside them and little stones for paper-weights'. Letters destined for the nobility were taken to the palaces, but the middle and lower classes, too, were besought from all sides. Rich and poor alike they responded, without stint and in every way imaginable, to the rule of charity. In no other country was that costly virtue honoured so largely.

The establishments of charity were uncountable. Voltaire found them as plentiful in the Rome he knew as triumphal arches had been in ancient times. Hospitals were more freely available here than anywhere else, very numerous and admirably managed according to the standards of the day. The biggest was the Santo

Spirito, where the huge galleries, hung with priceless paintings, could accommodate more than 1,600 sick, who were not only nursed, but succoured and amused. They had organ concerts and visits from a brotherhood who 'diverted them with discourse'. Almost every district had a hospital. In Trastevere there were two, Santa Maria and San Gallicano, one of them with 350 beds. Besides those founded and maintained by local charity, foreign nations, too, had hospitals of their own, just as they had their own churches.[1] This example was followed by Italian principalities and towns. San Giovanni in the Via Giulia was the Florentine hospital, San Giovanni Battista the Genoese, and Lucca had San Bonaventura. The big hospitals practised both medicine and surgery, while many of the lesser ones specialized, San Gallicano in leprosy, Santa Trinità in convalescent care, Santa Maria della Pietà in lunacy and San Teodoro in children's ailments. San Salvatore was the women's hospital and Santa Maria della Consolazione dealt with street accidents like a forerunner of our modern casualty departments, and was always full at carnival time. One of the leading confraternities, the Fate Ben Fratelli, nursed the sick in their own homes. There were twenty centres for the care of orphans and the aged, the largest and best run being the Ospizio di San Michele, founded by Sixtus V beside the Tiber. Two hundred old people lived there and twice as many orphans, girls receiving a dowry when they left. (A matrimonial future had been firmly indicated in the way they were taught to make their beds: two pillows and very definitely room for two.) The boys learned some trade. Any who showed artistic promise studied under the most celebrated singers and composers and the best painters, and so eagerly did they respond that the place produced several famous names. Attached to the Santo Spirito was the first foundling hospital in Europe, which had been there 400 years before St Vincent de Paul appealed to French mothers on behalf of homeless children. Even the much extolled Samaritan Hospital in London came two centuries later than the convalescent home of the Trinità dei Pellerini, while the lying-in hospital of San Rocco, too, was by far the oldest on the continent. This was a place for women in need of secrecy, where they could count on absolute discretion and conceal the fact of pregnancy by going there long before their time. If anyone at the

[1] The French church was San Luigi dei Francesi, the Spanish Santa Maria in Monserrato, Portugal had Sant' Antonio, the Germans worshipped in Santa Maria dell' Anima and the Poles at Santo Stanisláo.

hospital violated its rule of anonymity he was dealt with, none too kindly, by the Inquisition tribunal.

There was an appealing touch of delicacy about all Roman charity. The many convents where fallen women were helped back to better lives never mixed the hardened prostitutes with those who had yielded to a passing impulse only. Penitent whores were received by the Magdelene nuns who, feeling perhaps that penitence might be doubtful, saw to it that the confessor and the doctor were the only men who went near them. The Sisters of Our Lady of Loreto worked to reconcile separated wives with their husbands. There were even establishments for guarding young ladies—who were dowered when old enough to marry—from the perils of seduction.[1]

So active was the charitable spirit that there were two brotherhoods, the Santi Apostoli and the Pietà Divina, devoted to the relief of hidden misery. They visited needy families, gave the money that was wanted and disappeared without saying who they were. The confraternities of Saint' Ivo and San Girolamo paid for poor men's lawyers and the work of the Pietà dei Carcerati went far beyond ordinary prison visiting. They gave practical aid as well as comfort, tested the food and saw that the inmates were properly treated by the prison authorities. The brotherhood of St John the Baptist, attached to the church of San Giovanni Decollato, prepared condemned criminals for a Christian death. And the fear of a shabby funeral need never hang over the poor with more than one brotherhood, such as the confraternita della Orazione e della

---

[1] All the institutions providing dowries offered the alternative of marriage or convent and this choice was freely exercised, sometimes during the actual ceremony of endowment. An anonymous traveller has left us an account of such an occasion:

'I must tell you about a ceremony we saw two days after coming back from Naples. First, you must understand there is a voluntary fund, run by sixty gentlemen, to establish 350 girls every year, either by marriage or entry into convents. At the feast of the Annunciation the Pope and the Sacred College come to Santa Maria sopra Minerva where he, or one of the cardinals in his absence, sings High Mass and all the girls confess and take communion. They have white serge dresses, with ghost-like drapery over their heads, leaving only a little space to see through, sometimes only a single eye-hole. They go two by two into the choir where all the cardinals sit, and kneel before the Pope or the celebrating cardinal. A special officer stands at one side with a bowl full of small white purses containing fifty-crown notes for those who choose marriage and a hundred crowns for those who prefer to be nuns. Each girl modestly states her wishes, is handed her purse on a little holder, kisses it, gives a deep curtsey and quickly moves away to make room for the one behind her. The nuns-to-be wear wreaths of flowers as crowns of virginity and go first in the line. Only thirty-two among the 350 chose what St Paul tells us is the better course and would rather *maritarsi* than *monacarsi*.'

Morte, ready to bury them, under whose banners hooded princes and cardinals would follow the pitiful coffins with candles in their hands.

The homeless had many shelters, where they could live and eat until they found a lodging. If they stayed no more than a single night their clothes and shoes were returned to them cleaned and mended in the morning. At hundreds of refuges in Rome help was given to all who came and bread was nowhere refused to the needy. It was almost unnecessary for people to worry about their children's future, for the widespread provision of dowries made marriages easy to arrange. Yearly the Pope alone dowered 1,200 girls of good report and some part of the revenue of every convent and brotherhood went in settlements for daughters of the poor.

Where this sort of thing prevailed, work was clearly a waste of time. Given one day's bread, there was no point in bothering about the next and upon this oversimplified notion the Roman commoners based their admittedly uncomfortable lives. They herded together in their cramped lodgings, workers and craftsmen scraping a scanty existence, cheerful vagrants waiting for a miracle to produce their supper for them. Often a whole family shared one bed, as some still do today, much as we pride ourselves on progress. They fared poorly on pasta and cabbage and fennel and never had a fire in the house. All they earned or were given went on their backs and it was in gay clothes they walked on the Corso or sat in taverns over the light Castelli wines. Their women were ragged slatterns until five in the afternoon and then appeared well-groomed and hung with cheap trinkets.

The Roman of the lower sort had no military service to do or taxes to pay. Idleness saved him alike from brutalizing toil and from the 'unrest that political rights bring with them'. His head was stuffed with gossip. In this he was permanently free to indulge, as he was to enjoy perpetual festas and all the entertainment that was going. He lived in the sunshine in absolute liberty. So long as he could have the plain diet he liked, see processions and illuminations, take his evening stroll and sing his litanies to the Madonnas in their shrines, he was perfectly happy and asked for nothing more. Cushioned in so many ways, his poverty was a carefree condition and his class as a whole the heir to the plebs of the early Empire which traded all its rights for Caesar's *panem et circenses*. Imperial Rome exploited Europe and the Empire for the benefit of a million idlers and things were much the same in the eighteenth century, save that the city's do-nothings now lived on the world-wide oblations of Christendom. The Church had made their native place the capital of the universe and all the earth exalted their ruler and poured its money into his treasury. They did no work and the world worked for them. So it had been for twenty centuries. It was obviously the natural order of things. Pride was at the root of all their idleness. 'Since the rape of the Sabines,' it was said, 'nothing had ever surprised them.' They truly believed that they once personally conquered the universe and the lowliest of them never for a moment doubted his own superiority. Indeed, this seemed so very normal that they did not even try to justify it; they asserted it by implication, walking and bearing themselves in a high, heroic manner. 'When he lays aside his air of indolence, the commonest fellow comes to life with fiery looks and eloquent gestures.' It was the posing of his ancestors that once made the antique statues lifelike; he was posing now for his descendants.

The same pride kept the Roman from gross humour and from low debauch. He preserved a certain style, even in his least commendable activities. 'The degraded class we call *canaille* are unknown here,' writes a visitor, 'nothing vile is fit for Roman consumption.' In speech and moral standards the lower were identical with the middle and even with the upper classes. As Stendhal says, 'there is nothing mean or debased in the behaviour of the tailor or the baker, they would be quite at home if fortune ever bettered their condition'.

But pride did not prevent the Roman from appreciating jokes about his needy and precarious state. He shared it, after all, with many fellow-citizens and, as the popular proverb said, *Mal commune è mezzo gaudio*, 'an evil shared was half a joy'. And if the people did not exactly enjoy their sorry condition, they were at least readily amused by it. They crowded round the booths to hear the puppet-shows make their usual fun of working-class life and everyone had a good laugh at the sort of vexations he himself encountered daily. These performances, it is not always remembered, did not spare the rich and powerful either, who were mocked as heartily, but without resentment in the laughter. No one bore a grudge against the masters. Inequality bred neither hate nor envy, even in the poorest; they were only too pleased that the rich existed to be their benefactors.

People of such disposition were seldom miserable, and never

deeply so. Their imagination, stimulated by the hot sun, soothed by memories of past greatness and fed on music and church festivals, supplied every deficiency of circumstance. It was so powerful that anything they thought assumed at once for them the weight of authenticated fact; always their armour against the wretched present was the prospect of the wonderful future. The wonderful future itself, of course, depended more on the will of God than the efforts of men and this contention was, indeed, occasionally justified by the happier hazards of human life.

The lot of the poor was not, therefore, either continually or incurably depressed. A great man or a jubilee year might come along with a tide of gold in which they, too, could dip their fingers. They were sustained on hope and anticipation. The least of beings always knew the valet of some prince or cardinal good for contributions once in a while, with perhaps a more generous and frequent flow to come. New chances were born with every conclave, new perspectives opened with every move up in the Sacred College and the lottery nourished its expectations on all sides. Everybody awaited the favour of heaven in one form or another.

Of spiritual anxiety there is no trace. How could such a thing have penetrated the world of their imaginings? Their religion buried the past with facile absolutions, the life to come was gilded with its promises. Everyone had enough to eat, enough diversion and the right to live as he chose under a system which, having endured a very long time, would surely long continue. Worldly power was nowhere less respected, nor the support of the powerful anywhere more necessary or more sought after, though the seeking entailed no unpleasant competition. Influence was always exercised through servants, secretaries and monks and no one could tell just how important any particular contact was. Impossible, too, to guess just how far any friend might rise in the event of some cardinal's appointment or of an interregnum. Tomorrow the lowly priest could be a prelate, the minor prelate a wealthy cardinal; and the nobody you were chatting with today—what was to prevent his being valet or secretary to an official twenty-four hours later? So one was very careful. Everybody was very careful about everybody else and goodwill abounded. 'Every countenance,' says Dupaty, 'smiles on every other countenance.' It was not always from self-interest— Roman life at this time was chiefly charming because it was so friendly. Pride was unknown among the mighty and feelings of inferiority among the low; the classes intermingled in true patriarchal fashion. Nobles, prelates, burghers and commoners 'talked together with a cheerful accord it would be difficult to match elsewhere'. It was a many-faceted amiability. It was the Capuchin, armed always with his red umbrella and big basket, ready to help poor families; it was, as Louis Madelin describes it, 'the washing hanging from the Vatican windows, the palaces standing open to any menial's distant cousin, the great cardinal's snuff-box offered naturally to the unassuming *fratone*, the jesting between prince and artisan; the fishmonger casually setting up shop in the noble entrance-door and never thinking to ask leave; it was the typical neighbourhood of lordly mansion and low bar, of lavish, gilded churches and ramshackle hovels in one alleyway'.

Such things were possible, and had an air about them, only because priests, nobles, workmen and beggars all consciously belonged to one and the same family. Together they were Romans, people of the city of Rome. All were proud of the fact, with that emotion of ancient national pride that comes to the surface in the old formula, *Civis sum Romanus,* and which could still be heard, though now the context might be somewhat unexpected. Someone would go cleaving through a crowd of foreigners with 'Let me pass, I am a Roman citizen', or the bookbinder and the druggist, discussing their meagre livelihoods, conclude, 'Still, we are Roman citizens, we lead the world'. This love for their city, self-satisfied and exclusive as it was, was matched by no prejudice against outsiders, who were always welcome and sure of frequent, and at times excessive, honour. For all his irony and detachment the Roman was basically feeling, tenderhearted and noble, and his descendant of today, despite immigrations and the growth of population, is much the same in many ways.[1]

---

[1] Guido Piovene has recently written, 'One of the oddest turns in Roman history has come about in our own day for the very reason that the Roman people have remained a people in the classical meaning of the term, because they are reluctant to become bourgeois, and "prefer life to ideologies". Just because they are the people *par excellence* and retain so distinct a popular character, they have been adopted as a symbol by leftwingers and those democratic idyllists who, for example, would persuade us that Soviet life is fundamentally like the Roman—natural, with a dash of "antique" virtue, and "popular" in a folk-lorish sort of way. As a result we have the true conservative dream twisted into the dream of demos, a remarkable instance of the double thinking and intellectual deceit in which, regrettably, Italians have no equal. It explains why the Roman people became the darling theme of neo-realist drama. Not that they bother about what they look like on the comic stage. They are content to live, and from that content they draw their strength. Nothing

There is something catching about the Roman race and those who settled with them grew to resemble them and develop the same mentality. Only with strangers from the Abruzzi and the barren parts of Italy there came a fervour and a taste for toil that were to banish the old, happy-go-lucky Roman attitude into the realm of history.

---

they hear about themselves can interest them in the remotest degree. Anyone may clap any sort of hat on their heads, from the priestly *calotte* to the cap of liberty or any other disguise he fancies, and the Romans scarcely seem to notice. They go on living and pay no attention.'—*Viaggio in Italia,* p. 607.

CHAPTER THREE

ECONOMICS

If the Roman State were in financial chaos this was not in any way for lack of management. On the contrary, committees of management, under the nominal direction of the Cardinal Camerlengo, were attached in plenty to the Economic Congregation, though all they did was routine work with figures over which they had no control. Finance was in practice the affair of one man, the Treasurer, who by-passed the minister and settled payments in and out directly with the Pope. It would be wrong to say that he produced a budget; budgetary rigour and precision were far removed from the tentative and hopeful calculations of a papal treasurer.

The main source of income was of course the very large and very varied tribute coming to the head of the Church from all the Christian world, three quarters of it from France. We might suppose that an economy so secured would have escaped the scourge of public debt, as its citizens escaped taxation, but such was not the case, for the popes gave money away at a fantastic rate that made unceasing inroads on the exchequer. Each new reign brought in a whole new family to be provided for, its every member to be raised, often from near-poverty, to opulence. If the Settecento popes did not abstain from customary nepotism, neither could they avoid the duty of maintaining an ostentatious court; there was the duty, too, of giving alms and sustenance to the whole population and of regaling it with repeated festivities; and there were the public works which every pope felt impelled to undertake, not only for the Church's glory but his own.

And so the Romans paid taxes in the eighteenth century. These were light, it is true; even in the spendthrift reign of Pius VI they never amounted to eleven *livres* a head, hardly a quarter of what the French were paying under Louis XVI. The only direct levy fell on property-owners alone and the one indirect, the *macinato*, concerned the grinding of corn in the official mills and principally

69

affected the peasants. The Roman lower classes had nothing to pay at all.

Rather than burden their subjects with taxation the popes preferred to raise loans when money was needed and had two methods of borrowing from the public. They might offer for sale shares in Monte di Pietà, the municipal pawnshop of Rome, with a guaranteed rate of interest. This was sixteen per cent at the beginning of the century, but with constant falls dropped to two per cent under Pius VI. Such shares were called *luoghi di Monte*. Or there were the *vacabili*, annuities in return for capital made available, paid from the funds of the Dataria, or Vatican Chancery. They constituted a heavy burden, though in times of stress it would be lightened by an official reduction of interest. As for the national debt itself, its very size precluded any thought of repayment.

And yet, in spite of these problems, the government spent regardlessly; no other word can well express the absolute lack of method with which it embarked upon its projects. The Treasurer, an appointee of the Pope, obligingly threw his coffers open as required to any sort of charges, often sensible, sometimes unjustified, and without exception heavy. Nobody bothered to see if the money were there before they planned to spend it. When the cupboard was bare they bestirred themselves to fill it by yet another of the ever-successful appeals to the Catholic world. At the end of the century the Revolution cut off French supplies and with them the chief source of income; and when that happened, bankruptcy loomed. The circulation of gold dried up and that of paper money, in the form of papal promissory notes, increased. Napoleon's iron hand was needed before thrift and order were restored and the position stabilized again.

Papal currency bore the image, not of the Pope, but of the Church itself. The Saviour, Our Lady and the Holy Apostles were stamped on the silver and gold pieces. Louis Veuillot called it money that 'spoke of and to God, exhorting, teaching, praying; exhorting above all to charity with its lessons on the proper use of riches'. The coins indeed bore scriptural texts, appropriate to the character of the Pope who chose them, to the state of the Church or, more usually, preaching the love of the poor and the scorn of wealth. 'Being as dirt, I am the root of all evil,' announced a gold sequin. 'Redeem your sins with charity. The Lord loveth a cheerful giver . . . it is better to give than to receive . . . covet not silver and gold, nor set your heart upon them . . . if you look for salvation, love me not'; such was the uplifting language of apostolic currency.

But the gold pieces were rare and the silver scarcely enough for day-to-day business; paper money, circulated in large amounts by two financial houses, supplied the deficiency of hard cash. Those who wanted ready money would pledge clothing, plate or jewellery at the Monte di Pietà, to be sold in two years if unredeemed. The rich avoided the trouble and risk of keeping large sums at home by depositing them either at the Monte di Pietà or with the Santo Spirito bank and drawing on them at need. This, of course, was simply the operation of the long-familiar current account as we know it today. Both banks, the Monte di Pietà and the Santo Spirito, paid out their own notes which were invalid beyond the papal frontiers but as good as solid gold within them. It was this complete public confidence in the paper money of the Roman banks that first gave the financier Law the idea for his famous 'system'.

The coinage was reckoned in decimal values, the unit being the *paolo*. Ten *baiòcchi* made one *paolo* and five *quattrini* one *baiòcco*. The average equivalent value of the *paolo* during this period was a little more than ten sous of French money. What was called the *germinal* franc was given the same value as the *livre* at the Revolution and remained more or less stable until 1914, so we may say that the *paolo* was worth something like a fifty-centimes piece of the early years of the present century in France. The *baiòcco* equalled one sou and the *quattrino* a centime at the same values.

Rising in the scale, we come to the crown piece of ten *paoli*, comparable with the *thune* or five-franc piece in 1914. The sequin, which equalled two Roman crowns, was worth a French demilouis, the gold louis being usually worth about forty *paoli*. 'Usually' because its value varied a good deal during the century: thirty-three *paoli* in 1705, forty-five in 1765. This gives some idea of the difficulty in finding any sort of stable modern comparison, while dissimilar methods of production in the two periods also make such calculations anything but reliable. However, if we are content with a rough guide, we may take a differential coefficient of 300 for the rising values in France since 1914 and transpose into modern terms some of the payments and wages of eighteenth-century Rome. In this way we may reckon that a colonel in the Pope's army drawing fifty crowns a month had the equivalent of 250 *germinal* francs. The thirty crowns of a captain's pay represent 150 *germinal* francs a month.

Among government officials a salary of 1,000 sequins a year was exceptional. To earn so much one had to be one of the twenty-four *segretarii dei brevi*, majordomo to His Holiness or *maestro della camera*, all great offices whose holders ranked as nobility, with private chapels of their own. Lesser employments carried lesser pay and the ordinary quill-driver at the bottom of the heap received no more than a keenly calculated living wage. All official salaries were, however, supplemented by *mancie*. What these amounted to is hard for us to tell, but they would vary with the recipient's importance in the scheme of things, with his general adroitness and his skill in marketing what influence he had.

Manual workers were very poorly paid. A gardener, like a man in a workshop, could expect little more than fifteen or twenty *baiòcchi* a day, half what his French contemporary would earn. Lowest of all came the women who did spinning in their own homes; their five *baiòcchi* a day were starvation wages. Servants did much better. A liveried footman earned 50 *paoli* a month, a coachman or cook six crowns, but they were at the head of the domestic hierarchy. The customary tips made all these wages in reality much higher.

To form an idea of how earnings were related to prices, as well as of Roman standards of living, we may note that a *baiòcco* would buy a half-litre (or *foglietta*) of wine; a pound loaf cost the same and fillet of beef was four *baiòcchi* a pound. Two dozen eggs were ten *baiòcchi* and a three-pound turkey two *paoli*, that is to say one *germinal* franc.

Living, it will be seen, was very cheap and the government would always block any threatened rise in the cost of foodstuffs. If the harvest were bad the Pope kept the price of bread down; in 1773, for instance, Clement XIV borrowed for this purpose a million Roman crowns from the banker Cohen. Added to this system of subsidy and emergency imports were the strict controls aimed at maintaining price stability.[1] These at times could be excessive, with the result, well known in other places and periods when prices have

[1] State direction was here supplemented by the trade guilds with their severe compulsory rules. The consuls of the goldsmiths' guild, for example, destroyed jewels which they considered weakly made, the hatters forbade the sale of headgear 'that looks handsome but is of poor quality', and the mercers exacted their own heavy fines from any of their brethren guilty of fraud or cheating. All guild laws were designed to protect the public against fraud and to ensure fair charges.

been fixed too low, that goods disappeared from the markets. On July 16, 1771, Alessandro Verri writes to his father in Milan, 'Tell me something we are not short of. All prices are fixed and are now too low, so that no one wants to sell.' It was in vain that the prelate of the Annòna, superintending the markets, issued regulation after detailed regulation on conformity with controlled prices, despite the horrifying penalties. A baker who sold poor bread was strappadoed three times and had to pay a huge fine as well, and for passing off beef liver as calves' liver a butcher might go to the galleys for five years.

But there were all sorts of ways round the rules, the most common being the giving of short weight. Innocent XIII once took a notion to see for himself how the ordinances put out in his name were working and promptly learned how little they meant. Of nine loaves he bought from nine different bakers on his morning's walk and tested when he got back to the Quirinal, he found only one of proper weight. Shoppers, stung to reprisal, occasionally tried to steal the goods on display, or, more often, engaged in vociferous wrangles. Violence would follow and the police spent more time in restoring order than they did in checking the weights and prices. Since turmoil broke loose whenever they showed their faces they preferred to conduct investigations less directly, stopping housewives in the street to inquire how much their eatables cost and waylaying foreigners to make sure the hotels were not overcharging them.

And indeed the main market in the Piazza Navona could well do without their interventions, which would only add to the inconceivable confusion that there assaulted eye and ear. This was probably the most picturesque vantage-point in Rome for observing the life of the people, and certainly the noisiest, with the loud, continual chaffering and all the din of all the minor trades going on in the open air. Peasants who had come in with farm-produce— brown-cloaked men in pointed hats and women in red aprons —took their opportunity to buy odd things they needed from the hawkers, with much else that they did not need, foisted on them in an endless flow of sales-talk. Customers were shaved in the street at improvised barbers' shops, or took their letters to be answered at the public scriveners', where they found great difficulty in keeping their affairs to themselves, with all the bystanders joining in to offer advice. Charlatans made dramatic speeches to sell their wonder-working salves, drums rolled to drown the shrieks of too-

73

credulous patients having their teeth pulled out. Fortune-tellers and soothsayers inveigled confiding youth and maid, astrologers offered lucky numbers for the lottery; montebanks did their tricks and crowds gathered round performing animals. Musicians sang and peddled ballads, lemonade-sellers passed round. Near the Moro fountain an ingenious machine known as the *cavaletto* stood ready to dispense a mechanical thrashing to any offenders, whether market people or their customers. A Jesuit father preached from a platform near the central Bernini fountain. Old reports tell us that something amusing or unexpected was always going on. To quote one remarkable example, there was a fishmonger who on March 2, 1741, for six *baiocchi* sold to a carter from the Monti quarter the right to eat as many anchovies as he could with half a loaf of bread. An enthusiastic audience gathered to applaud and the mortified fishmonger had already watched him swallow 350 when the police arrived and put a stop to the performance.

Foodstuffs were cheap, despite constant complaints that they were far too dear, and food was not a heavy item in a Roman budget. They were a sparing people, the climate was no great stimulator of appetite and they were always filling up on ices. (The Romans would eat ices at any time of day. The French banker Bergeret once arranged to meet a cardinal at eight in the morning to go with him to his church and was astounded to find ices being handed round in large quantities and the antechamber full of ecclesiastics eating them.) Moreover, fasting on the vigils of the saints, the Ember week, and Friday fasts were scrupulously observed. Special dispensation was necessary to eat meat on forbidden days and not even for reasons of health was it easy to obtain. The butcher or eating-house proprietor who broke the rules was risking the galleys. A light diet prevailed, even among the comfortable classes. Red meat was never seen. The staple foods were vegetables, eggs, pastes, fish, stewed or braised meat always well seasoned with herbs, and cheese, often fried in the pan. There were, however, special dishes for certain festivals. Broiled lamb was eaten at Easter and *torta*, a cake made with ewes' milk. Eels and *pangellio*, a saffron-flavoured sweetloaf, were for Christmas. On St Joseph's Day there would be *fritelle*, or fritters, and during Lent the dry buns called *maritozzi*. Snails were served at the family meal on St John's Eve in memory of the saint's tribulations in the desert.

The lower classes did little cooking; they went instead to the nearest cooked-meat stall and then to another for the sauce. No

Roman housewife passed her morning bent over simmering pans. This lack of culinary skill may have been due to a 'holy and healthy' feminine idleness, but it should be added that neither police regulations nor accepted custom encouraged anyone to cook. People had a singular objection to the smell. Nobody minded the stink in the streets, but at this time a phobia existed about smells, especially nice ones, and cooking odours were relentlessly tracked down. To prepare tripe or cabbage at home was to invite the vengeance of one's neighbours and the attention of the police. Tripe for the whole town was cooked in enormous cauldrons set up in front of the church of San Marcello, while cabbages were boiled near the Piazza Colonna and sent round the various quarters by special cabbage-distributors. Roasting coffee in one's own lodging or courtyard was simply not to be contemplated. Coffee was roasted at the foot of the column of Marcus Aurelius on Monte-citorio. All the coffee merchants were to be found there every day and here the connoisseur bought his raw beans and had them roasted in his personal brazier in the shadow of the column.

Not even flowers were exempt from this distaste. Their perfume was mentioned with aversion as *puzza*—literally stench—*dei fiori*. But there were exceptions. The common people were fond of them, the women using them in their houses and to dress their hair. Lovers forced to conceal their love could always communicate by means of flowers strewn along a path and arranged according to a private language of their own. But flowers, in society, evoked an aristocratic disdain. Their scent was dangerous, said the ladies, and liable to make one faint. They were accordingly banished from gardens, where the only approved features were lawns and laurel or box hedges. Nor were they allowed indoors, any more than was fruit, though we must admit, after reading an anecdote told by Charles de Brosses, that it was often sheer affectation that kept fruit out of the house.[1]

---

[1] 'This antipathy,' he says, 'looks to me like a sort of inverted delicacy. I was at Cardinal Passionei's a few days ago when some nuns sent him the finest citrons I have ever seen. I put a couple in my pocket before going on to play cards at Princess Borghese's and thought of giving them to the unmarried daughter. But she said, "Oh, do hide them, Monsieur, take them away; Mamma will be quite ill if she sees them." So I took them into a further room and came back to my game. An hour later someone mentioned the citrons the cardinal had given me and Madame de Borghese had the vapours. She has recently had a child, it is true, but I had been sitting by her bed with the citrons in my pocket and she was as right as rain.'

INDUSTRY, COMMERCE, AGRICULTURE
AND THE ARTISAN CLASS

As we have already seen, the Roman State in the eighteenth century possessed neither industry, commerce nor agriculture of any importance, a threefold lack which meant that no comfortable bourgeoisie, such as quickened the economies of most other European countries, was able to arise here.

Everywhere else, even in Italy itself and in Milan particularly, a type of capitalist industry had come into being, a system, that is, of substantial businesses employing capital and workmen. But when this kind of thing was tried in Rome—by foreigners, needless to say—it met with severe discouragement. There were never enough raw materials and the most ambitious planning met its match in that lackadaisical labour force. Worst of all was the want of funds. Most of the money in Rome was frozen in ecclesiastical coffers and released only to build churches or found religious houses. In short, it always went on charity of one kind or another and those responsible would have felt they were misapplying it by investing in any profit-making enterprise. As for the nobility, rich as they were they could produce very little hard cash and what they had was drained away by needy dependants and dishonest agents. Bankers reserved their funds for paltry speculations. Business undertakings were obviously the last thing anybody thought of and the state itself did nothing to make them seem important. Official economic opinion stopped short of any desire to rouse the country from its hidebound mediocrity and, this being the case, it was certain that the smoke of factory chimneys would never pollute a Roman sky. The industrial complement consisted of a few paper-mills and tanyards, an oil-press or two, some petty soap-manufacturies and occasional silk-spinners; small-scale concerns, all of the old type and based on the individual workman.

Commerce had everything against it and was in no better plight. The Tiber was non-navigable. There were few ports, all more or less silted up and even Civita Vecchia was choked with debris and could take only small, infrequent ships. There were no roads except the ancient legionary ways, now cut in many places, out of repair and dangerous because of bandits. For want of organized transport it was impossible to send abroad the marble and fine building stone that was once quarried for classical Rome; the iron of Bracciano and the alum of Tolfa were hardly exploited. In fact, there was almost no external trade. Apart from the coarse silks known as *borgonzoni,* imitation jewellery and faked pictures, Rome exported nothing while the State, like a stern disciplinarian, kept even the irreducible minimum of import trade, limited in any case to foodstuffs, out of private hands.

Internal commerce, shackled by price-fixing and pointless restrictions, offered no better prospects for an incipient merchant class. The business world consisted of a collection of small men, many of them not even owning shops but using their natural eloquence to hawk their wares successfully from door to door. Many a flourishing concern was started in this fashion. But the dealers seldom achieved burgher status, despite the generous profit-margins that were everywhere the rule, for much of this profit went in commission. The meddling helpers appeared from all sides, each bent on deducting a share for himself. The owners of real shops, ever unruffled, made no effort to speak of. 'Oh, yes, I have what you want,' was the reply of one to a customer, 'but I can't reach it. Come back tomorrow.' The shops were usually dark and very untidy, their only attractive feature being the descriptive signs hung out by way of advertisement. The tailor would display a pair of scissors, a chemist the serpent of Aesculapius; the tobacco-seller had his long pipe and the barber his shaving-dish. The inns displayed a cock, a bear or a sun. The connection at times seemed rather tenuous. What, for instance, had the Pope's Swiss guard, noted by Maurice Vaussard, to do with the lace-merchants on whose signboards he appeared?

Agriculture was entirely neglected. South of the Tiber basin, between the mountains and the sea, stretched the waste of the Pontine marshes, a waterlogged wilderness, barren and unhealthy. In this baneful region, ravaged by malaria, a few scattered villages slowly sank away. Three quarters of the country, too, was unproductive limestone, though corn and olives were grown at Tivoli, vines at Frascati, chestnuts at Rocca di Papa and some fruit and vegetables more or less everywhere. But it was all on a very small scale, with tiny fragmented farms at the mercy of a variable climate and the vagaries of peasant idleness. Some districts, where the better land was more extensive, used a peculiar system anticipating that found in some parts of rural America today. When ploughing and harvest times came round all the oxen would be driven into Rome. There the farmers hired and took them to their own fields, where the season's work could then be finished in one day. 'These farming operations,' says Dupaty, 'are like rural mutual-assistance campaigns.'

Though Rome had nothing we should recognize as industry, she possessed her dexterous workmen and a whole galaxy of busy artisans. There was labour, highly skilled and plentiful, for every branch of building and the decorative arts. In more than 700 work-shops, in or out of their homes, were craftsmen to serve every need of their 150,000 fellow-citizens. They were, as we have said before, a body driven by no uncontrollable frenzy of activity, but there was accomplishment in all they did, and true artistic feeling. To these men we owe the perfecting of many processes and implements and some notable inventions. Solely because of their development of the art of mosaic, workmen who knew nothing about draw-ing were able to make the luminous, glittering copies of famous pictures that give St Peter's some of its glow and brilliancy. Damp would certainly cause fatal darkening of the originals in time and the copies, with their shining colours, were secure from all deterioration and faithful in every detail. They could also be scaled to their surroundings; Raphael's *Transfiguration,* for instance, was four times enlarged.

It was these ordinary craftsmen, too, who produced the idea of remounting pictures on new canvas that saved so many priceless works from ruin. The inventor of this process was a simple worker, entirely ignorant of painting. People thought he must have used magic of some kind and he escaped a charge of sorcery only by claiming to have received the secret from St Joseph to whom, 'in the guise of a poor man', he had given alms.

The Roman artisans were so proud of their work that eventually they all announced themselves as artists: artist shoemakers, artist farriers, locksmith artists and barber artists. The term was so far cheapened in the end that the least pretentious copyist would dis-avow it with the cry, 'I am not an artist, I am a professor'. Those in the true artistic trades favoured the name of *virtuosi*; Luigi Valadier, father of the famous architect, was a *virtuoso argentiere.* The wives of such artist-labourers belonged to a superior category of matron and considered themselves *eminenti*.

Many of these complacently self-styled artists, however, really deserved the name. Not only did they include the mosaicists, smiths and marble-cutters working on major enterprises together; there were, too, all the small manufacturers of the small objects so beloved of pilgrim and tourist. Engravers of cameos and precious stones sold off ancient monuments reduced to bourgeois taste. Bits of mosaic served as waistcoat buttons, necklaces of golden seals were common, scarab bracelets, combs of ivory set in gold, or clasps with lucky inscriptions. The copying of antique jewellery, like that of statues and pictures, was a flourishing business with a large and reprehensible sideline in forgery. This was brought to a high pitch of perfection by methods both empirical and surprising; last night's new bronze statuette, for example, emerged with the true rust of antiquity from its dip in a solution of salt, saltpetre, horse-dung and urine.

Rome had become one huge craftsmen's studio. There was un-doubtedly a great deal of tasteless stuff among the so-called artistic trash turned out for tourists, and much that betrayed a tendency to sham and 'artificial art'. And yet, as a whole, the work produced expressed the fundamentally aesthetic feeling native to the men of Rome. The love of the fine arts was so much a part of the air they breathed that many working people followed some artistic calling, often as pure recreation, in addition to their bread-and-butter jobs. There were few families unable to muster their amateur painter, engraver or mosaicist.

It was this side of their nature that inclined the Romans to occupations needing taste and address, towards work where the material and the imaginative could meet and mingle—the work of smiths and cabinet-makers and carpenters. They showed a marked preference for open-air employment and liked being fishermen or boatmen, laying roads or unloading ships. But they would not be coalmen or tailors, and left such business to the Genoese, while pastrymaking was, by general consent, the concern of no one but the Swiss.

The members of every calling, including the street-sweepers, town-criers, the grenadiers and even the singing-men in the churches, had a guild of their own. This was commonly very ancient and imposed rules, moral standards and social duties on all who belonged to it. The guilds united master, journeyman and apprentice in bonds of fellowship. (Workers in those days regarded their masters as benevolent guardians, not as enemies whose help it was best to reject and whose interests it was proper to ruin.) Each guild had its elected officers and a church, or at least some chapel, of its own in which to lodge the archives, hold meetings and keep the feast of its patron saint. Those both rich and pious enough would also maintain the twin institution of a brotherhood and here the members accepted very strict religious obligations, provided dowries and practised every kind of charity.

The trades were centred each in one district or street, where the guild name sometimes survives, as that of the hatters in Via dei Cappellari, of the locksmiths in Via dei Chiavari, the nailmakers in Via dei Catinari, the ropemakers in Via dei Funari, and so on. Clockmakers worked round about the Piazza Capranica and the ragmen near Monte Giordano. Pasquino's statue was surrounded by stationers and bookshops and the junk-sellers had a kind of flea-market in the Piazza Navona.

We have spoken already of the leisurely tempo of life in Rome. People never looked really busy as they went about the streets, even in working hours, but during the long interval of siesta that practically cut the day's activity in two, it might have been a city of the dead. It is well known that a noontide rest at home is necessary if one is to endure the summer temperatures in this part of the world, and to this sacrifice the Romans resigned themselves with great goodwill. Their siesta began after luncheon and lasted until five or six o'clock. Churches were closed, shops shut, workshops deserted. Rome stirred from profoundest slumber only when very little time was left before her early nightfall.

No one but a handful of foreign tourists dared defy the strength of the sun and the French had some claim to fame in this respect. Their heroic behaviour is proverbially celebrated, not without a tinge of mockery; already in the eighteenth century dogs and Frenchmen were supposed to be the only creatures moving in the Piazza di Spagna when the heat was fiercest.

The torrid summer weather could be matched by occasional very cold spells in winter and with every fibre of their being the Settecento Romans braced themselves to reject this fact. They declared, once and for all, that cold did not occur in the place where they lived and took against it no precautions at all. Carpets and hangings were rare, even in the most luxurious apartments. Windows were shutterless. Fireplaces were seldom seen and keeping them empty was a point of honour. One might exist, hardly ever more, as a purely decorative feature in some great room of a princely mansion; in ordinary houses the fireplace, if there were one, was for cooking, save when a small wood fire was lit, whatever the weather, on St Catherine's Day, as part of the celebrations. Fires indoors were thought to be unhealthy in any case. A few stoves, or *foconi*, might be found in sacristies and in the ante-chambers of cardinals where they were regarded as an old man's whim and just excusable. At home, women used footwarmers, referred to as their *mariti*, and chilly hands at social gatherings were warmed by passing round small china pots called *scaldini*, full of hot embers. The fact was that people would rather freeze than deny their set, ridiculous convictions.

In the event of snowfall the city was seized with acute panic and all its self-congratulations died away. Life went, as it were, into a state of suspense. The children stayed away from school, canons were excused church services, the studios stood vacant. Out of doors no living soul appeared. Numb and discountenanced, and happily never for long, Rome waited for the thaw.

Roman hours in the Settecento were reckoned 'in the Roman style', that is, from sunset. If the sun set at six o'clock, then the first hour was at seven, the second at eight, and so on through the twenty-four. It was the method of Antiquity and highly incon-venient because of the constantly changing time at which the sun went down. Watches should have been altered back or forwards every day, but people had fallen into the habit of ignoring dis-crepancies of under fifteen minutes and this minor manipulation meant that time could be stabilized for eight or ten days together. The essential adjustments were worked out in advance and small tables, printed on thin paper, were slipped into the watchcase.

But even with such an aid it was still most difficult for a stranger to know what time it was; though the natives, inured to the necessary mental gymnastics, found it all easy enough. 'The main thing,' they said, 'is knowing how many hours of daylight are left, and anyone can tell by looking at his watch.' Watches were set by the Ave Maria bell half an hour after sundown and standard time was taken from 'the Clock of the Roman People', a timepiece which worked only intermittently throughout the century. From 1412 onwards it was in the wall of Santa Maria in Aracoeli, above the round window to the left of the big door. It had its own main-tenance man, a well paid and hereditary official, but in 1705 it stopped and resisted all efforts of the experts to get it going again. They had to give up in the end and replace it, the new clock being fixed in the centre of the façade where marks of it can still be seen. This cost the town council 300 Roman crowns.

Unfortunately the new clock, too, went wrong almost at once.

The whole century ticked by as repair after repair was put in hand, each more extensive and less effective than the last. The Clock of the Roman People, sad to relate, told them the time only now and again, between its everlasting mending sessions. At last they decided on yet another replacement and newer and longer delays ensued. Someone had meanwhile observed that every town clock in Italy was in a town-hall belfry and so the clock for the Roman people was duly set up in the campanile on the Capitol. This departure stripped the Aracoeli façade of its sole piece of decoration and left it with the 'shabby old woman' look it has today.

To end our slight review of the Roman economy we should glance at the problems of written communication. Of all the public services the post was quite the least efficient. Foreign countries and all the big Italian towns maintained post offices of their own, independent of the central organization managed by the *generale delle poste*. The French office was in the Via Ripetta, the Milanese in the Piazza San Claudio and the Genoese in the Collegio Clementino Palace. None of them functioned at all well. The memoirs and correspondence of the French in Rome are filled with lamentation at the slowness of their post, its irregularity and grave deficiencies. Mail could take fifteen or twenty days to come from Paris, though it might speed up a little for important news. Thus the birth of Marie Antoinette's daughter on December 19, 1778, was known here on 29th. This was a splendid performance, in view of the bad weather, and the record was never beaten.

As for the service within the Papal States, its working was deplorable. The poorly maintained and dangerous highways may have been some excuse for tardy deliveries, but the disinterest of the officials played its part. They had their own typical answer to the difficulties of distributing mail in a town like Rome, with its unnamed streets and unnumbered houses. A postman was paid by the addressee at the rate of a *baiocco* a letter. He therefore took up his station in a wineshop with the post spread out on the table before him, and so long as each item was replaced by one *baiocco* and the whole lot collected quickly, it was nothing to do with him who picked it up. Anyone could put down a coin for any letter he fancied and nobody would ever inquire whether it were addressed to him or not.

THE LOTTERY

We should here include some examination of the Roman lottery, with its double effect on the economy. In the first place, it gave the Romans yet another excuse for doing no work, living as they did in eternal expectation of the ever-possible miracle that was to make them wealthy overnight. Secondly, it took out of circulation the immense sums they invested in tickets and as this money was never wholly re-employed its redistribution tended to disturb the balance of business.

Games of chance have a terrific appeal for any nation living mostly on imagination and feeding on hope, and they had been played at Rome, in every guise and combination, at all periods and by all classes. The lottery, that shortest road from rags to riches, was of course the greatest gambling game of all and might be called the Roman grand passion of the eighteenth century. It already existed in simpler forms before the State took it over. Anyone might organize a lottery and there were dozens of them, run openly or in secret, though none offered the gambler any guarantee and cheating was rife. This was wrong and a cause of scandal, and to stop it the papal government forbade the *lotto* altogether, matching the ban with dire penalties against those who disobeyed. All concerned, players as well as promotors, had the galleys in prospect and in 1731 Clement XII added the threat of excommunication to reduce the last hard core of determined punters.

Rome was a city of mourning, but the situation soon cleared. Barely six months later the same pope re-introduced the lottery, making it official and putting it under the management of the Roman State. This reversal was explained in an edict of his treasurer, Carlo Maria Sacripante, for, with the lotteries forbidden at home, the Romans had at once become devoted customers of those still functioning in many other towns of Italy and caused a huge drain of capital that badly affected papal finance. It was to stop this leakage, rather than with any thought of blessing the popular passion, that the Pope created the Roman lottery. Seemliness demanded that good works should benefit and the profits were to be divided between churches and charitable institutions. Also, at every draw, ninety poor girls were given tickets and if any of them held one of the five winning numbers she received fifty crowns on marriage or on taking the veil. The treasurer was sincerely resolved to gain nothing from the lottery and deliberately made its administration very costly, recruiting an army of under-occupied clerks to run it.

All preparations having been pushed through quickly, the first draw took place at the Capitol on February 14, 1732. At the top of the stairway leading up to the piazza a velvet-draped platform had been erected near one of the Dioscuri, and here sat the civic officers and great prelates. Conspicuous was a large silver urn containing the ninety numbered balls of ivory. An innocent orphan, dressed in white, made the actual draw and a purple-clad giant of a man called out the winning numbers in a voice of thunder, his announcements being greeted by a tempest of cheers and groans. In 1743 this ceremony was transferred to the loggia of the Palazzo di Montecitorio.

The lottery was a predictable success from the beginning. It cleared over 500,000 crowns in the first year and never looked back. It entered 'the very bloodstream of the Romans until it became the major preoccupation of all and the sole interest of many'. They all took part, grandees and beggars, women as well as men, with the princes of the Church by no means last among them. There was a draw every Saturday and the ticket offices were beseiged all week.

For a gambler, life's main business became the discovery of lucky numbers and how best to combine three such numbers in a *terno*. One could back a particular number, try for the first one drawn or a double, but the favourite forecast was always a *terno*. For this, three numbers were chosen and if they appeared, in the order named, among the five winners, the punter stood to gain over 5,000 times his stake. The composition was never left to luck; everyone had his private formula and went to exhausting lengths to demonstrate its certainty with rows of cabbalistic figuration.

Often this formula was revealed in a dream and there existed a specialist work, the *Libro dei Sogni*, to help with the task of translating one's dreams into figures. Some enthusiasts would multiply their chances by retaining as many as ten women a week to tell them what they dreamed. Each woman placed a given number at the head of her bed and any dream that seemed at all connected with this number was considered lucky. Others extracted portent from mystical pictures or *cabala*, provided by the experts. The Capuchins were supposed to know how the lottery worked and would be consulted for the most probable *terno*. 'If I were to make *terni* for everyone who comes,' one of them declared, 'I should have none left myself.'

But the best way of reckoning the chances of any number or *terno* was always the player's own fancy, based on his own intuition and the good or bad incidents of his own week. Seen thus as omens, the most paltry happenings lost any prosaic significance and passed into the realms of prophecy. Should you by chance see a man fall out of a window, you backed number 56 with no more ado. A drowned person as clearly indicated number 88. If one of your children caught fever, that meant the *terno* 18–28–48. Number 90 offered some consolation for amorous setback since the deceived lover, by taking the age of his faithless mistress and the day of the month when it all happened, might compose a *terno* with it.

Widely read and universally known by heart was the *Libro dell' Arte*, listing every imaginable circumstance together with its meaning as a number or group of numbers for the lottery. A cock crowing, a dog barking, a sudden noise in or out of doors, all were counted as so many hints from heaven and reduced to numbers. Omens were to be plucked even from assassination: there was the victim's age to think about, or how many teeth the criminal had who was executed during the week. The best bets were casualty and murder. If a fire broke out anywhere there was a stampede to the ticket office and before the results of any mishap were considered it was first analysed for its hidden *vera sorte*.

The *terno* once selected, novenas were said to make it win. Streams of people climbed the steps to the Aracoeli to entreat the intercession of the *Sacro Bambino*. Above all, having been openly advised to do so, they turned to the Virgin. Prominently displayed at the ticket counters was a verse to the effect that a small stake could lead to infinite riches and that, if they were prepared to risk it, it was hoped the Madonna, too, would do her best.

So intermingled was prayer with gambling that people bought masses for the success of a permutation and offered enormous sums to the priests to place the three numbers of a *terno* under the pyx.

In spite of all, of course, the day of the draw brought its inevitable disillusionments; but hopes were philosophically transferred to the week ahead and no blame attached to the selected permutation. 'My *terno* didn't come up,' the unfortunate player said, 'but it was a good one all the same.' This curious gamblers' mentality, persisting into the nineteenth century, was what Edmond About meant when he wrote of the Romans, 'I truly believe that by gazing at figures they become like Pythagoras and read into them all kinds of things that are not there.'

Certainly the lottery was of supreme importance to the whole population. An entire town spent its time concocting permutations and building castles in Spain. When he scraped his pennies to buy a ticket the poorest creature forgot his wretchedness in those bright dreams of fortune and found life worth living. An old woman once asked a mendicant friar for the winning *terno* and was advised to spend her money on bread and wine instead. Her reply was, 'Forgive me, but when the bread and wine are gone hunger and thirst will soon come back; with a ticket in my pocket I am rich till Saturday.'

Most people felt as she did and so the *lotto,* that food for hope and self-delusion, became in the eighteenth century an instrument of government. Priestly rule, as rule, may not have been up to much but psychologically it knew what it was doing.

THE GHETTO

The shortest account of the economy of Rome would be incomplete without some mention of the important part played in it by the Jews.

Of all rulers, the popes were most lenient towards them; no other sovereign allowed them so full a liberty of conscience. During the most fanatical periods, when they were hounded in every land in Europe, St Peter gave them shelter and protection. Not that Rome was for them another Promised Land. Here as elsewhere Jews were treated with contempt and forced to live apart, but there was no persecution and they knew neither exile, extortion, mob violence nor the stake. Ill-usage was always a matter of isolated incidents, condemned and checked by papal authority.

They were relatively few among the many foreigners drawn to Settecento Rome by the more or less light-handed government—about 5,000. Until the middle of the sixteenth century they had kept the privilege, which they possessed nowhere else, of choosing where they wished to live, but since Paul IV's reign had had to stay in a special district. The ghetto was walled round, with five gates and its main entrance in the present Piazza Giudea, near Giacomo dell Porta's handsome fountain. In an area that barely covered two and a half acres the inhabitants were disagreeably cramped together in dirty, narrow streets and rickety houses. These houses belonged to Catholic owners and to religious communities who fleeced their tenants shamefully until Urban VIII had ended the abuse by fixing reasonable rents and making it an offence to charge more. His Bull was still law in the eighteenth century, with the result that while the return on property had risen considerably all over the world, it remained constant in the ghetto at Rome. Since landlords also remained liable for repairs, the owners were ruined while their tenants could be sub-letting at fifteen times the nominal rent. A lease for them was an inheritance, their family fortune and their daughter's dowry. One has heard of situations not dissimilar today.

Within their ghetto the Jews lived according to the Pragmatic issued by the Camera Apostolica in 1661.[1] This was a sumptuary law aimed at stern control of the luxurious life which the Jews, paradoxically, lived in those unsavoury alleyways. It was forbidden, except for betrothals, weddings and circumcisions, to hold a feast for all comers with singing, music and dancing. The musicians at a ball must all be Jewish and might be paid only three *paoli* a head for the evening. There were rules, too, for women. No more five-string pearl necklaces or rings on every finger; no more nets of gold for their hair, or dresses with gold lace. Regulations as severe condemned the men to dark-coloured clothing.

By means of side-stepping and subterfuge they were all, of course, evaded. Laws, and sumptuary laws especially, are powerless against custom and these were doomed to failure. Nobody could make the Jewish bankers live like paupers when the Romans were so lavish with their borrowed Jewish money, and no Jewish woman was going to sit dowdily by and watch her Roman sisters in raiment that cost enough 'to run a small town'. There were infringements, then recognized exceptions, and now little was left of the harsh code save that Jews must wear the yellow head-kerchief, or *sciamanno*, and might not own horses or carriages, nor even work as coachmen.

When Clement XI, at the beginning of the century, cancelled the right to trade with Christians conceded by Sixtus V, a new, chill wind blew upon the Jews; but here, too, they gradually won free of these limits on their business activity. They adapted themselves to the ban with fair success, showing characteristic ingenuity in finding ways to by-pass and disobey it, and by 1730 had regained most of their commercial freedom. The list of trades they might

---

[1] This Pragmatic, originally valid for five years only, was renewed throughout the eighteenth century. Alterations were slight as to the letter but there was noticeable relaxation in the spirit in which it was interpreted.

legally follow was long. They could be clothiers, haberdashers, goldsmiths, jewellers, tanners, cabinetmakers, and so forth; and though not actually permitted to produce any article, they were past masters in the art of re-using old materials for such things as furniture, jewels, antiques and wearing apparel. What was more they had, as authorized old-clothes-men from time immemorial, considerably enlarged the meaning of that term. Sole established dealers in bric-à-brac, they pushed their handcarts through the town to the familiar cry of 'Heb! Heb!' But these rag-merchants possessed whole streets in the ghetto and always, in front of the shops, clothing of every land and fashion was piled up, from Abruzzi peasant garments to the grandest of court costume. There was furniture, too, in plenty, some of it magnificent. Under cover of the second-hand trade they carried on an extensive business in carpets, gems, *objets d'art* and precious stuffs. There one was sure to find all one could want or wish for and the shops, spilling their generous trays of merchandise out into the street, drew the Romans in fascinated crowds.

The Jews did not confine themselves to their permitted occupations, nor even to those the police pretended not to know about. They had others, where most of their many customers were women, for they sold potions, amulets and magical prescriptions for any and every ill, bodily, spiritual or romantic. They would tell fortunes and for a fee cast every spell in the Cabbala. Benedict XIV, in an edict of September 15, 1751, forbade them 'to reveal the whereabouts of anything that was lost'. St Anthony, obviously, was feeling the competition.

Disqualified from the possession of land and more or less penalized in business, the Jews, with their undeniable knack in such affairs, concentrated on the money market. They handled any kind of transaction, from small credit to high finance. The numerous pawnbrokers operated in semi-secrecy in the rear of unobtrusive shops, but large sums, whether secured or not, were a matter for the great bankers. These were always powerful men, some of whom were known to furnish the popes with occasional timely loans. Their rates of interest fell short of usury and, considering the risks they took, were not even excessive. The Jewish banker was never regarded as the 'monster thirsty for blood and gold, the heartless Shylock' he was often claimed to be.

Such bankers were the barons of finance, living in luxury, but the rich merchants too were comfortable enough. The highest ranks in Rome were not above attending feasts and celebrations at more than one well-to-do house in the ghetto. 'If the popes,' commented Rodocanachi, 'had on the one hand to protect the Jews from ill-treatment by the lower classes, they had their work cut out on the other to prevent their mixing too intimately with the richer citizens.' This is borne out by the story of a marriage-banquet in the ghetto at which the house collapsed under the weight of guests, with many deaths and casualties. The list of victims was surprising: it included one precentor, a well-known canon, several *abbés* and quite a number of socially prominent Christians.

CHAPTER FOUR

CRIME AND PUNISHMENT

The judicial system was without doubt the weakest feature in the papal administration and the least suitable to contemporary life, subject as it was to a hopeless tangle of peculiar laws that paralysed it completely. Of law courts there were enough and to spare. Apart from those of the Church itself (the Inquisition, Index and the rest) they existed in such diversity that no plaintiff could possibly tell to which he should apply for a hearing. They had so multiplied because every authority in Rome was at the same time a judge. The Governor, the Senator, the Cardinal Vicar, the Treasurer and the Camerlengo, each division of the great departments of state and all the Congregations had individual courts for cases affecting their interests or their employees. There was even a revenue court for St Peter's, while the Holy Father's majordomo judged suits brought by or against any member of the pontifical household. This complexity meant, to begin with, that litigants might well look to more than one tribunal, with endless bickering over competence, while scandalous irregularities arose from the whole eccentric organization. Indeed, there was nothing to prevent opposing verdicts being returned by different judges on one and the same question.

The appeal courts could supply no remedy beyond that of unreliable revision, for they were as numerous as the lower courts; they had evolved on the same defective lines and no one knew exactly what their province was. The highest such tribunal was the Rota, so called from the round table at which it met. Its findings had the force of law but there was much that lay outside its jurisdiction. Others who could hear separate appeals were the Camera Apostòlica, the Congregations of Immunità and Buon Governo, the Signatory Court, the Assessor of the Inquisition and the Governor of Rome. By some strange departure, contrary to all established principle, these courts gave first hearings to certain kinds of case and so occasionally found themselves considering appeals from decisions they themselves had made. The simplest suit could be dragged out for ever amidst all this overlapping and confusion and made to last for ten, twenty or thirty years. Some came up again and again and were repeatedly postponed.

Such a system was calculated to undermine all those resorting to the law and most unlikely to leave the judges with any great sense of fulfilment. They, of course, being men of the Church and passing constantly from one sphere to another—from justice to finance, from diplomacy to the cure of souls, lacked the legal spirit as much as legal learning. Convinced that 'the light of a priestly conscience' would guide them easily over the gaps, they gave their judgments according to individual temperament, mood or predilection; even, sometimes, according to their own best interests, for venality was not unknown among them. They were aware, to say the least, of those pressures any lawsuit must engender, and it was never their way to immerse themselves in fatiguing inquiry nor to mull their decisions at great length. They were, in short, light workers, whose natural tendency not to overdo things was reinforced by the lavish allowance of non-working feast days and by the fact that when the courts rose they rose for five good months' holiday.

But had the judges made ten times the effort, they would still have encountered one insuperable difficulty. The canon law which was the law of the land had never been codified and was to be consulted only among a welter of Bulls and Decretals that no one ever tried to attack, so enormous was the coil and so chaotic the arrangement. Decisions rested usually on plain jurisprudence. In presenting and in settling a case, lawyer and judge would argue from some ruling of the Rota more or less applicable to the matter in hand. The Rota, however, had unfortunately assembled rulings in one hundred large folio volumes which comprised a somewhat impenetrable collection. Each side, all the same, would manage to find something among the hotch-potch to contradict the other, leaving the poor arbitrator to make his choice on the inspiration of the moment. It may have lessened his qualms to know that judgment was declared with no introductory summing-up and need not be expounded. Such latitude left the judges free to be indulgent or severe as they thought fit and the best of them acted in sheer simplicity of heart, totally convinced that the equity of the Lord must see that right prevailed.

The Lord's equity took human form in the person of the *auditore santissimo*, the Papal Auditor who stood for the highest and at the same time most arbitrary authority of the law. He represented the pontiff, and by extension God Himself, as sovereign judge. He might reserve any case and the fact that his intervention alone overrode any previous verdict could be providential for a losing side. Having perhaps gathered more influence in the course of a decade or so, such a side might return to the field with a better chance of winning.

Under a system with no fewer than seventy-two avenues of appeal from any ordinary sentence, and where appeal-court decisions were themselves open to revocation, amendment or suspension by the supreme arbiter, it was clearly most difficult to obtain a definitive verdict. Those who managed it, after years of litigation, were by no means at the end of their troubles. Before the decision so painfully arrived at could be implemented, it had to face a barrage of delaying tactics made available to the reluctant debtor in Rome. There were indeed so many ways of postponing an evil day that it was hard to choose between them. When a defaulter had exhausted the patience of the bailiff's men or their eighteenth-century equivalents (a patience easily prolonged by the artful combination of little gifts and influence), he could always fall back upon a moratorium. This was a circumstance furnished very frequently by custom and the law. He might not be sued during an official festa, and some festas lasted for two months. The bailiffs were never sent round if his wife were pregnant, nor for forty days after the birth, time enough for the fortunate father to think of the next move. If the worst came to the worst, he went to ground in a convent on the orders of his confessor, and made a retreat during which he could not be disturbed, however long it lasted. Debtors could also take sanctuary in any house displaying the arms of a cardinal. Such houses were numerous, easy to get into and no questions were asked as to what anyone was doing there.

We need not be too scornful that the bad payer enjoyed all these advantages; there were even more for murderers, as we shall see. Nor do we have to push comparisons too far to find parallels in our own day to some shocking Settecento practices in Rome. How easily, for instance, could tenants avoid paying rent if they so wished. Cornered and threatened with eviction, all they need do was to let their premises to some insolvent friend and then stay on as guests. To get rid of them the landlord must say goodbye to his back-rent and pay compensation to the undesirable occupant, who promptly went off and played the same trick somewhere else.

Of criminal justice we need at this point say only that it was no better administered than civil. But before we consider all its missing links and oddities we may usefully describe the quite extraordinarily permissive atmosphere surrounding the criminal, and especially the criminal guilty of murder.

THE GAME OF KNIVES

The Romans, said Dupaty, 'lived peaceably without check or curb from justice or police, and this was due to no force of law and order, but to the absence of anything that might provoke disorder'. Certainly order reigned in the eighteenth-century city. Serious theft was rare, burglary rarer and rioting unheard of. In contrast with the country roads, where the brigands defied every pope's determined efforts to destroy or win them over, those in Rome were safe. Even at night one could walk about at any hour, without fear of attack or robbery. The worst to be expected was a meeting with a watch-patrol, who were most particular about taking the names and addresses of all nocturnal strollers, whom they could thus question next day should anything untoward have happened in that part of the town. It was best not to try to avoid their inquiry, for they had long, hooked pikes with which to stop anyone who looked like running away. If need be they would also trip people up by throwing short staves against their legs.

But the safety of the streets was due less to the, admittedly relative, vigilance of the law than to the simple Roman scorn of thieving. To steal so much as a handkerchief was to arouse the most violent hostility and a pickpocket caught in the act was pursued at once by the crowd. Unless, of course, the victim laughed about it, in which case all the witnesses laughed as well and stopped trying to be policemen, a role they also abandoned as soon as a real policeman appeared on the scene.

Stealing was so rare because the physical wants that lead to it were less strongly felt here than anywhere. The general sobriety of life told against petty larceny. The working man got all he needed by his not very strenuous toil or from that vast network of aid and charity. Crime for the attainment of extra wealth, such as large-scale theft, or swindling or the rifling of shops and warehouses, was almost unknown because the passion for getting rich quickly was non-existent. Riches were no real help towards ambition; one rose in the world by rising in the Church. Neither want, idleness nor ambition, then, could make a man a thief, any more than women could, for as standards grew laxer, women were easily come by and not at all expensive.

But if thieves were scarce, the murderers abounded. Several killings a day took place in Rome, five or six as a rule and more at festa times. There were 18,000 in the last five years of the century and only the so-called 'atrocity' of French law was to cure the evil.

These murders were usually the result of brawls flaring up among the lower classes over romantic rivalries or insults exchanged while they drank or danced. Depending on how serious things were, the threat might be that of a slight wound or a plunging dagger but it was never an idle one among these hot-blooded people. Anyone resenting a look or an ill-judged word had only to cry 'Draw your knife!' and the duel followed. The crowd formed a circle, each contestant rolled his jacket under one arm and flew at the other. There was no pause for injuries, but when one was gravely or fatally hurt the victor took to his heels, assisted by the bystanders and even by the friends of his victim. The latter, if merely wounded, never denounced his assailant. In this he was prudent rather than magnanimous, since if he did so he would certainly never live to see his own recovery.

This, then, was the game of knives, with its own code of honour and the knife instead of the fist. It was the instrument of vengeance and in Rome vengeance did the work of the law. It was the duel of the common people and therefore the killer was not regarded as evil or dangerous. If a man were killed by a knife-thrust in the public street an 'unavoidable accident' was said to have carried him off and to wish anyone such a death was the worst and most solemn of curses. So usual was assassination, so ordinary a part of life, that it furnished the everyday Roman oath, *Sia ammazzato*, which meant exactly nothing. Children blew their father's candle out at the Shrove Tuesday festivities with undesigning shouts of '*Sia ammazzato il signor padre!*'—'Let's kill father'. It was even employed as a compliment and Goethe relates how Angelica Kauffman overheard an admirer say, '*Sia ammazzata la signora Angelica, la prima pittrice del secolo*'.

It should be noted that not all 'unavoidable accidents' were the result of spontaneous dispute. Many were premeditated. People turned to the use of crime because the state of the law implied its use. Where it was impossible to obtain legal satisfaction for injury a victim's family were driven to execute their own justice. The seducer whose betrothed had too easily believed his ill-found promises would find all her male relations with drawn knives facing him in a row. How many murders must have been done because the murderer saw no other way and considered right was on his side; how many differences, how many purely family discords, must have been settled by the game of knives for lack of any other means! The people recognized the knife for an instrument of justice they handled for themselves.

As well as being quarrelsome, the Romans were great grudge-bearers and did not easily forgive. At all levels of society the vendetta was in their eyes a moral obligation, though the upper classes employed subtler instruments than the *coltello* to be rid of a pest, a jealous lover or a faithless woman. True, it was no longer 1650, that heyday of the poisoner, but they still resorted to *aqua tofana,* the mysterious brew that would kill in two years at the rate of a drop a week. The gold knives, poisoned on one side, for dividing fruit and killing with the lethal half, were not yet relegated to the curio shops. A heritage from the Renaissance, and still occasionally used, were the notorious death-rings for scratching the skin of a woman's hand; what looked like a caress was a sure means of revenge.

Such refinements belonged to the last stages of intrigue in high life. Among the commons retaliation was a more direct affair, the affair of the knife. In many Roman churches, notably in Santa Maria in Trastevere, might be seen the strangely-decorated walls and pillars which were, and still are, hung with knives, daggers and stilettos of every kind, even the pins the women wore in their hair; and all these steely weapons record the penitence of those who were dissuaded by their confessors from intended murder. Or so the sacristan will tell you. All too probably, alas, they hang there in thanks to the Madonna after the deed was done.

There would have been less crime if criminals had felt less secure. Had they truly feared that the law in its rigour would come down upon them, or the executioner cut their heads off in the end, their performance would have lost some of its verve and liveliness. But the Roman State, which more than any other required a firm police and a stern justiciary, had neither. These flaws were supplemented by the idiosyncrasy of a public which, looking upon the law-breaker as a kind of unfortunate hero whose due was fame rather than disgrace, paralysed the police and made a mockery of justice.

The bandits who infested the neighbouring countryside were popular heroes and ballads were sung about their exploits. Despite their vicious extortions everyone believed they robbed only the rich and were very kind to lesser folk. Their adventurous life was delightful fodder for the Italian imagination and the country lad gained more esteem by turning bandit than he would if he went to the Pope as a soldier. The government was constantly hampered in its long struggle against the brigands by the sympathy they inspired and the popes, after humiliating frustrations, fell back upon frequent amnesties as a method of controlling them. The brigands, rich with loot, would then go back to their villages, buy land and houses and marry the prettiest girls in the district, who naturally took them in preference to honest stay-at-homes.

The same admiring attitude shielded the urban wrong-doer and even led to practical co-operation with him; the shared approach to the whole question of crime produced the most incredible tales of active partnership. In 1719, for instance, a girl had her father thrown from a window for withholding his consent to her marriage. She had found two gentlemen, so we are told, 'of the first families in Rome', happy to perform this murder though neither was the fiancé in the case, neither even knew him and it concerned them not at all.

After the crime there were always three hopeful prospects for the criminal—those of not being captured, of not being condemned and, if condemned, of being freed without delay by the intervention of a monk.

Most murders were committed in public, by the light of day, but most police reports end with the words, 'The guilty man fled and so escaped'. His flight would have been abetted by all who saw the drama, for they were always on his side. The common cry of *povero cristiano* never referred to the man stretched in his own blood on the ground, but to the man who put him there; the pity he should have aroused was given to his murderer instead. The assassin was always in the right, the victim in the wrong, a fact which tended to impede police inquiries. There were never any witnesses. Nobody had ever seen anything. Killing was a private matter, the business of murderer and victim alone. This notion was so firmly rooted that forgiveness by the latter, however

96

ambiguously expressed, meant that official justice could no longer
intervene.

It was an article of popular faith that the officer of the law was
everybody's enemy and collaboration with him was frowned upon
accordingly. A crowd might be engaged in thrashing a thief caught
redhanded, but turned as one man against the *sbirro* who presumed
to try to take him into custody. Honour forbade not only the
denunciation of a criminal but even any assistance in arresting him.
An honest man simply did not stoop to being a policeman. This
ostracism sprang from the boundless, never-to-be-modified abhor-
rence inspired by the police, their agents and auxiliaries. The
sbirro was a vile creature through and through and *figlio di sbirro*
the worst insult to throw at an enemy. And indeed the police by
their activities justified the notion. They were often old lags themselves, drawn from the scum of society. Ill-clothed, ill-paid, going
about everything in the most unsavoury way, they raised more
dread in honest men than they did among the criminals. Small
wonder, then, that popular sympathy went to the 'noble murderer'
rather than to such villainous constables.

And yet Rome, as far as numbers went, was heavily policed.
Seven hundred uniformed officials served the city area alone,[1] apart
from those by no means lowly specimens employed by princes and
nobles to keep order in the districts where they lived. Yet despite
this strength, the police force only rarely managed to arrest the
evildoer, since places of refuge were so easy to reach and the crowd
so willing to assist. And at this period the town was full of places
of refuge, beginning with the sanctuaries. A villain sheltering
beneath the cross was out of danger and the officer bold enough
to lay a finger on him would be excommunicated; this custom was a
survival from the classical world and the sure asylum of its altars.
With a church every few yards, domestic chapels on all sides and

---

[1] A host of police spies or, as we should say, informers, were also kept on the
payroll to check evidence and ferret out offenders. Secret agents were everywhere, in every house and in the shops and bars; the common saying went that
where six or seven were gathered together one at least was sure to be a spy. This
extra force was of little help in tracking down the lawbreaker or in criminal
investigation; its activities were confined to the giving of information of an
administrative or political kind and for both it was highly efficient. When a
Roman was asking for some place of benefice the relevant authority had no need
to start inquiries, for the information would be to hand already. The candi-
date's previous doings, his tastes and habits, had been carefully, almost daily,
noted and would be on the file, together with his attitude towards the Church,
the police regulations and the law.

convents everywhere, the delinquent had no trouble in finding a bolthole. To make it easier still the term 'sanctuary' carried the widest possible interpretation. A cardinal's residence was sanctuary, and even the person of a servant of God encountered in the street. The assassin who could seize a monk by the robe was in harbour. The police entreating the *fraticello* to prise him loose were wasting their breath and he reached the door of church or convent safe and sound.

Whole districts round the embassies were also forbidden territory to the police. The popes tried hard to limit this immunity, based on very ancient custom, to the palaces of ambassadors and the houses of the chief members of their staffs, but all negotiations came to nothing. The diplomats jealously defended their privilege, never hesitating to set their own guards upon any *sbirri* who ventured over their boundaries in the course of duty. The very quays along the Tiber had become inviolate, in case a hunted man threw himself into the water. That he should die unshriven was the most terrible thing imaginable and pursuit was called off if the quarry threatened suicide.

All these safe areas led Charles de Brosses to suggest that '*les pauvres diables de sbires*' ought to have 'a detailed street-map of Rome to show them just where they were allowed to chase a criminal'. The children even invented what they called the Church Game, in which one player was the assassin and the others police, trying all ways to catch him without setting foot in a refuge.

The right of asylum could have some odd results. The story is told of a culprit who, having taken shelter in the porch of a church beside the Cancellaria, kept up a continuous bicker with the porter of that palace. One fine day the porter, determined to end the nuisance, seized his gun and aimed from his doorway as at a couching hare. He missed and killed instead an unfortunate *abate* who happened to be passing. Immediately he re-ensconced himself in his own lodge and the situation then froze, for the police could touch neither murderer nor intended victim, murderer as he was himself.

Malefactors sheltering in the churches brought with them all they needed for a life of leisure. Often there were parties of ten or fifteen people; the food was good and the company at bed and board —*non sine candida puella vel puello*[1]—could be quite gay, and

[1] Not without a pretty girl or even a boy.

worshippers would occasionally find the holy water stoup full of wine bottles set out to chill.

CRIMINAL JUSTICE

Yet despite all these dismaying facilities, a criminal might actually be caught and handed over to one of the countless tribunals with some part to play in the task of keeping public order. These were even more numerous than the civil courts, for some had both penal and civil jurisdiction, while others heard criminal cases only. There were so many branches and the distribution of responsibility was so tangled, that a man might come before several courts on the same charge. Judged by one, he could never be sure, even after serving a sentence, that another would not re-arrest him; the principle of legal limitation was unknown and he might live all his days under the threat of a new charge. It was always possible, too, to be pardoned by one court, or by several, and still be kept indefinitely in prison.

There was no penal code, only a very contradictory collection of *bandi*, or decrees, as issued by the Secretaries of State. Towards the middle of the century Cardinal Valenti, Secretary of State to Benedict XIV, put some sort of order into the jumble by listing all crimes and misdemeanours with their corresponding penalties. His list contains some curious provisions. Breaking into a convent of nuns merited death, even if nothing were stolen and nobody alarmed. Kiss a decent woman in the street and you went to the galleys for life. The strappado was inflicted for blasphemy, with five years in the galleys for a second offence. Fomentors of quarrels, including those who merely prevented reconciliations or caused a truce to be broken, might be executed. So might those who carried arms, even catapults or weighted canes; on this point the law was very harsh and a pistol found within six feet of any loiterer was presumed to belong to him. A galley-slave's career would follow the uttering of personal libel or the affixing of defamatory inscriptions, even on houses belonging to known harlots. Pasquinades were punishable by death. Yet the pasquinades were more caustic and more frequent than ever and nothing is heard of any action against the authors. Never had so many women been kissed in the street and the tale of assassinations sufficiently indicates that no one hesitated about carrying daggers, knives or even firearms.

The arsenal of pains and penalties failed to cow anyone for the simple reason that its threats were often mere figures of speech. They could vary with the station in life of the accused (*secondo la qualità delle persone*) or be left vague in the original pontifical edict. Even when the punishment for some crime or misdemeanour was precisely defined and legally laid down it remained at the discretion of the court's presiding prelate, *ad arbitrio di Sua Eminenza*. Ecclesiastical judges were by no means an oppressive body, nor did the popes, conscious always that they represented upon earth a God of mercy, urge them to severity. Rather they disarmed the penal laws by the precepts of leniency they passed to one another down the years. No one paid the full penalty but proven criminals and flagrant murderers, priest-killers and blasphemers; insulting the Madonna, we shall see, was as serious as poisoning one's mother.

The court with the greatest and least merited reputation for harshness was that of the Inquisition. Certainly in Spain, in the hands of fanatical monks, the Holy Office was still terrible; but in Rome it consisted of high dignitaries of the Church, sat under the Pope himself and was automatically proof against excess. Its only work, in fact, was to trace and punish anyone who wrote against religion or practised sorcery or magic. A code was published in Rome in 1730 by one of its officers named Pasquelone defining the offences that it dealt with:

'Magicians are those who by spells cause any man or woman to be possessed of an evil spirit; who imprison the devil in a ring, medallion or other object; who own triangles, circles or other charms; who gain the affections of a woman by magic words and potions.'

How little the terrifying tribunal actually did may be inferred from the fact that in 1765 there were only four inmates of its prison in Castel Sant' Angelo.

But if the courts were mercifully inclined, the same cannot be said of the police. A patrol catching a criminal in the act was liable to carry out sentence then and there and hang him without further trial. They were also allowed to inflict corporal punishment on their own authority for certain minor misdoings. It was they who usually and with their own hands operated the *cavalletto,* an instrument already mentioned and seldom idle for long. It was a simple, practical piece of machinery made of two humped wooden boards on four legs, sloping from back to front. The offender was placed in the 'saddle' and thrown head downwards to receive the requisite number of lashes on his naked back. The *cavalletto* was a permanent feature, standing like a sentinel policeman wherever large crowds met—near the market, where cheats could be dealt with on the spot, on the roads off the Corso during carnival, where it was handy for courtesans daring to wear masks, outside the theatres for troublemakers hissing the play (and a very good way too, as Santo Domingo says, to ensure that a feeble play did well). It could also help—if help is the word—the criminal condemned by a court in the normal way, with his crimes detailed on a notice round his neck and the bystanders counting as the cane fell twenty or fifty times on his shoulders to the sound of applause and *lazzi*; for the cheers would be just as loud for the kindness of some passing cardinal who exercised his right to stop the punishment 'with a wave of his hand'.

Imprisonment ranked as a lesser penalty than flogging and there were as many prisons in Rome as charitable foundations. The main government departments had their own and political prisoners went to Sant' Angelo where they were never very numerous, as we have seen. If the Pope were dying they were joined there by all persons held under common law, for in the fortress there was less chance to start a rising while government was more or less in abeyance during the interregnum and rash attempts were probable. Normally Sant' Angelo, like the Bastille in Paris, served chiefly as a place of detention for young men in love or in debt and a general worry to their families.

The biggest and best organized of Roman prisons were the *Carceri nuove*, where the occupants were segregated according to age and sex and, an innovation for the period, those awaiting trial did not mix with those condemned already. The penitential system of the Papal States was the most advanced in Europe and it was in Rome that the use of cells was first begun. Prisoners nowhere else enjoyed such comforts and were in fact so well treated that prison could hardly be thought of as a punishment at all. What was more, they never stayed there long, whatever their original sentence may have been. The popes took care to empty the gaols from time to time by general or partial amnesties, giving these in the end 'as often as blessings', a mercy which more than any other commended them to the love of their subjects.

Those guilty of graver misdeeds were sent to the galleys after being paraded through the town for the benefit of decent citizens, with crime and punishment placarded on their backs. The Roman records mention some such exhibition nearly every day. On April 27, 1727, the central figure was a tobacco-smuggler with a sign saying, *In galera per contrabando.*[1] The following October two young men were on show in front of the Gesù *Per irreverenza ed impertinenza usate in chiesa.*[2] One wretch was exposed to the jeers of worshippers throughout the services of Sunday, August 8, 1728, labelled, *Per bestemmie ereticali, dieci anni di galera.*[3] Such examples, taken at random, give some idea of the sort of thing that brought one to the galleys. Bigamists incurred the same penalty and were led through the streets on donkeys.

The *galleotti*, of course, never rowed a papal galley at sea, since the Pope possessed no fleet. They were not even cut off from ordinary life, as convicts were in other lands, but worked in the streets of Rome where passers-by were full of kindness and consideration and not a few would stop to shake hands and bestow a coin. It seemed to them unreasonable to admire a man as a killer and despise him on a road-gang.

The situation of the galley-slaves created a truly disturbing paradox. These men were well thought of, well treated, better fed and housed than most good-living workers, and paid for their work into the bargain, though their slackness was proverbial. Should one of them wish to visit his wife a warder took him home, where he was welcomed with enthusiasm and friends and neighbours met to greet him. One devoted wife, so the story went, arrayed her ten-year-old son in a complete galley-slave's outfit for the occasion so father and son could glory in the uniform together. The galleys, in short, furnished a dangerous example of punishment that was no punishment, a risk anyone could run without hesitation. The convict who grew tired of it all could, moreover, mend matters for himself by a simple escape or an easily-obtained remission of sentence.

And yet, despite the climate of indulgence, the number of crimes and of capital sentences meant that some executions had to be carried out and they were always famous occasions. There would be a curious announcement in the form of a notice, written in black on a white background and posted at the corner of the Via Lentari,

---

[1] Sentenced to the galleys for smuggling.
[2] For irreverencies and impertinent behaviour in church.
[3] Ten years in the galleys for heretical blasphemy.

not far from the Pasquino statue. It invited the faithful to earn plenary indulgence by prayer in the nearby church for the soul of the man to be executed at such and such a time and place, and also requested prelates, auditors of the Rota and cardinals to stay indoors that day. This was in case the criminal, meeting them on the way to the scaffold, should demand a pardon which could not be denied.

Contemporary opinion required that the spirit of Christianity should always soften the rigours of the law. In many churches the Holy Sacrament was exposed at dawn on the day of an execution and communion held for the wretched victim. The Pope himself said a long prayer for him in his private oratory. The brotherhood of the Misericordia, whose church was San Giovanni Decollato, made it their mission to comfort his last moments and help him to a Christian death. As soon as the time was fixed the prior and several of the brethren, in their white robes and hoods, went to the prison, urged him to penitence, wept and prayed with him. Should he refuse the sacraments they got the execution postponed. The Misericordia had the privilege of setting free one condemned criminal every year, a right which was occasionally granted to other confraternities for the feast of a patron saint. The fortunate beneficiary was led in procession to the brotherhood church of his deliverers where, instead of facing priest or altar, he knelt to one side, 'so that all might see his countenance'.

Some of the prisons held a ludicrous, if not blasphemous, charade before an execution. The condemned man was taken before an image of Christ which, by some mechanism, leaned from the cross, threw its arms round him and pressed him to its bosom. This, it was thought, might impart inner strength for the ordeal, and with the same intention a crowd of penitents followed the cart to the gallows, chanting the Miserere.

There was no set place for the scaffold. The Piazza del Ponte Sant' Angelo, the Campo dei Fiori, the square in front of the Pantheon, the Campo Vaccino (as the Forum was then called) and the square of St Peter's itself, served in turn as the scene of the grim ceremony. One execution in a hundred took place in the Piazza dei Santi Apostoli and the star criminals of the year would be reserved for carnival-time, when they were despatched in the Piazza del Popolo by executioners dressed as *pulcinèlli* and derisive jesting was traditionally the last earthly sound they heard. A death-sentence was carried out by beheading, a method which had finally replaced hanging and throat-cutting and been perfected by the use of various mechanical devices, forerunners of the guillotine.

The mob gathered to watch but, save in the outrageous time of carnival, were drawn less by sadistic curiosity than by anxiety for the victim's salvation. They wanted to know whether he had confessed, whether he had taken the sacrament. From all sides arose cries of 'God bless you; we are praying for you; we shall have Masses for your soul, we shall look after your wife, your mother, your children'. Once when a boy of sixteen protested his innocence on the gallows they shouted back in unison, 'Think of your soul, my child, nothing else matters'.

The practical Romans, however, would not neglect the moral and exemplary opportunities of capital punishment. They took their children to the spectacle and give them a slap as the head was severed. 'Take that,' they said, 'and just remember that's going to happen to lots of people better than you.' Which done, they went off and adored the Holy Sacrament.

CHAPTER FIVE

WOMEN AND LOVE

RACIAL TYPE AND COSTUME

They were a handsome people, sound and healthy. Young Romans always married among themselves, or looked no farther than their near neighbours in the countryside around, and so preserved the purity of their race. The type recalls that seen in classical medallions. The men were sturdy without being ponderous, proud of bearing with black hair and fervent eyes. Of the women Chateaubriand was to say, 'you would think, to see them, that antique statues of Juno or Pallas had come down from their pedestals to walk about the temples'. This was certainly true of some of the Roman women and applied to the Trastevere beauties who used to model for the painters—to those, at least, who appear as Olympian goddesses or allegorical personages in pictures of the Neo-Classical school. But the many eighteenth-century artists who portrayed the life of the people have another and much more varied female type to show us. Their women are far from displaying the chill loveliness, the hard-cut lines or severe mien of their sisters in the grand canvasses, and have none of their affected, formal air. Their chief attraction, on the contrary, lies in a sort of pliancy, in the free and easy look that Frenchmen such as Lalande thought, no doubt mistakenly, 'indecent'. All contemporary evidence—and modern observation too, for the race is little changed—agrees in praising their splendid, shining black hair, wonderful teeth (due, it seems, to the pure Roman water with its equable temperature) and their marvellous eyes, so brilliant they could burn with a glance. These eyes, their greatest charm, were never lowered. 'You cannot make them drop their eyes before yours,' says Dupaty, 'they have the boldest way of looking at men.' Their complexions had the fresh tint of health, glowing and warm and heightened with delicate colour: 'they always seem to be blushing slightly, which takes off from the brazen air'.

The beauty of Roman women flowered very early; they were roses, never rosebuds. A girl was in her bloom at fifteen. Overweight would blur line and feature soon enough; the pretty head, so cameo-fine, grow clumsy and the whole figure flabby. Only the shoulders improved in this thickening process, a fact of which the coquettes were well aware and took every advantage.

Costume varied a good deal with rank, but more in taste than in the quality of dress or ornament. The upper classes looked to Paris for their fashions. The time had been when France had imitated the elaborate Italian styles, but the current later set the other way and the rule of Paris was so absolute that the exquisites of the Settecento now insisted that their tailors use French cloth. Goldoni in his *Femine Puntigliose* shows a woman refusing to accept a dress because it is made of Italian material.

The men were as infatuated as their ladies with the approved modes of Versailles. They wore coats of French pattern, wide across the chest, with long flowered waistcoats, short breeches, silk stockings, and lace on their shirtfronts; they had swords and powdered wigs and tricorne hats. The only trouble was that they were twenty years behind the current Paris cut.

But it was different with the fashionable women, who were careful to keep up to date. Their panniered gowns were set off with gold and silver trimming, all their adornments were the latest thing from the trinket-shops of Paris. Upon their heads soared those amazing powdered coiffures, those confections of hair and plumes and birds, that nodded so gracefully at the château of Versailles. The French vogue was so much the rage that its very absurdities were adopted without hesitation, though some of them had a purely local fitness and made no sense at all beside the Tiber. Thus the Roman ladies went about *à l'enfant* whenever Marie Antoinette was pregnant; and in the days of the Revolution, little as its tendencies were relished here, headdresses were seen *à la justice* and *à l'humanité*, though never *à la guillotine*. That style got no farther than Milan.

The French liking for scent, heavy make-up and rouge struck no root in Rome. French women certainly overdid the use of rouge and here it was absolutely prohibited. A visiting Parisienne who persisted in the habit would quickly realize she was offending against convention and be forced to give in and do as the Romans did, though it usually meant a dreadful sacrifice. When the Duchesse de Nivernais was French ambassadress she took a long time before she could resign herself.

Their horror of rouge and their phobia against scent did not mean that Roman women wore no make-up. Creams by the dozen stood in rows on their dressing-tables and a perfumer in the Piazza di Trevi did very well with the assortment of thirty he sold in a charming box with pots in separate compartments. But such preparations were only slightly scented and so sparingly applied that they were never obvious. The possessors of those naturally lovely skins could afford a light hand with make-up.

As for scent itself, the ladies of Rome wore none, perhaps in reaction from Renaissance times when the craze for perfumes came from Spain and they wore far too many. Now the craze was dead and Frenchwomen arriving drenched in musk and ambergris had to stop using it or find that they were definitely unwelcome in the great world.

Society women spent a lot of money on dress and competed, as they always do, for leadership of fashion. The burden on a husband's income was enormous. Two hundred crowns—perhaps thirty thousand new francs—were often given for a ball dress, sometimes more. This may not seem too terrible to patrons of the Paris *haute couture*, but it was enormous in days when a hundred crowns bought a pair of fine carriage-horses or paid the coachman two years' wages, and such comparisons, however arbitrary, are our only way of forming some idea of conditions.

These *toilettes*, in which the great ladies appeared as so many marquises by Fragonard or Boucher, were full-dress affairs, kept for gala evenings at the theatre or elegant *conversazioni*. For every-day, women shed their irksome finery together with the whalebone corsets that made them look so stiff and unnatural. But they still wanted the Parisian look and what they called their 'casual clothes', too, were Paris-inspired. This was why women of the upper class seemed so very different, in gait and contour, from the middle- and working-class women who were faithful to traditional local costume.

The difference was quite as marked among the men. If they were not of the nobility, and not in canonicals, they wore the brief velvet coat, often merely slung across the shoulder, and broad bright sash, with breeches to match the coat and coming below the knee, coloured stockings and shoes with wide buckles. The most popular kind of hat was the high round sugarloaf, such as pos-tillions on the *diligences* used to have in France, always of a brownish grey. Some trades demanded special headgear. The men who drove the wine-carts had pointed hats with cocks' plumes, and labourers took pride in their berets with tassels dangling to the shoulder.

There was more variety of dress for women than men among the working folk, a variety more of colour than style. Invariable was the beribboned velvet bodice, slashed at the sides to show the bright laced silk beneath. Sleeves were wide at the shoulder and narrowed to a tight wristband. The silk skirt came to the ankles to show embroidered stockings and buckled slippers. Hair would be held in place by the wide tortoiseshell comb and silver pins big enough for daggers. (And as daggers they were sometimes found among those votive offerings at the feet of the Madonna where the repentant sinners left them.) Plaits often hung in a green silken net to the shoulder. Women went about bare-headed, putting on a small muslin veil for church and a broad grey felt hat for the country, the sort one sees in old Castelli wine-labels or the costume-drawings of Pinelli.

Gay already in coloured material, women's apparel was also set off by very bright trimming. There was lace on the bodice and an embroidered apron often covered the front of the dress. Heavy gold ear-rings were worn and big necklaces of gold or coral, and the young girls put flowers in their hair. All Roman women, even the humblest, took trouble over their appearance. It was after siesta-time when they dressed up, but then life and colour came into the streets as they preened on their balconies or strolled along the Corso.

LOVE AND MARRIAGE

As might be expected love, with all its attendant charms and complications, played a great part in the lives of people who so delighted to enjoy themselves in every way. Conditions were ideal for profligacy: idle women, men of all classes with nothing to do, and both paying more attention to the externals of religion than to moral law. Fashionable society, too, had set its fashionable example. The smart Romans were in the grip of a Gallomania that looked beyond the costume and coiffure of Versailles to include the manners of the French nobility and their passion for amuse-ment. Louis XIV's reign came to its staid, strict end in 1715 and the reaction in Paris was an outburst of licence which Roman society imitated in the craving for distraction. It was a craving that spread to all levels and grew so strong as the century advanced that Venus, as Louis Madelin put it, became 'the second sovereign of Rome after St Peter'.

This liberty of manners reached such a pitch that the French themselves, who became much steadier after their Regency days, were to marvel at it. Marmont, Napoleon's future general, came to Rome in 1790 and said in his memoirs,

'Roman society, I found, was very gay and devoted exclusively to amusement. The freedom of the women passes all belief and their husbands permit it, speaking cheerfully and without embarrassment of their wives' lovers. I heard M. Falconnieri talk of his wife in a quite incredible way; he made a distinction between possessiveness and true feeling, which alone meant anything to him. In my role of young man and foreigner I was only too glad to benefit by the consequences.'

The consequences, indeed, of so accommodating an attitude in romantic matters were defined in a manner cruelly precise by another visitor. He says of the women of Rome, 'My God! You have to get up early to find them by themselves.'

It was no joke. Libertinage and adultery had become accepted features of life. The Church might condemn them from the pulpit but they had its tacit toleration as inevitable results of human nature. Dupaty, amazed at such indulgence, heard this explanation from a priest: 'It is for religion's sake we are lenient about love; people would forsake religion if we were more severe. We have tried it more than once, with most discouraging results.' Another said, 'The compulsory celibates have to be considered; there are so many of them here and it would be dangerous to dishearten them.'

Ecclesiastical thunder was reserved for harlotry. Not only had the courtesans fallen from the high social standing they enjoyed at the Renaissance, but their trade was now hampered by stringent regulations. Advent, Lent and Holy Week were close seasons, as were Sundays, festivals and fast-days. The police were allowed to confiscate and sell for themselves the furniture and clothing of offenders and the monstrous privilege made them eager watchdogs. Year by year the Church produced its fantastic prohibitions, growing ever more severe against the prostitutes. They had long been forbidden to wear disguise at carnival time, but soon they might not ride in carriages during the day nor emerge from their houses at night. Mere vexation was the object of rules like 'No talking together', which, it seems, was meant 'to remove occasion for exhorting each other to debauch'. More seriously, they were not admitted to communion, nor buried in holy ground. They might not make wills and their property went to girls' convents. Thus the Church put the prostitute beyond the social pale and outside the fellowship of Christians while its tolerance of dissolute behaviour in every other guise certainly encouraged the lowering of contemporary standards.

It may have been because of this tolerance, perhaps too because of the opportunities and outright complicity to be found on all sides, but love, in this time and place, was rather different from love anywhere else. Climate and conventions gave it a character all its own. There were few obstacles to toughen it, little disapproval to make it seem more precious, and so, unless it were a real affair of the heart (which it often was), love was only a whim, a pastime. Always, however, it was treated as a natural phenomenon with no mystery about it and freely discussed, like rain or good weather. More freely, indeed, with nobody beating about the bush or striving for decency. 'If you can say anything to a woman, you can say it all.'

Woman was in any case quite well prepared for anything she might hear. The mother of any *ragazzina* of fifteen spoke openly before her of the joys, sorrows and distresses of her own love-life and mentioned with no more reserve the state of the girl's affections. The neighbours were told all about it—'My daughter can't eat or sleep, she's in love', as though she were merely in a fever. And girls were very often in love, from puberty onwards. They all had their young men who passed to and fro under their windows and gave them something to dream about. Their mothers did nothing to curb the silly infatuations and would even lend a hand if need arose. One of them, when her daughter fell ill, finished a love letter for her: *Finisco io la lettera della mia figlia, la quale non ha potuto andar avanti per un gran male.*[1] But let us make no mistake; convention set a limit to such idylls, and a very narrow one, and these obliging mammas took care that it was not exceeded. What was called *fare all' amore* was only flirting of the most innocent kind, an intricate game of stolen glances and little, secret presents.

[1] 'My daughter is very ill and could write no more, so I am finishing her letter.' The story comes from Gasparo Gozzi's memoirs.

The girl who allowed a man to speak to, or, still worse, walk beside her in the street was throwing away her reputation. An admirer was permitted nothing beyond the *discorso,* or converse, at the window or the doorway—the *lenes sub nocte susurri* of Horace.

It was a fictitious sort of loving, but the girls were perfectly happy with it. The five or six successive romances they could thus enjoy were as entertaining as a novel, and afterwards, if all went well, they would be married. A mother's chief care was, in fact, to teach them how to get a husband, no easy skill in a town swarming with professional bachelors, and five women to every eligible man. Speed, too, was essential. To be an old maid was a disgrace and one that could very soon befall, long before what the French consider the crucial age of twenty-five. Success lay mainly in arrival at the altar pure, if not in heart (the heart's virginity being more difficult to preserve), at least in body; and this was required by male possessive instinct rather than for any moral reason. The sky changed once a girl was married. Then the most barefaced conduct could not damage her good name and women did as they liked, regardless of public opinion and secure from ridicule. Hearing nothing spoken of but love, surrounded by bad example and enticement, they brought a kind of innocence to immorality. Constraint and even conventionality were as foreign to them as deceit. What transparent simplicity in the refusal to dance, *'Il mio amico non lo vuole'*—'my lover says I mustn't!'

Marriage was considered indissoluble: *Quod Deus conjunxit homo non separet.* Yet though this venerable pronouncement in canon law remained valid, many marriages were annulled for all that, usually on the grounds of the husband's impotence. On this subject, and for the purposes of the inquiry, there were recognized distinctions. It need not be *erga omnes*; a 'relative and particular' impotence sufficed. A man might prove fruitfully victorious elsewhere; it was enough that he feel aversion towards his wife and be unable to consummate his marriage. Such an aversion, it was accepted, could declare itself over a period of time and demonstrably fertile unions might therefore be annulled after the birth of several children. But this happy outcome was to be reached only after long, expensive lawsuits with all their attendant scandal.

A much simpler solution existed for domestic troubles. Marriage, among the aristocracy and the comfortable middle class, was the result of negotiation, turning always upon some point of family advantage. Affection had nothing to do with it and couples were as a rule ill-matched in tastes and age. It was no more than an institution for settling one's children and one's property. The well-born young man, being incapable of taking a solemn or even a serious view of life, found this outlook harmonized exactly with his own. Had you suggested to a Roman that he love one woman all his days, he would have objected that you were removing a good part of his reasons for living at all. When a bridal procession entered the church the thought of lasting fidelity never crossed a single mind. It could happen, of course, that a man was in love with the girl he married and his situation was then that of a lover in regard to a mistress, but this would soon pass. Faithfulness may not have been entirely unknown but it was certainly not in fashion and a pair were strangers very soon. They came to an amicable agreement and went their separate ways, neither suffering from what the other did.

And this inevitable break marked the moment for a new character to come upon the scene—the *cavaliere servente* or cicisbeo, who gave perfect form and balance to the marriage. Cicisbeism, which spread to the whole of Italy and was current until the nineteenth century, was introduced in Rome by the gentlemen who came with the Borgias from Spain. Usually of the same age and rank as the husband, the cicisbeo was often some poor friend or relation, though he could, too, be a possible financial benefactor. He bore the reassuring style of *amico della casa*. This courtly personage, like someone from the days of chivalry, served his lady in the most attentive manner, escorting her to church and squiring her round the town, standing ready to offer his hand and whisper in her ear at parties. (The name cicisbeo is possibly derived from the word for 'whisper'.) The *cavaliere servente* cocooned his partner in delicate care and small politenesses. He brought a pleasant atmosphere into her life and protected her from worry, and from herself, and other people. He kept her happy and amused. He followed her like a shadow from the time she got up, when he was often allowed in the room, until she went to bed at night. At this point, since married couples did not then sleep alone, the husband took over, having left her to her gallant's care all day. That valued auxiliary might have pulled up the lady's garter or 'run his finger inside her bodice to smooth down her chemise' and her husband might, inadvertently, have seen him doing so, but he would never dream of raising an objection. He was only too delighted that someone else should pay his wife the attentions he himself was lavishing elsewhere.

The man for this equivocal role needed a battery of talents. Fosco gives a list:

'To wear the latest fashions well and know at least the titles of the most talked-about novels from France; always to carry round a stock of nick-nacks and a spare brush and comb; to make a perfect bow and dance a faultless minuet; to gamble so that she can win, and lose a lot of money in the process; know all about everything that doesn't matter and be perpetually disengaged.'

Considerable liberties and near-surrender were the prerogatives of the cicisbeo. Did he ask anything more than this *amitié amoureuse*? Society, by general consent, emphatically agreed that he did not. The *cavaliere servente* was by definition a gentleman, no husband would court ridicule by the display of jealousy. One married man expounded the ethics of cicisbeism thus: 'Here in Rome it would be shameful for a woman to sit beside her coachman on the box, but we know it is the English way and if we see an English woman doing so we do not blame her. There is no disgrace in it, for her.' Another, when asked how he could be sure, in the circumstances, that his children were his own, wisely replied, 'It is enough that they are born into my family.' Those bold enough to claim that there was no smoke without a fire stood revealed as unsubtle spirits, incapable of appreciating the beauty of half-tones. Charles de Brosses, with his sly Gallic wit and coarse Burgundian relish, saw the cicisbei clasping their ladies closely, 'with not a hairsbreadth between them', and was sure they were 'ten times more married to them than their husbands were'. To which charge public opinion responded with one voice that such liaisons were so open and lasted so long that of course they were innocent.

Lasting they certainly were and everyone, beginning with the husbands concerned, did all they could to foster them. The want of a cicisbeo was very awkward for a married man, forcing him personally to offer his wife the civilities that made life tolerable. It was an axiom that 'husbands knew nothing about love' and the man who wished to cut any sort of figure did well to keep this tenet in mind. Let him arrive anywhere with his own wife, or himself hand her into her box at the theatre, and he was in a fair way to being considered tied to her apron-strings and utterly foolish. If the lady and her cicisbeo had a quarrel it was the husband's duty to reconcile them in the name of domestic concord. Should a cicisbeo tire of his bonds and withdraw, the lady received visits of condolence from her friends and her husband shared in the affliction. It was all an accepted element in life; cicisbeism was the natural outcome of an artificial morality engendered by idleness and inertia.

The Church, as we have said, did not expressly condemn it. Among the highest ranks it was as open as the day. Princess Braschi, leader of Roman fashion, was to be seen escorted to church by her attendant, while the prince her husband followed behind and never offered her his arm. Quite often a woman was authorized to have a *cavaliere servente* by her marriage contract in a clause no more unusual than others by which girls sought to protect themselves against what they considered the infringement of their liberty in married life. Most common is one binding a man not to make his wife live in the country, which to a Roman matron would have been the depth of horror.

The tolerance of the Church did not extend, of course, to marital infidelity. There was in Holy Week a special sermon, delivered in private and to married women only, warning them against this sin. The preacher read a long list of the 'transgressions, great and small, their sex might possibly commit and each of his flock might search her conscience for what applied to her'. The high-born ladies who heard this sermon at the church in the Piazza Sciarra on the Corso had to come out and face their lackeys and coachmen, all giggling together at the sight of their woe-begone expressions. But the lecture awakened scruples only of a fleeting nature, that cost the *cavalieri serventi* very little effort to dispel.

Cavalieri serventi should not be thought of as a purely upper-class amenity for they were found also in the middle and even in the lower ranks. It was the smart thing for any woman to be seen on the Corso with her cicisbeo and every woman had one, the shopkeeper and the hairdresser with the best. It seemed better to do without bread than do without a *cavaliere servente,* notes the *abate* Chiari. The institution had adapted itself at all levels and middle-class wives often employed several of these attendants at a time. Most adroit of all were the ladies who had three, *il bello, il brutto* and *il buono*—one for love and one for errands and one who paid the bills.

Foreign observers have left many accounts, humorous or reproachful according to taste, of the libertinage of Rome at this period. Mostly it took the form of adultery, since women, for reasons we have stated, kept out of mischief until after they were married. But marriage set them on the royal road to licence.

Madame de Staël was to consider 'English infidelity itself more moral than Italian marriage'. And indeed in the eighteenth century adultery was flaunted in Rome with arrogance and pride. Custom encouraged it and the men indeed provoked it by some of the things they did. On this point a Frenchman named Legouz has an illuminating tale. He had, at some social entertainment, been expressing admiration for a certain Signora Montorio, although she was admittedly too thin, too dark and scarred with the small-pox. But he thought these defects largely compensated by gaiety and wit and a glance that went, as he put it, 'straight to the heart'. He detailed her charms to the listeners and added, 'That is the mistress I want. I have not as yet met Signore Montorio, but I intend to see a lot of him, in his home; and I shall be so very polite that he'll have to be a real boor if he doesn't ask me to dinner twice a week.' Scarcely had he finished than a stranger stepped from the shadows—Count Montorio himself, who gravely declared, 'I have never had any illusions about my wife, Monsieur. God made her ugly, she was ugly when I married her and so we go on. It never occurred to me that anyone would fall in love with her and I really am delighted that a clever, fastidious man should come so far and find her attractive, more so than the beauties, even. Pray be so good as to dine with me tomorrow.' The result of course was obvious.

With husbands behaving in so detached a fashion, wives were certainly encouraged into amorous intrigue and the cicisbeo's presence could not always discount a handsome face and engaging manners. Cash and influence, too, were powerful weapons of seduction and Montesquieu notes that men who sold their wives for money and patronage were all too numerous. Another result of the prevailing indulgence was that a lady with a lover rarely tried to hide the fact. Love was something that happened; one could not control it and it gave one certain rights. Only in Rome could a woman who, like all her kind, would certainly pride her-self on birth and breeding instruct her servants to turn away callers with, '*La Signora è innamorata*'. Pleasingly enough, the other aspect of this freedom was the duration of the love affairs and the constancy more or less demanded by public opinion. It was excusable and even laudable for a woman to have a lover, but it would not do for her to change him very often. A short liaison did the lady no credit; she was then 'a weak creature who didn't know her own mind' and unfaithfulness was frowned upon. The coquetry of French women, some of whom collected a whole train of adorers, was considered the height of indecency. Such things a Roman husband never would permit. He was little prone to jealousy, as we have seen, but his wife might have a lover only if she stuck to him.

These ways, once again, were not confined to good society but extended to the common people, though here immorality was more obviously a matter of profit. No less than among their betters, marriages were based on interest. Poor girls were often given dowries by some brotherhood or charity organization and, says Charles de Brosses, 'let a girl of the people get the patronage of the bastard son of some cardinal's apothecary and she can count on five or six dowries from five or six different churches and promptly loses all desire to learn to sew and spin'. With the lure of ready cash she would find someone to marry her easily enough, but the money was soon squandered by a young lady who fancied fine dresses and gold necklaces and never thought of doing a hand's turn. The poor man would have all their expenses to find while she sat at the window and watched the scene outside. This exercise produced its own temptations and soon the husband found it quite natural for his wife to contribute to the budget by the not inexpedient means of a little judicious harlotry. 'My wife wants dresses, let her earn her dresses.' This basic, underlying argument was admitted by all and carried no tincture of disgrace. They acknowledged it even in Trastevere, a sort of separate nation where they took love very seriously. There the man who, more out of vanity than jealousy, would kill a wife suspected of having a lover in their own world, cheerfully accepted the fact that she received trifling sums from a gentleman, or was managing to place the home under the wing of some distinguished person thought to have local influence. There were plenty of skilled procurers about to make all the arrangements and many a Roman family lived on the attractions of the lady of the house. The complacency shown by husbands and fathers is partly accounted for by the great extremes of poverty and riches. Where the huge majority were very poor and a tiny minority held all the money and power, gifts that meant nothing to the givers looked like the wealth of Midas to the needy recipients. Coming as dowries they figured comfortingly as family insurance;

Montesquieu is not alone in telling us how rich and important men with low-born pretty mistresses would pay them off with a dowry.

But these evil courses were not universal, nor genuine feeling impossible to find. True love existed in Rome as everywhere else. There was a great deal of laxity, all the same, leading perilously to moral disorder and even to superstitions of the most extraordinary naïveté. The *Bocca della Verità*, the big moon-face under the portico of Santa Maria in Cosmedin, was believed to be the surest instrument for confounding a suspicious husband. The stone mouth would snap shut, they said, if an unfaithful wife put her hand inside, so anyone with a suspicious husband had only to confound him by this simple means. Time was when Roman women were required to prove their chastity by grasping hot iron or walking over burning coals. What progress had they seen along the paths of tolerance!

CHAPTER SIX

RELIGION

FAITH, BELIEF AND SUPERSTITION

Religion in the eighteenth century bore once again the character it used to have before the Reformation: it was accommodating. In 1785 Dupaty rightly calls the Romans those who, of all people, fear least and hope the most. The temperature of their faith, he adds, is 'mild as their own skies'. The young Casanova observed on his arrival that no other Catholic city pestered one about religion less. He likened Romans to 'workers in a tobacco field, who can help themselves to as much as they desire'. Mainly they helped themselves to their own good pleasure, for theirs was not the nature to embrace a regimented existence. They did not become involved in too many scruples, nor fall in with practices of a demanding kind. They were innocent of hypocrisy nevertheless, and fundamentally religious; but they happened not to be Puritan northerners, afraid of annoying God if they went for a walk on Sunday.

This liberty was theirs by virtue of the custom of starting afresh after every fall, so that sin never weighed heavily upon them. A good Easter confession wiped the whole slate clean. They were on a footing of the greatest ease and amity with the priesthood, who had always been free of their houses and joined in their family life, and from this intimacy they extracted a little reasonable give and take. It is only fair to add that some of the priests seemed to encourage the idea, shepherding their sheep on the principle of 'Do as you please but tell us about it afterwards'. This process would cancel out the past and look after the present at negligible cost, while as for the future, things were simpler still. The Romans were convinced that every saint in heaven was busily watching over every tiny detail of their lives. They therefore consigned all things to this holy protectorate and put in special requests for emergencies, taking care to petition a saint only within his or her proper sphere of influence. San Rocco guarded them against the plague and Sant' Emido from earthquake, Santa Bibiena cured aching heads and San Biagio diseases of the throat. St Andrew warded off apoplexy, St Anne assisted women in childbirth. Every saint in the calender had his own clearly defined speciality and even his preferred intermediaries. It was well known, for instance, that San Luigi da Gonzaga passed on messages to God only if they were endorsed by a Jesuit and so letters for him were left in a particular box at the Gesù. The malicious declared that this made the good fathers free of domestic secrets, but people wrote a great deal to the saints, all the same. Of all holy persons, the Bambino at the Aracoeli received the largest mail; even now letters pile up daily at his feet from every part of the world. The Bambino is an olivewood figure of the Infant Jesus whose face was painted by miraculous means. He is richly dressed and the most gorgeous carriage in Rome is kept at his disposal. In the eighteenth century the wealthy made sure he came to their bedsides when they were gravely ill and two Franciscans escorted the wonder-working image in its splendid vehicle. The sufferer's fate could be read in the face of the Child. If it remained pink he could hope for a cure, but if it turned the colour of ashes the case might be considered desperate. Whatever the verdict, image and bodyguard stayed with the sick man (who was paying all expenses) until he was either dead or better. When the Bambino was not out on a mission the faithful in numbers climbed the 124 steps to the Aracoeli on their knees to beg his assistance, finding it completely natural to bring their problems to him. It was the same with all the saints. People were on such happy terms with them that they would ask blessing on questionable dealings and on their wildest flights of fancy as confidently as for more respectable projects. Ticket-holders expected a lucky *terno* in the lottery, girls expected husbands and lovers a more friendly attitude from mistresses.

But the great popular devotion was directed to Mary the Mother of God. The people thought of all the heavenly powers as having bodies and faces and so tended to disregard the Holy Ghost, whom they could not picture in bodily form. What face, moreover, could captivate like the Virgin's? The Jesuits, who knew all roads into the human heart, had noticed long ago that young men prayed more fervently before a beautiful Madonna, and this was true of everyone. Our Lady was worshipped in a frenzy of tenderness or, as the common phrase went, *con amore*. She had seventy-four churches in Rome, to say nothing of chapels in private houses, and even these were not enough for her adorers. Nowhere in the city was she absent, from the palace to the poor hovel where, painted in relief in her small niche, she had replaced the 'good old pagan Hermes'. The eye encountered her at every turn, on the walls of shanties and carved above noble doorways, and at nightfall a group was always gathered praying at her feet. She was in the courtyards and the corridors, in cattle-sheds and stables; she graced the shop and tavern. No work was done, no enterprise or business launched, but sheltered under the image of Mary.

Domestic Madonnas and those in the street might be simple things, but in the churches they were magnificent. Richest of all was the Madonna del Parto, shining still with her diamonds, rubies, topazes and pearls in Sant' Agostino, bowing under the weight of gems, with the wall invisible behind her for its incrustation of precious, heart-shaped votive offerings. It is a treasury that outshines the Bernini high altar, dazzling as that is, and quite eclipses the little-visited tomb of Santa Monica.

In the popular faith of the day Mary was the chief power in heaven. Everything came from her, it was she who made the world. A dying man was said to be on the point of seeing her, a beggar denied alms but blessed in her name gave thanks as though for golden generosity. The civil law protected her. When two peasants came to trial on the same day, one for insulting Mary and one for killing his mother, the same court gave each the same term at the galleys and it is fair to assume that the matricide got home before the blasphemer. But custom took care of her in every way and she did not need the law. One true story among thousands will illustrate the veneration in which she was held. About 1750 a widow left her jewels to the Madonna del Parto and the monks of the church had hung them round the neck, ears and arms of the holy image, when the human heirs contested the will and won their case. Those good fathers neither troubled to appeal, nor set any long drawn-out legal machinery in motion to invalidate the new verdict. To the family demanding the old lady's jewels they said simply, 'Come and get them.' And no one was found brave enough to despoil the Madonna, the law officers themselves refusing, 'with the sign of the cross', to lay a finger on her.

This strong public feeling against both profanation and mere irreverence sprang from a devotion that was universal. During this century no breath of impiety would blow on the sturdy Roman faith from the free-thinking *philosophes* in France, Rome would produce no inquiring cynics. If the practice of religion could, from being so much a matter of course, become a habit, it was nevertheless a habit so deeply rooted that it entered the people's inmost soul. Here must lie the explanation of their apparent indifference in church; no one showed much emotion, even at great ceremonies. And yet these drawing-room churches, those opera-house ceremonies, were the vehicle of a religious concept that had a mystical value and grandeur of its own; this voluptuous worship suited the needs and temperament of its practitioners. Movement, splendour and outward lavishness stirred their imagination. The Romans sought in their churches the reflection of eternal bliss, the exact presentment, even, of anticipated paradise. They did not come to hear about penitence and meditation, piety on the Jansenist model was not for them. These were people who lived through their senses, to whom an etherealized faith could mean nothing. They had to hear and see and touch religion. Its services must be imposing, the papal benediction fall to the sound of trumpets and the roar of cannon upon the city and the world. These ideas did not affect the humble devotions offered to the Virgin at the dark streetcorner, at the little railing with the consecrated flowers, but the mainstay of faith had to be something visible, something one could listen to, something concrete.

Non-Italian Catholics who had felt the fascinations of harshness and taken the tinge of Puritanism were offended by this type of facile worship, with its avoidance of all that was vague and abstract. To them it seemed a perversion of the true spirit of religion. They did not understand what popular religion was, nor how the people brought their spontaneous interpretation to its dogma, alive and instinct with poetry. Not until Renan, who found that 'the Madonnas conquered him', was anyone to recognize this 'unique gift for the ideal' in the religious life of Rome.

But the preachers seized its spirit to perfection, for they, too, addressed the senses. A sermonizer at the Aracoeli, urging his congregation to the Lenten fast, helpfully indicates the best recipes for cod and macaroni. Another, enraged to see the audience drifting away to puppet-shows, brandishes a large crucifix, shouting *'Ecco il vero pulcinèlla'*.[1] One would lay his flat cap on the pulpit's edge and harangue it as though it were Jean Jaques Rousseau in person. 'And what have you to say, my fine Genevan philosopher?' he would demand, and when it had nothing to say he claimed an easy

[1] 'Behold the true Punchinello!'

victory. 'You are convinced, I see,' he cried and clapped it on his head again.

The holy orators had their own technique, with voices running the gamut from bass to falsetto and a performance constantly animated by physical activity. They made great play with their caps, taking them on and off like lightning. They went to and fro in their pulpits 'like pendulums' from one side to the other and every gesture was exaggerated. The Capuchins were said to be the most demonstrative, rending their beards, beating their hands together and uttering frightful groans. Dogs were never seen at a Capuchin sermon, for they all ran out of church.

Could any Roman have resisted so agreeable a faith? So little demanding, so lenient towards backsliders? On one thing only did it really insist, the performance of the duties at Easter. Everybody confesses at Easter, notes a traveller, 'even the confessors'. And everybody, willy-nilly, took communion. The priests lived closely enough to their people to know just who was absent from the Lord's table and the list was published on St Bartholomew's Day, accompanied by a decree of excommunication for all who remained obdurate. They were, in the circumstances, very few. It was anything but creditable for a pastor to acknowledge rebels among his flock and all laboured to return blank lists. They did this mostly by persuasion, though other and surer methods might be resorted to. The surest of all was revealed by a Roman parish priest:

'Personally,' he said, 'I never have a list to send in, but if I have warned a parishioner in private and publicly summoned him and he still neglects his duty, I have him sent to prison. I kept one inside for six weeks last year and he communicated in the end.'

But everyone in Rome was so religious-minded that coercion was pointless and such persuasion extremely rare.

It is not surprising to find that this compliant faith was unsevere towards superstition. The clergy seem to have been tolerant on the grounds that folk 'swallowed a little religion with the rest', as one of them put it. But some of the popular amendments were certainly questionable, as when Christ was seriously criticized for having delayed His baptism in Jordan until the age of thirty. There were also peculiar interpretations of the Bible, such as that the money-changers were driven from the Temple to teach us the somewhat original lesson that God forgives every sin save that of desecration.

Secular things came to play an increasing part in the festivals of the Church. When the junketings of Easter drew near the butchers made figures of Moses in lard for their shops and Madonnas all of butter appeared in bowers of garlic sausages. A huge show of eatables at Epiphany turned the Aracoeli steps into one great groaning board with every conceivable gastronomic allure, and Easter Day was marked by a vast consumption of *zuppa inglese* to the glory of Holy Church. And it was neither Father Christmas nor St Nicholas who came with toys for the children on Twelfth Night, but a non-religious fairy creature known as the Befana.

The power of direct intervention in human affairs was extended, in superstitious belief, beyond the saints to other people, some benevolent and others, more numerous, who brought ill fortune with the evil eye. This dark force of the *jettatura* was averted by carrying a small horn-shaped piece of coral and pointing it at any such unlucky person one might meet. For the *jettatori* could be recognized and were themselves aware of their peculiar abilities and much embarrassed by them. So Stendhal relates of the Duke of Bisagno that 'when a peasant caught sight of him and dropped a large basket of cherries, the duke rushed up, crying, "I never looked at you, my friend, I do assure you" '.

Spell-makers were feared and the mysterious portents of coming calamity dreaded even more. A wall collapsing, a tree uprooted by the wind, a swift rise of the Tiber, were all signs from above. If a clock struck of its own accord, as did that of San Biagio during the night of September 2, 1726, the whole town fell into mortal apprehension. This kind of thing led straight to infantile credulity and the belief that nothing ever happened except by miracle. Miracles, consequently, were apparent on all sides. Few Madonnas were not credited with miraculous intervention; they had all at some time moved their eyes or sighed or sung a litany. Few crucifixes had not shed their tears of blood. The thing might be a prophecy of misfortune or a token of protection, but it was in any case a miracle; people flocked to see it and all the local wineshops prospered on the proceeds. Until the day, that is, when religious authority signified its disapproval, for it had seen too many of these marvels and was usually sceptical. But still the neighbours went on believing in their Madonna's miracle and stood ready to deal with anyone who cast a doubt. Not that anyone dreamed of doing so and, as for the priest, if he had reservations he kept them to himself for fear he might offend her.

Popular imagination would occasionally fix upon some object whose miraculous nature the Church, unconvinced or even hostile to begin with, had to accept in the end. It was thus that popular insistence made a saint of the French ascetic Benoît Joseph Labre, whom they considered an intermediary with God. Dressed in rags and wallowing in a carefully cultivated and repulsive state of filth, he spent his time making countless Stations of the Cross in the churches and mortified his flesh in all imaginable ways. An exemplary love for all created things included the very lice on his body and when he died of starvation on the steps of Santa Mari dei Monti on April 16, 1783, a spontaneous wave of disturbance swept through Rome. He had been a saint, he had worked miracles. Multitudes came to cut scraps from his shroud and pull the hairs from his head and beard for relics and soldiers had to guard the body. The fact that it had not stiffened, too, was held to be miraculous. His funeral on Easter Day was accompanied by astonishing demonstrations which the Church was unable to control. When the Pope allowed the process of canonization to begin well in advance of the specified canonical delays, he was admitting that the miracles ascribed to Benoît Labre were true.

Less discerning, perhaps, was the vogue for Cagliostro, but that bizarre personality was the talk of the town when, having escaped justice in Paris for his part in the Queen's Necklace affair, he came to Rome and fell into the arms of the Inquisition. Cagliostro was an immoderate creature, crook, wizard and adventurer in one, claiming to have spoken with Ramases of Egypt and watched the trial and crucifixion of Christ; he remembered the fire in Nero's reign, he had seen the first crusaders off to the Holy Land. Here there was to be no saint-making, but endless speculation as to his relations with the devil. It was the undeniable whiff of sulphur that lent some faint, unfortunate import to the masonic movement which English Protestants in Rome had previously tried, unsuccessfully, to establish.

RELIGIOUS FESTIVALS

The festivals of religion, as was natural in a 'religious' capital, were many and magnificent. Including Sundays, they numbered officially 150 at the beginning of the century and though they became fewer as the influence of Jansenism increased, there were still 120 listed in 1770, a liberal slice of the year for holidays. All these were holidays of obligation, when no work might be done. On others, the traditional feasts of some one church or district, the faithful could work if they wished, but it was improbable that they took advantage of any such concession. All the trade guilds, too, held ceremonies of a religious nature in honour of the various crafts.

Festivals always caused much excitement and drew enormous crowds. People supported them, of course, as good Catholics, but also because they loved parade and merrymaking. It was certainly a holiday atmosphere that was generated on these occasions in the vast basilicas. Dupaty catches the right note in his journal: 'I heard the opera called Vespers and saw the lighting-display of Benediction', phrases which exactly evoke the great ceremonies. And these brilliant ceremonies used to full advantage the elegance of Baroque, revealed in all its splendour of gilding and jasper and precious marbles as the colour and pageantry of divine service unfolded in the jubilant light. Unknown here was the dusk that fits the Gothic shrines, or the downright gloom of some of the chapels in Paris. The radiant Roman light reached into every corner and made the forests of candles superfluous, though 14,000 crowns' worth were consumed at one daytime celebration in St Peter's. The churches shone with great stands of tapers, the altars flashed like huge hearth-fires. It was all rather like a party, or a gala night at the opera.

The theatrical element was seen again in the feast-day decoration of a church's internal architecture, in the velvet hangings and tapestries stretched along the walls and pillars, in the massy gold ornament of choir and altar. The floor would be strewn with flowers and often servants waited at the door with posies for the women as they came in. The posies might be special offerings from the wealthy local patrons of the church who, in their more chivalrous moments, liked to present them in the name of some lady whom they wished to compliment. Can it be true, as some claim, that the congregation was ever given ices and light refreshment? One is tempted to believe it, so casually did they behave as services went on.

And the services went on amid the greatest confusion and disorder, with everybody pushing towards the front and quarrelling frequently for places, so that their noisy outcries interrupted the undertone of private conversation. New arrivals hurried to their friends with lengthy greetings and people hailed each other across the benches. Nor was all this agitation a tuning-up process only; it continued throughout the Mass, though comparative silence would just prevail for the elevation of the Host. The rest of the time they all fidgeted and talked and strolled about and paid no attention to what was going on. The fact of being in a holy place had not the slightest effect on what they said or did. It might as well have been a theatre.

The accompanying music strengthened this impression. Several orchestras would perform in turn and listeners clustered round to hear what was often a secular programme, for sacred music had no monopoly in church, where operatic overtures and even comic opera were played without misgiving. Foreigners were apt to find this rather shocking and Bergeret was taken aback by the light selection when he went with Cardinal de Bernis to a service at the Lateran. 'Full of pretty things,' he wrote, 'but none of the concord of true church music I was hoping for. This,' he adds, 'is no place to come in search of that sanctity whose very source we might expect to find here'. No one was helped towards solemn thoughts by the behaviour of the women, either. Those who did not drive up in their carriages as though to a playhouse were at any rate escorted to and from the door by a footman, often specially engaged for the job at ten *baiocchi* a day, and their attire was hardly sombre. At most they put a filmy veil over their hair, but never concealed their faces and indeed gazed round 'with the utmost boldness' at the men.

It was only as Easter drew near that church services ceased to be occasions for the senses rather than the spirit. Holy Week in Rome was the great magnet for Christians all over the world and drew a huge concourse of pilgrims. A new emotion descended on the worshippers, an atmosphere of reflection and austerity upon the city. Entertainments were closed, the streets fell silent. Papal troops carried their arms reversed, the drums of the guard were slackened and gave out a muffled sound. All was penitence. The women wore black. Their trinkets and jewellery disappeared, their lovers were sent away and for the time being the men, too, forwent their pleasure-seeking. The holy water stoups were empty in the churches, the altars bare of candles. People of all classes flocked to the confessionals.

When Palm Sunday came the Pope blessed and distributed the traditional palm-branches in front of St Peter's and for a week the evocative, liturgical ceremonies unrolled with all their symbolism in a stately pageant of the Passion, Death and Resurrection of Christ. The Tenebrae in the Sistine chapel lasted from three to seven, a full four hours during which the candles were extinguished one by one; the office was supposed to end in darkness, though the penetrating daylight prevented this in practice. It finished with a great scraping of feet on the floor to simulate, also in imagination, the entombment.

On Holy Thursday outside St Peter's the Pope washed the feet of the poor. Often the guards were knocked down and troops and sightseers came to blows with fists and gun butts as people fought to watch him. The ceremony over, the crowds surged into the Apostolic Refectory where he served a meal to the beggars with his own hands. In this commemoration of the actions of Christ he was imitated in all the hospitals by the great ladies of Rome who put on the black dress and white apron of nuns to wash the feet of three or four hundred poor women and serve them, too, at table. In the same costume they mingled with the long procession of beggars.

Saturday, Easter Eve, was one of the most important religious occasions, for families were then visited by monks and priests who blessed their houses, previously scoured and cleaned from attic to cellar—a symbolic stripping of the old Adam in readiness for a new life. Every room and every piece of furniture was sprinkled with holy water. Next, the chief business was the preparation of the Easter meal, a huge cake of cheese and eggs which lasted the whole family a week, and roast kid in memory of the paschal lamb. The clergy all ate real lamb and the Holy Father sat down to the animal which had been dedicated for this very purpose on January 21st in Sant' Agnese fuori le Mura.[1] The rites of Easter Sunday were one blaze of pomp and splendour where the Church paraded its entire

[1] 'A ceremony is held every year in Sant' Agnese on 21st January when the priest, among his canons, blesses two young lambs wreathed with flowers and placed on the altar. He then gives them to the master of ceremonies of St John Lateran and they are taken to the Pope, who blesses them in his turn. The Camerlengo hands them over for fattening to the nuns of a convent chosen by the Pope. Their wool is used by the senior Apostolic Sub-Deacon to make the pallia and at early vespers on St Peter's day these are laid on the tomb of the saint and left there all night. Later they are kept among the relics until they are needed for patriarchs, archbishops or metropolitans. The pallium is the strip of wool with four black crosses which the Pope wears over his shoulders, fixed by three big pins with diamonds in their heads.'—G. Robello, *Les Curiosités de Rome.*

magnificence and pope, cardinals and prelates were seen in all their spectacular retinue of state.

Austerity melted away from Rome as the hour of Easter struck. Rockets, firecrackers, singing and dancing came back into their own with the promptitude of bad habits. Already on Holy Saturday the city had kept a feast which, though known as the Madonna of the Hams and thus nominally associated with Our Lady, was pagan through and through. The pork-butchers crammed their windows with sausage and hams festooned in gold paper and greenery; the Maddona sat enthroned among the polony and the people wandered about to admire the displays, compare the lighting and decide which exhibition really made their mouths water.

Many of papal Rome's religious festivals had the same sort of echo of some local observance going back to ancient times. There was, for instance, the Rappresentazione dei Morti in the cemetery chapels in the week of All Saints, when the Dies Irae was sung in the presence of full-size waxen models of corpses, and sometimes of actual corpses collected from the hospitals. Beggars made a point of attending and if sufficiently infirm to arouse the pity of worshippers were taken inside the chapels to provide inspiration in the background. Their companions meanwhile formed a long double line up to the doors outside, all rattling their wooden bowls together. On December 26th the martyrdom of St Stephen was enacted in the highly appropriate setting of San Stefano Rotondo where the frescoes are all of tortured saints, all horribly realistic, with nothing to be seen but tongues torn out, breasts sliced off and limbs being roasted.

Every household had its miniature crib at Christmas. The bourgeois families would use a special room for it, making mountain scenery and waterfalls and trying to outdo one another for the best effects. They went round to see the cribs of neighbours as well as those in the churches, the best of which was that in the Aracoeli. All Rome flocked to visit it, and to hear the children preaching. During the whole octave of Christmas the heirs of Bossuet, aged from eight to ten, took turns to pipe from the pulpit, while their parents dissolved in tears of joy and the audience drank in their platitudes as words of wisdom.

Epiphany brought its splendid tableau of the visit of the Three Kings, a magnet for huge crowds of peasants who sat all day on the Aracoeli stair, munching chestnuts and discussing miracles. Another picturesque occasion was that of January 18th, when the

1   *The Pope giving beads, medals and Agnus Dei's to pilgrims*

3   *Trinità dei Monti, by Van Wittel*

4   *Basilica and Piazza di S. Pietro, by Piranesi*

5   *Piazza di Spagna, by Piranesi*

6   *Bridge and Castel Sant' Angelo, by Piranesi*

8   *Via Scelerata*

10 *The site of the ancient Roman forum, by Piranesi*

11 *The Colosseum from the south-east, by Van Wittel*

12   *The Rotunda, after Piranesi*

13   *The Pope deputing three cardinals to open the Gates of*
St John of Lateran, St Maria Maggiore, and St Paul

a

b

c

14 *a. Benedict XIII*
  b. Clement XI
  c. Clement XIII
  d. Clement XIV
  e. Pius VI

d

e

15　*A Roman Catholic ceremony: the blessing of the nuptial bed*

16 *The Jubilee proclaimed in St Peter's Church*

17   *The Pope at the close of the Jubilee, placing the first
stone to shut up the Holy Gate*

four-footed population of Rome gathered in the square before Santa Maria Maggiore to be blessed in the name of St Anthony. Oxen, horses, asses and mules arrived in numbers, all decked with ribbons. Domestic cats and dogs were welcome. A priest in stole and surplice scattered holy water on them and their masters would give a cheese, or something from the farm, to show their gratitude.

So closely did the sacred mingle with the profane that the people marked the feast of St John by dancing all night round the tall red porphyry obelisk in the Lateran piazza. They danced, too, round Santa Maria Maggiore on certain other feast days and when a nun took her vows the solemnity would be followed by the chocolate and ices of a lavish collation.

But a general and most engaging piety was evident in the celebration of the Quaranta Ore, a festival that saw the twelve months round. At the beginning of the Church's year, the first Sunday in Advent, the sacrament was exposed in the Pauline chapel of St Peter's, where it remained until the Thursday. It was then removed to St John Lateran and subsequently to all the patriarchal and several other churches. In each it was exposed for the length of forty hours while offices were sung continually and local members of the Company of the Holy Sacrament, who were everywhere in Rome, kept vigil at night. The year and its journeyings ended together at St Peter's, to begin again immediately.

Of all religious spectacles Rome loved a procession best. Processions, with the greatest figures of the Church making their appearance to add to the excitement, always drew the faithful in great crowds. On Corpus Christi day the Pope himself led the procession round St Peter's Square beneath Bernini's colonnade.

'The Pope, in his immense robe of cloth of gold [says Fernand Hayward], was carried on a sort of platform, with the Host in a glittering monstrance. Since he was often an old man and easily tired, he used to sit on a little stool with the big cloak draped round to look as though he were on his knees before the Holy Sacrament.'

All the many processions had interesting traditions of their own. That on St Mark's Day, April 25th, glorified the Most Serene Republic and the Venetian ambassador took part in great pomp with all his banners flying. On the octave of the Nativity the captured Moslem standards were displayed in memory of John

Sobieski's victory over the Turks in 1683. Dowries were given to the 120 girls who walked in procession on the anniversary of Lepanto. In Holy Week the *penitenti* with their pointed hoods and white or purple, blue or yellow robes, filed by with hardly a break. Their backs were bare and they scourged themselves rhythmically with knotted cords which, however, produced more noise than damage.

The people loved their own local processions best and these were always the most attractive. Each district had some pageant of its own and long before the great day a drummer went round for contributions by way of preparation. Hangings decorated the houses on the route and kneeling in the dust the population lined streets sanded and strewn with myrtle. Bugles and fifes kept time for the participants, children dressed as angels spread rose-petals about and hawkers sold pieces of watermelon. It might all have been happening in the reign of Sixtus V. The single district of Trastevere had two processions. The bottlemakers paid for one of these, known as the Bocoletti, when they raised a large altar by the Tiber and loaded it with flowers and people came in flat boats to look at it from the river. The other, that of the Madonna of Mount Carmel, was something of a sporting occasion, for the huge cross and banner at its head were so heavy that only the toughest men could carry them and bevies of local beauties came to applaud the chosen heroes. When thirsts were quenched in the thronged taverns afterwards talk naturally turned on the strength and relative beefiness of the bearers. The inevitable arguments as naturally led to fighting and bloodshed—all part of the tradition.

Here we must mention the illumination of St Peter's that crowned the saint's festival and was the time-honoured climax of all religious celebrations. Visible from every part of Rome, it was a spectacle such as no other city in the world could show. The crowds gathered well before dark and an orchestra would play in the Piazza to wile away the time until at last a pale gleam was perceived along the cornices and 1,400 lamps showed every line and angle of the building, from the colonnade up to the tip of the cross on the dome. This was in itself a marvellous sight but the great illumination came as the bells rang an hour later; then the whole mass in all its detail was lit up by almost 6,000 fire-lamps.[1] It was

---

[1] Paper lanterns were used for the first stage and for the later, brilliant illumination, jars packed with wood-shavings and turpentine.

as though the dome caught fire. The huge church, the wide piazza with its double colonnade, were all 'on fire'. To one spectator it was like 'a dream, or fairytale', and Bergeret recalls 'the impact of that tremendous surge of light, reducing the previous glow to pinpoints and blotting it out in seconds'. The miracle was wrought by no fewer than 365 technicians, hanging on ropes, keeping out of sight and working incredibly fast. How they did it was their secret, the culminating achievement of a nation who were past masters in the stage-management of festival occasions.

Having enjoyed this illumination of St Peter's, the crowd went on to watch the fireworks at Castel Sant' Angelo. The best way was to take a boat and float gently on the river with the whole show reflected on the water, the light rippling over Hadrian's mausoleum in falls and torrents of fire. When the eruption of Vesuvius was the chosen theme the building would disappear in cascades of incandescent lava, volcanic flames reared into the heavens to drop as burning rain. Discharging mortars added their din to that of the rockets and it seemed, said someone who saw it, as though 'nature were crumbling away in sublime and terrible uproar'. The display ended with the famous *girandola* of 5,000 rockets all set off together, flooding the sky over Rome in a vivid fantasia of light.[1] Castel Sant' Angelo played its part in all religious revelry and may be seen, gaily decorated, in contemporary prints, with the flag-staffs and big, bright-coloured flags on the battlements.

There was so close an involvement of religious with everyday life that some festivals had come into being which, though officially pious occasions, served really as the flimsiest excuse for rural rides. Such was the festa of the Madonna of Divine Love held on Whit Monday at a small church thirteen kilometres from Rome near Leva on the Appian Way. The Romans who flocked there in any conveyance they could find were, if the truth were known, more interested in having a day in the country than in doing reverence to the miracle-working image. Early as they arrived the peasants from the nearby villages would be there before them; they came the previous evening and spent all night singing hymns. The townsfolk, however, brought another atmosphere. The women picked flowers for their hair, picnics were spread and everyone had a good

---

[1] As Algarotti said, the English used their gunpowder for firing cannon and the French for firing mortars, but Italian gunpowder was damp and what little dry stuff they had they put into bunches of fireworks.

time without ever going near the chapel. After dark there was a festive homeward drive and the singing was somewhat inebriated at times. The wagons raced each other and when they collided the disaster led to the customary exchange of insults in the moonlight.

The feast of the Annunziatella, with its gay outdoor meal near the Porta San Sebastiano, was very similar. And at Genzano on the octave of Corpus Christi, though the sacrament was borne through the streets for the festival of the Infiorata, most of the visitors from Rome were there to see the processional carpet of flowers, patiently and perfectly created by the villagers. That ceaseless intertwining with religion, in fact, brought as much honest pleasure as spiritual meaning into common or garden existence.

BIRTHS, MARRIAGES AND DEATHS

It is surprising to find that these people, with their innate love of formal display, married and baptized so quietly at home. But they had not always done so and the present simple mode was the result of overwhelming luxury in other days when the popes, with varying fortune, tried again and again to apply the control of sumptuary laws. The latest of these dated from 1661 and were no longer in force by the eighteenth century. Still, they had bequeathed some habit of moderation, though not one that sprang exactly from Christian humility.

There was no longer any ostentatious entertainment for a christening, but not everybody minded this for it meant there were no presents to buy. The newer and less extravagant way was to send simple gifts of food to the young mother. However, if the *padaglione delle puerpere*[1] were a slight sort of offering, it arrived in such state that its slightness was easily overlooked. No nobleman or cardinal would fail to send a *padaglione* when a female relation was confined, a structure of such complication that it could fairly count as a *macchina*. It was a kind of set-piece filled with every variety of pasta—*taglierini, tortellini*—and with capons and chickens. There was nothing very exotic about it except for the custom of sending it to its destination with an imposing escort through the streets. A *padaglione* reached the house to the sound of trumpets, preceded by a host of retainers in gala livery and four ushers in black ceremonial dress to hold the onlookers back with their silver-tipped staves. Every now and again the trumpets fell

[1] A present for those in childbirth.

silent and a crier stepped forward to announce the donor's name and titles and those of the lady he desired to honour.

Sumptuary laws had also reduced the number and value of wedding presents, so that only small personal ornaments were now permissible. The Jews had got round the rule by putting costly gold lace on the slippers, garters and stockings that a young couple received, but the Romans forbore to follow their example. Like that of exhibiting the trousseau, which would have led to great excesses, the custom of wedding presents was allowed to die. Marriages were celebrated in private, though some time after marrying their daughter a noble family would hold a large reception where, says Lalande, 'all the diamonds and all the loveliest clothes in Rome' were to be seen. In order that wealthy girls going into convents should not miss this important parade, a grand and very temporal fête was given when they took the veil. Here the chief attractions were the buffet, with its load of pastries and ices, and the recital of rhymed compliments composed by friends and relations in the young nun's honour.

Weddings and baptisms, then, were family affairs, but funerals offered a spectacle varying in splendour with the social position of the dead. The Romans regarded death as a due debt. Unexpectedly, in view of their extreme care to do nothing that might hasten the inevitable reckoning, they put a good face on it. Their attitude is neatly stated by a character in one of their plays: 'I don't want to bathe in the river, you get drowned; I don't want to get on a horse, you fall off; and I don't want to go to war, you get shot at.' This was many people's rule of life, but to the fact of death there was general resignation. The devout were prepared for it by the repeated warnings of their religion; almost every sermon contained some exhortation on the subject. It was vividly evoked in the churches at All Saints and everyone knew the Capuchin church near the Piazza Berberini, ornamented entirely with bones. As Edmond About described it, 'there were arm-bones in sheaves and baskets made of shoulder-blades, and pelvises hung up like chandeliers with candle-holders cut from the tops of skulls'. Another church, dedicated to the Good Death, boasted similar decoration.

Tastes of this sort had dictated Roman funeral custom. Burials were in church or convent cloisters and often inside the churches themselves, though the practice was neither hygienic nor legal. But

Rome at this period honoured its laws more in the breach than the observance and this particular breach meant that priests collected a tax for permitting it; the notion of having a cemetery outside the town would have seemed the height of impiety. A body was usually carried to rest on a simple bier with the face exposed, so that chance observers, taking a remarkably detached aesthetic view, exclaimed, '*Che bel morto!*' or '*Che brutto morto!*' in utmost unconcern. Funerals were generally at night, by torchlight, and cowled *penitenti* followed with candles in their hands and chanting as they went. On reaching the church the bier was laid on the ground and the penitents, kneeling round, let light shine on the dead face for the last time. They then extinguished their torches and 'left him to the dark'. It was a moving and dramatic ritual, performed always to perfection for, as it was once analysed:

'The chief actor cannot fail. The others may rely on their costume (the long, enveloping robes of the *penitenti*, with slits to see through), and on their torches, first bright then smoking; and the imagination of the audience does the rest.'

No relations were ever included in that audience. When hope was abandoned for a sick man his wife, his children and his brothers left the house, sometimes the town. Ostensibly they were going away to give him peace and quiet but it was really because the dying were supposed to have the evil eye and the superstitious Romans dreaded it. All service to the dead was bought and paid for. The poor man was escorted by a handful of *penitenti* to his grave; and to the imposing cortèges of the rich or powerful the religious orders sent as many representatives as seemed called for by the rank of the deceased. They were joined by his servants, his empty carriages, occasionally even by his dogs ('if their hearts incline them to it', as was once wickedly said), but by neither friend nor kinsman. Perhaps to do him honour, perhaps in idle curiosity, a crowd would watch some great man's funeral go by just as, the day before, they filed past his body lying in state beneath a canopy, the candles blazing round it.

The funeral of a cardinal was a major event that stirred the whole town. Bergeret was present when the old Cardinal Caval-chini was buried and says the flurry rivalled that of a race day at the carnival. The body was brought from the Dataria to the church of the Holy Apostles in a huge, ill-marshalled procession led by the bands of *penitenti* in their various-coloured robes and hoods. They took nearly an hour to pass, with their candles and banners, and were followed endlessly by the different orders of monks, singing each a different hymn in somewhat distracting want of harmony. Then came a wide gap in the cortège and a long wait of fifteen minutes before the dead prelate was borne along on a hearse draped with banners with his coat of arms, his face uncovered. A throng of church dignitaries, mounted senators and the members of his household came with him. It was too disordered a train to be either impressive or grandiose, inspiring Bergeret with no ambition to die a cardinal. He watched from a window of the French embassy with 200 other guests bidden for the occasion by Cardinal de Bernis, who varied the monotony of the scene by eating a 'prodigious quantity' of ices. The day after his burial a dead man was forgotten. He was stated to be in paradise and further comment was a solecism. A few noblemen were the only people who, faithful to old custom, ever wore mourning and calls of condolence would have seemed merely peculiar.

CHAPTER SEVEN

SPORTS AND PASTIMES

The Roman populace had always loved enjoyment and its basic aspirations were well summed up in the old formula of *Panem et Circenses*. In the eighteenth century the bread, as we have seen, came from the inexhaustible charity of papal government, while festivals of all kinds had replaced the circus games. They were so frequent that a Frenchman visiting Rome in 1785 could report to a friend, 'Every night there are public celebrations here.' Excitement was not confined to religious feasts alone, for in contemporary Rome any pretext served for a procession or a march-past, illuminations or fireworks. The election and coronation of the pontiff naturally disrupted the whole town, but his shortest outing would draw a crowd to line the route and gaze upon a retinue that far outshone anything the Renaissance popes could have produced. Never a day went by but some cardinal, seizing the grand opportunity to display all the glory of his scarlet trappings, found he had to drive about the streets with a tail of friends and dependants in full and festive array accompanying him to the church that he proposed to honour. For the entry of an ambassador or the visit of any notability, for a city magistrate's taking office and for other, quite minor, doings the gay processions paraded with banners and uniforms before a large and ever faithful concourse.

The aristocracy of Rome liked to pay its own lavish attentions to foreign sovereigns and marked their coming with luxurious fêtes. They never, in this period, surpassed their reception of Queen Maria Carolina of Naples, for whom they contrived superb entertainments; the Pamphili family's concert was a milestone in Italian musical history. There were games and dancing all over the town, with wine flowing in fountains before the illuminated palaces.

The various ambassadors, careful for their national prestige, saw to it that when they had anything to celebrate they celebrated brilliantly. Their ceremonies sounded in Rome the echo of events in the outside world and the Romans would find themselves involved as a result in rejoicings that were really nothing to do with them at all. The French were especially so very brilliant that their great occasions were perhaps more splendidly signalized here than at Versailles itself during the eighteenth century. When a Dauphin was born to Louis XV and Marie Leczinska the public triumphs were dazzling. Three orchestras of eighty musicians in the Parisian colours played for dancing on the Piazza San Marcello among the most profuse exhibition of ices and refreshments ever yet beheld. And in 1745, when the Dauphin was betrothed to the Infanta Maria Teresa, dancing went on all night in front of the Farnese Palace with twenty cardinals looking on. The building stood clear against the dark, outlined in lamps, with every window specially decorated and adorned. For Louis XVI's coronation bands were stationed at intervals along the Corso which was illuminated as far as the Piazza Colonna by light-standards in the form of fleur-de-lis.

In 1752, when the Duc de Bourgogne was born, the Duc de Nivernais decided that there was not enough room to hold the celebrations in the Embassy. He arranged to borrow the Farnese Palace from the Spanish ambassador, put in painters and upholsterers and had them working for three months to turn its state rooms into a glorification of the royal house of France. After the Te Deum in San Luigi dei Francesi and racing by Barbery coursers for a *palio* of a superb piece of Lyons silk, the splendours of the reception at the Farnese went on all night. There was a play, then a banquet, diversions and a magnificent ball. The nobility of Rome were present in force, bands performed on the piazza outside and crowds from all over the city came to enjoy themselves.

The most picturesque ceremony of all the Roman year was that of the Chinea—the palfrey—on June 29th. The Grand Constable of the kingdom of Naples, always one of the Colonna family, presented the Pope with a white palfrey as tribute in the name of his sovereign, redeeming it immediately for 1,200 Roman crowns. *La cosidetta chinea* was no more than an old white mule, but richly caparisoned, its shoes coated with silver leaf. It came in a wondrous procession from the Piazza dei Santi Apostoli to St Peter's, with papal attendants mingling among the lackeys and lancers and the mounted soldiery in glittering uniforms.

The gifts were delivered in the midst of the huge nave after Vespers. Attempts, usually vain, were made to get the animal to kneel down and the Pope blessed it. Both were supposed to arrive at the centre of the church at the same time and this presented difficulty. It would never do for the Pope to have to wait for the palfrey, the mysteries of etiquette made such a contingency unthinkable. To avert it, messengers were sent one after another to regulate the Constable's procession whose progress was marked by gunfire from Sant' Angelo.

At the starting-point in the Piazza dei Santi Apostoli a huge 'machine' was erected outside the Colonna Palace with the set-piece of rockets to be let off after dark. This framework would of course go up in flames but it was a solid structure, big enough to serve as a theatre where live actors, or more-than-lifesize puppets, gave musical plays on the glorious history of Naples and the greatness of her kings. Contemporary paintings show us what these extraordinary machines were like, architectural fantasies with allegories and symbolic figuration.

The set-piece followed the play and then the machine was burned to the applause of the audience. After this everybody danced and ate their sorbet-ices all night long on the piazza while a grand assembly, the most distinguished of the Roman year, went on in the Colonna gardens, lit up *a giorno* for the occasion. The cardinals all wore their *cappamagne* of purple silk and the ladies court dress with their hair in towering, complicated coiffures.

This lovely fête of the Chinea was discontinued in 1766. It had led to serious differences over protocol and it was thought better to offer the tribute more simply for the future; and in 1788 the King of Naples freed himself from the obligation altogether.

Illuminations and fireworks were taken for granted as a part of any nocturnal celebration. The palaces were always lit up and lamps hung in the streets, while fireworks were the high point of all religious festivals and formed an interlude at every public ball. The firework men strove all the time to think of novelties and make their set-pieces ever more astonishing. Those they produced for the Chinea were renowned but they could do even better, as for instance with the enormous structure set off before the Palazzo Farnese for the Dauphin's betrothal. It showed the union of Love and Hymen in the temple of Minerva and was hailed by the crowd with long-drawn cries of wonder. But the real masterpiece of the Roman pyrotechnicians, made for the canonization of St Catherine of Bologna, was never used. They set it up on Michelangelo's cornice above the Farnese and at the last minute decided not to light it because of fire danger to the palace.

All Rome took part in these great festivals, while there were many others of a homelier nature, whose gaiety was confined to one district or even to a single street.

In the upper reaches of Roman society, where the parade of wealth was seen as a duty of rank, life was of necessity a thing of splendour. The princely palaces were, on certain occasions, the scene of magnificent assemblies with all kinds of entertainment— concerts and, more especially, great balls with *maestri di sala*, acting more or less like cotillon leaders, to direct activities. The foreign ambassadors bid strongly to outdo the princes and the bankers in all this glory and Cardinal de Bernis, straining to bedazzle Rome with his receptions, would have been dismissed as a lunatic for giving anything of the sort in Paris.

The luxurious displays offered pleasure to ordinary folk no less than to their betters. Abundantly, their delights overflowed from salon and garden for the neighbours' benefit and the neighbours took good care not to miss them. Bands played at every crossroad, the would-be pedestrian found people dancing in his path, the fountains ran with wine. It was customary for a newly elected cardinal to give a fête, known as a *facciata*, the day he received his hat. Haunted by the remembered magnificence of the Medici, some of the cardinals made a stupendous thing of these triumphal tableaux, piercing through walls and knocking houses down to accommodate the enormous settings for pageants and pyrotechnics.

So the commons flocked for their share in rich men's revels, but they also had traditional junketings of their own and here the aristocracy, feeling perhaps that one good turn deserved another, would join them. The Ottobrate offered such an occasion. October, month of the grape harvest, was a time for rural pleasures and the festivities, entirely pagan in origin, recalled the Bacchanalia of the antique world. From the working-class districts the people would pile into rough wagons and make for the country. They wandered in the fields, singing verses improvised by the Trastevere women, who were famous for their skill in the art. It was they who, like so many bacchantes in pretty clothes, eyes alight and hair flying in the breeze, kindled the Ottobrate into a carnival wildness. Flutes and tambourines played to the songs and laughter, everyone drank the new wine at the inns, orchestras struck up and young folk danced the *saltarella*. Then in the evening the noble villas were specially thrown open and they all went to dance there on the lawns. The Pamphili, the Borghese and the rest chose this season to show their beautiful houses to their friends, and their ladies, in the true Roman way, took part in homely merrymaking.

The Trastevere people also celebrated the Ottobrate nearer at hand, in Rome itself, on the Testaccio hill which had always been a favourite spot for local outings. Pig races held there during the Renaissance are hardly the happiest illustration of the classical tastes of that period, but the cellars of the man-made hill—one great heap of fragmented pottery—formed the main attraction in the eighteenth century. Here the tavern-keepers dispensed the white Castelli wines in generous quantities.[1] Groups of young people drove out together and even for the short journey from Trastevere the carriages were beautifully decorated with flowers. They drank and danced and sang songs reminiscent of the carnival lyrics of Lorenzo de' Medici.

Another treat the Romans adored was that of the naumachia held every Saturday night in the hot weather on the Piazza Navona. By a cunning arrangement of underground hydraulic machinery the square could be charmingly transformed into a sheet of water, immediately covered with gaily dressed craft, some with bands on board. Water jousts were held on the improvised lake, and historical pageants, and at the end the great family carriages, often camouflaged as Venetian gondolas, went plunging in among the boats. The horses would be chest-high in the water and the coachmen, urged on by surrounding small boys, did their best to make them snort and splash their neighbours and the fun was always good-humoured. Every window in the square was festooned with flowers and carpets. The gentry hung over the balconies to enjoy it and the people at the water's edge spiced the entertainment with *lazzi* and serenades. At nightfall flat-bottomed boats floated about with men holding torches, the light gleaming on the water and the palaces around. Coins were thrown in and urchins scrambled for them. At intervals the torches were extinguished, a brilliant moon was seen high in the sky and its light filled the piazza. And though it was a make-believe moon, hung by invisible cords and worked by hidden mechanism on those palatial rooftops, the illusion seems to have been complete.

The festival in the piazza came to an end at midnight, to be continued with the cheerful suppers known as *sabatine* in the

[1] Every landlord in Rome had his cellar at Monte Testaccio. The hill was like an ice-house and wine from it kept cool for seven or eight hours.

nearby inns. Tables had to be set in streets and gardens to accommodate all the customers and the picturesque district round the Piazza Navona rang with music and singing into the small hours.

Religious or profane, the festivals punctuated the whole year 'like arches and flag-standards on some triumphal route'. Every single day marked some memorial or anniversary from the past, was sacred to some special saint or relic or recalled some old tradition. Majestic or endearing, the pageants continually unfolded, the people were continually free to enjoy them and this pursuit of pleasure reached its climax with the Carnival.

THE ROMAN CARNIVAL

A walk along the Corso was at any season the favourite diversion in Rome. From the end of siesta until darkness fell all the Romans with nothing to do, and all those looking for free entertainment, strolled the length of that elegant thoroughfare, something short of a mile. The beauties flaunted along in open carriages the better to see and—what was more important—to be seen, with their dashing cavaliers prancing round them. The burgess women were cramped in hired cabs but they, too, had a fine escort of gallants. A solid crowd of pedestrians followed behind or wandered on the pavement. The sole object was to take the air and make a good appearance, for this promenade constituted a sort of detailed social inspection and no one could hope to succeed who did not observe the rite. If a well-known woman failed to turn up everybody speculated on what had kept her away. Interested spectators hung out of the windows, greeting the gentry or their own friends, gossiping and appraising the women's clothes. The commons came in hordes to admire the coaches and wave to any lackeys or drivers they happened to know. Up and down the Corso the parade went on, from the Piazza Venezia to the Piazza del Popolo, at which point it was usual to halt and sit in the carriage for a little while, listening to the music and eating ice cream.

This was the promenade which the whole city stampeded to join when Carnival came round, all ranks and conditions together, and it then became the most exuberant fête of all. Pleasure-seeking ruled there for eleven days. The Romans were seized by a passion for excitement, a furious appetite for amusement to be found nowhere else. Such was their madness, so universal their fever, that the Turkish ambassador could only think that its abrupt ending on Ash Wednesday must be 'the effect of the mysterious powder the Christians sprinkle on one another's foreheads'.

The masking, the *confetti* battles and the races were the three great sources of this wholesale mania. The beginning of Carnival was announced by the bell on the Capitol, rung only for this purpose or for the death of a pope, and there, round Marcus Aurelius on his horse, the opening ceremony was held. The Senator emerged from his palace at the bell's summons, robed in cloth of gold with the Conservatori in attendance. Next came the Governor of Rome, preceded by a thunderous brass band. The procession that formed up and passed along a Corso already packed with masked onlookers from one end to the other, contained allegorical floats, furbished richly with tapestries, flowers and branching greenery and drawn by plumed horses in embroidered trappings. It was a point of honour with all the noble families to produce one of these chariots. In 1779, for instance, the Colonna took as their theme the different regions of Italy and the Borghese had priests at an Indian sacrifice. Prince Chigi's float presented an assembly of the gods, based on the frescoes at his Villa Farnesina. Neither the nobles nor their wives were above appearing in person. Prince Ruspoli figured as a sultan in 1711 and Prince Rospigliosi was a Polish magnate in 1735. The Marchesa Gabrielli, an unchallenged beauty, was once an odalisque and the Duchess of Gravina-Orsini was enthroned as Diana the huntress. Her tableau aroused great curiosity, being made like a mountain but so cleverly constructed that no one could see how it moved. But the palm of the century for Carnival display went to the art students of the French Academy for the Sultan of Mecca's Caravan which they drove along the Corso in 1752. Attired in splendour, janissaries and three-tailed bashaws, eunuchs and oriental envoys followed a float where six sultanas, two of them negresses, sat in state. The production was a terrific success and Benedict XIV himself was said to have hidden behind a curtain to watch.

After the floats came the coaches of the aristocracy, gilded and wreathed with flowers, the coachmen flourishing beribboned whips; then the long files of citizens, in carriages whose ornament, though less prodigal, was often more imaginative.

Maskers appeared from all sides the moment they heard the bell announce that Carnival had begun. Everybody except churchmen, Jews and prostitutes might wear disguise, and any costume save those of priest or monk. Moors and satyrs were seen, dervishes in turbans and Turks with pipes, sceptred kings and sham beggars, English sailors, tearful Jews, syphilitics, even assassins, and all the wide choice of delicate or comic masks from the *commedia dell' arte*. Caricature and exaggeration of all kinds were allowable and the most piquant encounters of all hinged upon the fact that so many women were there dressed up as men.

The masquerading was vivid and lively because everyone stuck to his part. Harlequin knocked his head against the wall, Punch devoured macaroni, Pierrot was suitably moonstruck. A fake lawyer would threaten people with some libellous lawsuit, accusing the men of farfetched crimes and reeling off fantastic lists of all the ladies' lovers. A theatrical Spanish captain boasted of imaginary heroisms, to be brushed aside by Punch.

The crowd joined in the mock disputes and laughed at the antics of the *quacqueri*, the comic-opera comedians who stood about in noisy groups ready to provoke something ridiculous. The women carried little switches made of rushes to push away anyone who squeezed them too hard and would often chase such an offender off to the applause of all around.[1] Every remark led to some comic exchange. 'Everyone you meet,' reports the English traveller Matthews, 'is sure to be amusing. I have heard more wit in a day of Carnival than anywhere else in a week.'

The revelry was sanctioned by secular and ecclesiastical authority alike and full and unrestricted advantage was taken of the fact. The Corso became one enormous masked ball and so long as you enjoyed yourself it did not matter who the others were. You joked with everyone, everyone joked back and nobody asked questions.

This same complete medley of rank and manners persisted when the *confetti* battles raged on the Corso, 'confounding all mortal men together', as Madame de Staël said, 'turning the nation upside down as though there were no social order any more'. They all fell into a frenzy—duchesses in their coaches, women on foot, girls at their shop doors and beauties at the windows or in the big stands

---

[1] Usually without male escort, they were left to look after themselves and very efficiently they did so. The rush brooms that warded off unwelcome attentions could also castigate those who were not being attentive enough. 'In this case,' writes Fernand Hayward, 'they would crowd up to their victim of the moment and flick the little broom continually under his nose. It was vain for the poor man to look for escape, the little broom came and tickled him wherever he turned. He could not run away in that dense throng and it was asking for trouble to make a determined resistance, for masks enjoyed the protection of the police.'

in front of the Ruspoli palace. Indeed, they were almost demented and Goethe said one evening in Carnival that he 'had spent the day with lunatics'.

The ammunition for these mock battles had once been blown egg-shells filled with evil-smelling powder, but later real sugared almonds—*confetti*—came into use. This pleasant custom was still found at the beginning of the eighteenth century, but gradually the sweetmeats were replaced by small missiles about the size of peas, made of a volcanic rock called *puzzolana*, rolled in plaster and whitewashed. This grapeshot, by no means as fragile as what we should call confetti, was launched through cardboard cornets similar to those used in backgammon. Delicate persons protected their faces with light masks of copper mesh and ladies sometimes took refuge behind whole masks moulded from the flawless beauty of classical heads; but for the most part they preferred to show their own features and disdained any such precautions. They might, however carry handmirrors, not so much to attract attention as to parry the flying pellets. It was of course the pretty ones who received the heaviest bombardment and went home more than a little battered. Among other and less dangerous ammunition their admirers also threw bouquets of spun sugar with love-letters attached and such attentions could not, in etiquette, be ignored though no one was obliged to respond.

The whole process of throwing things was governed by a strict set of rules. Only maskers might throw pellets indiscriminately; other people could attack no one but the maskers and servants had to leave each other alone. The neutrality of the Church was to be respected, for its members confined themselves to the role of spectators. The police stood watchfully by with their *cavalletto* in readiness and those who overstepped the mark paid the penalty without delay, though the *sbirri* rarely had to punish anyone save prostitutes with masks on.

The plaster shot was sold at every street corner and the residents of the Corso sent *facchini*[1] out in the morning to lay in ample stocks. So much was used that the road was white after a battle and in the blanched carriages the occupants looked like millers. But these were minor drawbacks, soon forgotten in the delirium of festa.[2]

---

[1] Porters.

[2] The sweetmeat battles continued into the next century. When Madame Récamier suggested having them in Paris, Delécluze replied, 'Certainly,

It is not difficult to conjure up that scene on the Corso with the battles in progress against the clamour of *lazzi* and greetings, with people calling and singing and shouting for joy. In the background was the ceaseless crossing and re-crossing of carriages, the long paper darts curling out of windows to entangle passers-by, the tumult of the colourful crowd, the sills hung with carpets and tapestry, the balconies full of pretty women. Weary contestants might for a moment break away from the cheerful hustle of the Corso and recruit their strength at stalls in nearby streets where the *friggitori* fried mountains of fish, vegetables and macaroni in oil for famished customers. The ice cream sellers made a fortune.[1]

But the climax of the day, the hub of the Roman Carnival, came with the races, the magical, compelling races run by the Barbery coursers late in the afternoon. Fifteen barbs—horses of the Berber breed—were released at the foot of the obelisk in the Piazza del Popolo to rush in wild career to the Palazzo Venezia. They would be mad with excitement, unbridled and riderless, full of oats, stimulated beforehand by drugs such as scandalize the racing world today, ropes over their backs studded with rowels to spur them on and fireworks going all along the course. Manes streaming, with smoking nostrils and glowing eyes, they hurtled to the goal and swept down anything in their path. Vehicles were pulled into side turnings and people pushed back against the houses, but in vain. The crowd was itself at boiling-point and surged off the pavements in perilous invasion of the track to see that frantic galloping at closer quarters. The animals knocked and tumbled men over, dragging them to the ground, and trod them underfoot but never slackened speed. Horses fell, hooves threshing as the chaos grew, or leaped among the crowd. There were casualties, often many

---

Madame, if you want to lame a quarter of the population every day.' And it seems a reasonable reaction when we remember that the accidents were always caused by foreigners, who were less playful about the whole thing than the Italians.

[1] The jollifications overflowed from the Via del Corso to the streets around, where concerts and dancing were liable to start up at any minute under the placid gaze of those settled outside the taverns with their glasses of chilled wine. 'You would see, too, fantastically garbed figures trailing imitation sugared almonds at the end of fishing rods, with twenty urchins after them all eyes and gaping mouths, who would earn a rap over the knuckles for forgetting they had to catch the almonds with their teeth alone.' *Un Parisien à Rome et à Naples*, a travel-book by J. J. Bouchard.

casualties, but no one stayed to see. In the yelling, the stamping, the near-frenzy, nothing else mattered and danger was forgotten.

The horses came like a whirlwind into the Piazza Venezia, where the officials sat in state on a decorated platform, and were stopped by means of outstretched cloths. After this, and not without argument and objections, the winner was declared. The Senator presented the owner with the cloth-of-gold *palio*, glorious prize of the contest, and the victorious animal returned to his stable with this trophy on his back, 'prancing superbly through the streets'.

By this time it was nearly dark. Soon, at the stroke of the Angelus, everyone crossed himself and took off his mask, a point on which the police were adamant. Not a few, resuming mask and disguise, would go on to one of the many nocturnal balls of Carnival. Whether for invited guests in the palaces, paid for in the theatres or free at one or other of the assembly rooms, these balls were always unrestrained and gay. Gayest of all were those of the Thursday and Tuesday before Lent, although, falling as they did on the eve of the Friday and Ash Wednesday fasts, they were supposed to end at midnight. Roman ingenuity, however, was equal to the problem with a little apt manipulation of the timetable. They altered the figures a trifle and put their watches back and went on dancing till dawn on the lee side of propriety.

The last night of Carnival was the night of the *moccoli*. These were the small tapers, thin and flexible, which were lit at dark as though to make the merriment last a little longer. In an instant the Corso and its surroundings were full of a thousand twinkling pinpoints and the game consisted in keeping your own taper going while putting out your neighbours'. There were risks in the mock warfare; fingers were burned and clothes, when not singed, were sure to be marked with melted wax. But everyone laughed and enjoyed himself as the encounters went on, with chases and invasions of carriages and clambering on the shoulders of people trying to keep their lights above the danger-line on the end of tall canes. Princes, prelates and ambassadors, transported with excitement, would struggle with the best. Elegant ladies consigned embroidered sleeves and Indian shawls to ruin to put the nearby candles out and through the open windows people were to be seen continuing the game at home. The unruffled householder looking forth, safe and sound with the front door locked, would find his *moccolo* assailed with a damp handkerchief on a long pole by some master tactician, himself exposed to vengeance from his victim's neighbours on the floor above. Nothing was disallowed in the game of tapers save the use of kitchen bellows, condemned as unsporting. Every trick was greeted with lighthearted laughter and the whole atmosphere was friendly. But it was the final burst of Carnival. Tomorrow, Ash Wednesday, everyone went piously to church.

Besides their outdoor feasting and the delights of Carnival, Roman folk managed to vary their leisure hours with assorted amusements of their own. They were much given to gambling and even the lottery could not assuage their thirst for getting something for nothing. All kinds of games of chance were played in the convenient cool of the wine-shop, on the parapet of a bridge or in the open street; games of skill, of dice and cards, some akin to the brain-teasers which enlivened the *conversazioni* of more elevated circles, others of ancient popular origin. Most interesting was the game of *morra*. The Roman legionaries were devoted addicts of *morra*, which may go back beyond their time, for there exists a Greek bas-relief showing the wilful Ajax and the wily Ulysses playing it, with Nestor for an umpire. You threw out the right hand with several fingers doubled back, calling as you did so the number of fingers shown. Your opponent had to imitate the gesture immediately and lost a point for every mistake or hesitation. It was simple enough, but played at such a rate that nobody was ever sure that the second man followed correctly. It led to terrible disputes and an observer could easily believe the fervid gamesters about to cut each other's throats; and sometimes the observer would be right.

Card and dice games, the usual tavern pastime of the wine-drinkers, were also very apt to end in quarrels and fighting. Blows could follow insults resulting from an unconsidered glance, a tactless word or a simple disagreement over the fall of dice. Certainly the wine was not to blame, for the light vintages of Frascati and the Castelli were innocuous enough, as Horace and Seneca had found them long ago, and were drunk sparingly in any case. But the Romans, sober as they were, were both passionate and hot-tempered.

Another very ancient game was the *passatella*, a version of the classical Roman eating competition which by the eighteenth century had become a drinking matter only. Each member of the party paid his share of the wine on the tavern table but was never sure of getting it, for only the *maestro del vino*, chosen by lot, could say who was to drink. This temporary monarch was all-powerful, swilling as much as he could himself and appointing a subordinate to fill the glasses at his command. Every glass was held out, but might be excluded from the round if he said, 'No drink there.' The outcasts came in for much laughter and mockery and not infrequently took offence.

Paradoxically enough the Romans, so easily roused to violence over trifles, were also very fond of poetical contests, Sunday events in the dingiest and most pugnacious bars in Trastevere. Here the poetry fanciers met to improvise and sing their poems in recitative to the strains of the mandoline. Their themes came generally from ancient history. One would sing about the Trojan war, another the death of Nero, a third the reign of Augustus. They issued challenges and competed in groups and the winner was chosen by public acclaim. It all resembled the old literary tourneys of the Middle Ages, though the verses, despite the easy rhyming of a language where most words ended in *e, i* or *o*, might not be of the best. Nevertheless, the poetical note was struck and an ornate vocabulary used. We are told, indeed, that language so far removed from that of everyday was astonishing to hear from men and women so completely uneducated.

Though this was no games-loving century and disliked taking physical exercise according to rules, the young men of the aristocracy would play pelota with their bare hands against a wall as the Basques do now. The court was sometimes the wall of a palace, such as that which has left its name in the Via della Pilotta beside the Palazzo Colonna. The players backed themselves to win considerable sums and there was once a Knight of Malta who lost 250 Roman crowns on a single game.

The one team game was football, imported from Florence and a distant ancestor of the *calcio* that delights Italian crowds today. The teams were large, as many as twenty-five or even thirty a side, and played on special grounds. One by the Vatican walls had huge stands for ordinary spectators and boxes for the nobility. The temperature of this game, too, was raised by heavy betting and the hissing and applause matched anything heard at the theatre.

Often as the commons came to blows after gaming disputes, their amazing appetite for violence was still unsatisfied. The inhabitants of the Monti quarter round Santa Maria Maggiore had a terrible reputation and the Trasteverini, with their claims to direct descent from the ancient Romans and the appropriate energy they therefore displayed, were most inflammable. Some outlet was needed for the forces they disdained to spend in work and set battles between gangs offered a regular, organized safety-valve for natural pugnacity. Their field of action was at Monte Testaccio, where nobody disturbed them, they had plenty of room for manœuvre and stones, always the ammunition in these mortal scrimmages, were lying to hand. If separated by a police patrol the combatants merely waited for it to leave and went on fighting until darkness fell.

And yet the favourite amusement of all, dancing, was peaceable enough. Much of it took place to the accompaniment of orchestras provided by the nobility on gala nights, and even more often spontaneously at crossroads. Here a handful of amateurs with guitars or mandolines would play the *tarantella* or *saltarella* and the young folk needed no second invitation, keeping time as they danced with tambourines to the traditional street-songs of the quarter.

THE SOCIAL SCENE

We have described the glitter of the princely fêtes but, far more than by these stupendous displays, the tone of society was set by what Montesquieu calls a 'special kind' of gathering, purely private and personal, which did not, however, preclude the pleasures of mutual admiration.

We must first note that ceremonious dinners, contrary to the custom of other countries, were seldom given here. In contemporary France, for instance, to live in style or to cut a grand figure meant no more than keeping a good table. But the Roman nobles showed their taste and their magnificence in quite another way. They could of course on occasion provide most splendid feasts. When Prince Borghese received Queen Maria Carolina in his Pincio villa sixty-eight guests sat down to a banquet surpassed only by the Duke of Braschi, whose menu included a sturgeon weighing 150 pounds. In 1769 the Corsini entertained the Austrian Emperor and 300 people ate off gold plate. Some of the banquets at the Palazzo Colonna are straight out of the Arabian Nights and notable too were the little suppers at the Duchess of Fiano's.

But this sort of thing was the exception in Roman society, which tended to look askance at the persevering dinner-party host. Cardinal de Bernis was fond of saying that he kept *l'auberge de*

France at the crossroads of Europe; he welcomed forty guests a night with every refinement of his national cuisine and the bishop of Bayonne, Auditor of the Rota for France, followed his lead with an equally distinguished table. Yet, sincerely as the two Gallic emissaries were admired for other reasons—and the Cardinal was even nicknamed King of Rome—their hospitality was not understood. The noblest Romans were merely astonished that 'a couple of sensible men, who had done so well for themselves, should go to all this trouble keeping open house'. In the opinion of Prince Antonio Borghese it was because 'they both started life in a garret and magnificence was such a novelty they could not have enough of it'. He may have been a little jealous, but clearly, to him and his friends, all this eating and drinking was the luxury of parvenus.

And there was indeed a striking difference between the attitudes of Rome and Paris. Every year on December 13th the French ambassador would invite 150 people to a lordly feast by way of commemorating the conversion of Henri IV. The Duc de Saint Aignan, aware of Roman prejudice against these very expensive foregatherings wished to stop them and use the money as dowries for poor girls instead; but his court formally disapproved his suggestion and sent definite orders to proceed as usual. It was never an occasion which advanced his country's credit. Degenerating into a public festa, as anybody might have expected, it gave rise to the ludicrous scenes kindly reported for us by President Charles de Brosses. The President says:

'This dinner is one of the most interesting sights here. A hundred and fifty of us were seated at one scroll-ended horseshoe table. There were seven or eight cardinals, Ottoboni, Aquaviva, Alessandro Albani, Corsini, Tencin, etc. and Canillac, who dearly wishes he were a cardinal too; all the presentable French residents and leading foreigners; many of the Roman nobility, especially the pro-French among them. Four *maîtres d'hôtel* and their assistants served the meal, each contingent wearing a different coloured ribbon and each using a different door. Before I sat down I counted forty-nine epergnes or stands on the table, all full of citrons. The Duc de Saint Aignan told me afterwards that some of them had cost eight hundred *livres*. They marked out where the rest of the fruit was to go for dessert, in two rows of low crystal dishes. As for menials, we were absolutely overwhelmed with them and a *maître d'hôtel* came and asked us to see that no one changed our plates except a man in our host's livery. He was well-advised to do so, for the banquet is a real field-day for masters and servants alike, conducted in the boldest and most shocking way. No sooner was food put before us than a horde of strange footmen bore down carrying plates and demanding this and that for their employers. There was one in particular who attached himself to me as the most promising member of the party. I gave him a turkey then a chicken, a cut of sturgeon, a partridge, a slice of venison, some tongue and some ham, and always he came back. "My friend," I told him, "everyone is getting the same, why doesn't your master eat his own food? He certainly likes it, I never saw anyone with such an appetite." Detroy, sitting not far from me, said, "Don't be silly. All he asks for his master he's taking for himself." And I could see that the more restrained of the lackeys were indeed vying with each other in the amount they could cram into their pockets, even wrapping the truffled poultry in napkins to keep their fingers clean, for the linen was worth taking too. The cleverest ones were whisking the dishes away. You could see them filing out of the room and taking them home under their *ferraiuoli,* the big cloaks they wear. The better-organized, to avoid having to go all the way to their own houses and leave at the height of the mêlée, had wives and children posted on the staircases as intermediaries, ready to carry off the victuals to their miserable abodes. And I was told as a fact that their masters indulged in pilfering too; if any Italian gentleman fancied anything he simply sent his servant home with it, thus adopting the dish and its contents together—an appalling thing. It made me furious. When my rascal turned up again I gave him only sweets and sauces, which put him off and he went to someone else.

'Later the ambassador told me that he lost between twenty-five and thirty pieces of his dinner-service every year at least and, even more annoyingly, things he has borrowed as well. He reckons that the affair costs him nearly twelve thousand *livres,* apart from this.'

Disapprobation of grand dinners did not mean that the art of cookery was not assiduously cultivated among the upper classes. The Pope set an example of finer points by serving at his Holy Thursday dinner for the cardinals 'fresh cherries from the kingdom of Naples, grown on trees forced with manure and hot water'. Cardinal de Bernis' cook tells how he often found himself up against his brother cooks from the great patrician houses as he combed the markets for the fattest birds, the finest fish and the most perfect fruit for his master's table, and that men from the cardinals' kitchens were not the least of his competitors. But all this delicate cookery was for family consumption only or the entertainment of intimates and played little part on the social scene. However, it was polite to offer one's friends any speciality as it appeared in the markets, as a compliment, and it was quite proper in this case for the recipient to pass it on to one he judged more worthy. When the fishmongers' guild gave Benedict XIV a giant sturgeon caught on June 2, 1725, he sold it for the benefit of the poor.[1] It was bought by the *abate* Lanace and given to Cardinal Spignola. He sent it to Cardinal Cascio, who gave it to Prince Borghese. The prince sent it to the Duchess of Bracciano and the great fish ended its travels at Frascati, where she happened to be spending a holiday.

The basic social function was the *conversazione* and the name conveys an exact idea of what this was. On a day previously fixed one or other of the noble houses opened its doors to a chosen few who met to talk together. Invitations were necessary but otherwise the host did nothing beyond making the arrangements and preserving the formalities and it might have been a public entertainment. Each family had its special day. Some received several times a week, the Borghese every day. Indeed the daily choice was wide and some socialites made brief visits to one house after another: there were places where one must be seen.

Timetables varied. The *conversazioni di prima sera* began when the Ave Maria sounded, just as darkness fell; they were held by cardinals and by the *mezze dame,* ladies who, though not of the highest rank themselves, yet received cardinals and aristocracy. At the second hour, two hours after the Ave, the grand *conversazioni della seconda sera* began which went on late into the night. The scene was the chief salon of the palace, so closely hung with pictures that, said a French guest, they 'wearied as much as pleased the eye'. There were marble tables with their load of figurines and crystal vases, and upright chairs, covered in silk or velvet, ranged round them to welcome visitors. Not that many visitors ever sat in them, the privilege of doing so being reserved for a few great ladies, ambassadors, cardinals and princes. Other people remained stand-

[1] For centuries the fishmongers had had to give to the Conservatori all fish exceeding the measurements inscribed on the wall of the old Portico of Octavia, now the entrance to the church of Sant' Angelo in Pescheria near the fishmarket. The guild of their own free will had turned their former obligation into the custom of sending exceptional catches to the Holy Father.

ing in groups and moved and mingled as they wished. There was plenty of room, for large pieces of furniture were rare and the architects had designed them, when present, to reproduce in wood the decorative stone columns and pilasters of the walls. Only the mingled colours of marquetry cabinets gave an occasional brighter glint and presiding at one end of the apartment would be the infrequently used, monumental fireplace. The ladies had a *cassetina,* a kind of foot-warmer for the hands, with which to defy the cold until the crowd was large and active enough to take the chill off the air. For there was always a good attendance and a hum of noise, through which the servants circulated all the time with wafers, biscuits and ices. Guests had been known to eat fifteen ices consecutively.

There were no strangers in this world. Its inhabitants saw each other constantly, they knew the whole history of one another's fortunes and mishaps. Everything that happened was food for gossip, but the fact still left them free to do exactly as they liked. Foreigners found this a most attractive line of conduct and, however incurious, were soon abreast of all that was going on. They were readily admitted to the round of *conversazioni* and quite at ease there, French people more than most, for Roman society adopted Versailles ways so eagerly that they possibly felt they were still at home. Everyone, too, was friendly and polite to them. The lackeys all in a row gave the newcomer a distinctive bow as he passed along between them, an attention they balanced off next day by calling round for a *mancia,* the tip it was never prudent to refuse in Rome. Nor was this first visit by any means their last; they might be expected back on all the great feasts, on New Year's Day and indeed on any pretext, good or gloomy. As de Brosses records,

'If their employer has a cold, and even if you know nothing about it and care less, round they come when she is better, so you may rejoice together. They rejoice continually, in fact—the happiest band you could meet, and all at your expense.'

Entertaining, among these people so careful of outward appearances, was naturally hedged about with rigid ceremonial. The rules were variable, since each family made traditional modifications of its own. For example, each would have a different list of those who were greeted by a gentleman in waiting as they left their coaches before entering the palace. Distinguished foreigners could add enormously to the complications of protocol. The majordomo, in whose department all such problems fell, did his best to avoid any awkwardness, but he had no easy task, surrounded by pitfalls as he was. Courtesy was to be measured out with care. Visitors were left to wait for longer or shorter periods according to rank in a whole set of rooms devoted to the purpose, passing from one to another only as announced by special ushers. Their names underwent curious distortions in this lengthy vocal transference and Montesquieu was to hear himself called successively Montedieu, Montieu and Mordieu before ending up as Forbu. This difficulty of foreign names was eventually solved by reducing them all to unspecified *Signori forestieri*. Ladies were conducted to their seats and care was taken not to separate a lady from her escort; only during the to-do consequent on a cardinal's arrival might a couple briefly be divided.

Conversation, obviously, was the staple fare at these assemblies and the priests were always there in force to uphold and lead it, refined and cultured men who set the standard of talk. This was never constrained by their presence; colourful jokes, animated wrangles and even wild bursts of laughter might be heard; the youngest females and the most elevated churchmen listened without the flicker of an eyelid to expressions of the coarsest kind. The cold dignity the Italians call *sostenuto,* and which the French, said Stendhal, mistook for distinction, would have seemed unbearably affected.

But conversation was not the sole charm of such parties, each of which had a character of its own. Some were of a purely worldly cast, others more intellectual and some were musical. Twice a week Cardinal de Bernis offered these delights combined and his Tuesdays and Saturdays passed for the most agreeable in Rome. The host, with his passion for wit, let the witty talk run to all lengths while ease, frankness and simplicity reigned in a setting of comfortable magnificence. In one room an excellent orchestra accompanied the best of the *castrati* and women singers; another was set aside for the gossip of literature and enlightenment; a third for politics; there were some nooks, even, where the theme was love; and everywhere the plentiful ices and the 'nimble, deferential' lackeys.

Every social function had its corner or its special room for cards. Though all popes had condemned gambling as the devil's invention none ever succeeded in uprooting the habit from among the nobility, lay or clerical. In Renaissance times play was so deep that in one night Cardinal Riario won from Innocent VIII's nephew, Franceschetto Cibo, enough to build the Cancellaria Palace. By the eighteenth century the *abate* Benedetti could say that 'chastity was not really the favourite Roman virtue, nor gambling really the worst vice'. Card games of all kinds were played everywhere. Some of the names, such as *stoppa* or *tre sette* no longer convey anything to us, but others, like *trenta e quaranta* and *banco fallito* are still known, as is that of the *minchiate,* the chequered tarot cards, ninety-seven of them, big and thick, said to have been designed by Michelangelo. This was a lively game, full of banter and cross-purposes, but stakes were small. It was *faraone,* ancestor of baccarat, that involved the large sums. Nothing was less like a modern baccarat table than a faro game in a Roman palace. Bets were laid in every sort of coinage, in *baiocchi* and sequins, in Spanish pistoles and Portuguese currency, but no money changed hands and no chips were used. Players noted their position after every hand by entering sums won or lost on scraps of card, gains on the coloured side, losses on the plain. By turning to the appropriate side one saw how one stood in any given currency. This remarkable accounting-system did not lead to utter confusion, as might have been expected. At the end of the evening each player told the banker, I have lost or won such-and-such a sum. Nothing was disputed, cheating unheard of. Debts were not as a rule settled straight away, but at the first opportunity; that is, at the next meeting. If this were to be delayed, the loser sent the money, with a polite note on the back of a playing card.

Women, no less than men, were besotted gamblers. Husbands, lovers, sometimes both, were ruined. Princess Chigi once borrowed 24,000 crowns from her own cook to clear an evening's debts.

If we have said little so far about women it is because women were restricted to a decorative role in this society. It was odd, said Montesquieu, to observe in Rome a town that took its tone, not from the women but the priests. No one, certainly, paid much regard to what the women thought and they were such limited creatures that many subjects doubtless were beyond them. How could it be otherwise when everyone, from fathers and husbands to the nuns who brought them up, was firmly convinced that 'a girl's best education is to have no education'?

Female learning was not a total blank, however. There were women who lectured publicly at the Academies at a time when

155

others could not even write and had an amanuensis to answer letters for them. Yet to none of them did such things make any difference. The bluestocking was not vainglorious because she knew Greek and if the illiterates did not exactly boast of their ignorance, neither were they ashamed of it. Naturalness and simplicity were the most charming, and the least to be expected, traits of women in good society of the time and foreigners, especially the French, used to reproach them with the want of 'the grand air that people talk such nonsense about'. They had no grand air because they had no affectation. They were great ladies and saw no need to draw attention to the fact by assuming the lofty graces that Stendhal likened to 'the label on the pitcher'. They came and went about the huge, brilliantly lit salons whose ornament they were, saying what they wished to say and laughing when they wanted to. They had, besides, a large degree of freedom, as is proved by their attitude to love. If further proof is needed there was their informal way of welcoming visitors before they even got up in the morning. The English traveller Brooke tells us how he called on an illustrious lady early in the day, was asked to wait, and received the explanation that she had thought it best to put a shift on before he came in. Not every lady would have bothered. They slept naked and if company arrived pulled up a—very flimsy—sheet and claimed that less was then revealed than by the deeply plunging necklines of their *abiti da società*. When Madame de Genlis came to Rome she is said to have held friendly converse with Cardinal de Bernis while in her bath and thus outstripped the custom of the country.

THE THEATRE

The Romans adored the theatre, but when the eighteenth century began possessed no playhouse big enough to seat a large audience for drama or opera in the comfort and elegance that is part of the treat. The special character of the government meant that things beside the Tiber were far behind the capitals of Europe and most other towns in Italy in this respect, for the popes, understandably, had preferred to build churches rather than centres of mundane entertainment. None had felt called upon to imitate Charles III, or Charles Emmanuel of Savoy, who gave the great court theatres to Naples and Turin. The princes of Rome limited their efforts to equipping small domestic stages for private performances; papal bias discouraged them from combining to raise a public theatre as the Lombard nobles, with their effective system of co-ownership of the boxes, were later to do at the Scala in Milan.

But the Roman people had all the Italian's inborn love for music and the children grew up with it. Their parents sang at their tasks and walking past the studio-workshops they would hear master and journeyman singing part-arias together. There was a whole galaxy of composers blazing new trails in music and a genuine dramatic revival was in progress. It was becoming impossible for many reasons to keep plays and operas hidden away in holes and corners; as people began to feel they needed theatres the public interest was to override the Church's disapproval.

The popes, indeed, though they did not actually encourage the opening of playhouses, took account of the temper of the times and ceased their calculated obstruction of any private projects. Several large theatres were built as a result and justified by the most enthusiastic support.

The largest was at one time the Alberti, or Teatro delle Dame, near the Piazza di Spagna. It was rectangular in shape, the three sides of the auditorium consisting of six tiers of boxes. Since the sides were set at right angles, the occupants of the farthest boxes had to crane their necks painfully towards the stage. The Alberti's chief rival was the Argentina, where the special feature was an enormous chandelier that vanished into the ceiling when the play began. The house was then plunged in total darkness and enthusiasts wishing to follow their opera scores had to bring their own candles and sit there rather like persons attending a Benediction service.

The rivalry of these two great Roman theatres went far beyond any mere commercial competition designed to catch the public interest. It unfolded in a long series of tragi-comic episodes, one of which will suffice to show what passions were unleashed in the struggle for leadership. The Alberti had been having a triumphant success with one of its tenors—a *bravissimo* tenor, it was acknowledged—and the opposing camp of the Argenti were mad with rage. One evening they hit upon the plan of taking a dog into enemy territory, teasing it unmercifully and releasing it to bark the place down just as the tenor launched into his star aria. The time taken to catch the infuriated animal and the confusion of the chase of course broke the spell and put the singer off; he faltered and could not regain his audience. The next few days were even worse, for he had to sing against a claque all barking away to remind him of the dog and drown his voice at one and the same time. Protests only provoked renewed jeering and neither performer nor performance could survive. The director of the Alberti had to dismiss his singer and take his opera off.

All the same, it took ten years of constant and unmannerly strife before the Argentina emerged as the premier theatre of Rome. It had superior elegance on its side, as well as the remarkable fighting spirit of its supporters, and provided the better background for playgoing, which was an entirely social activity in those days. It even managed to attract official blessing too; at least, the Governor of Rome seemed to regard it as an official theatre, attending first nights and functioning with goodwill as its protector, patron and master of ceremonies. They waited for his command to raise the curtain and gave no encores until he signalled with his handkerchief, though the gesture was merely conventional and by custom he always allowed whatever the audience asked for. On those around he lavished courtesies. During the first interval his servants in their gorgeous liveries, preceded by an attendant with a big candelabrum, went from box to box carrying ices, preserves and fruit on silver trays. Another detachment circulated with similar offerings in the pit, which welcomed them warmly and swept the trays bare in no time.

Musical plays were the favourite fare and these only were given at the Alberti and Argentina. Other forms of drama flourished at other houses, notably the *Commedia dell' arte* (wonderful acting, it was said, in shocking plays), in which the Italians had long been acknowledged masters. In these unscripted comedies the actors improvised on the bones of a plot in a flowery style, all puns and extravagant jokes—a firework display of misunderstandings, clowning and cudgelling, with no attempt at coherence. The people always loved these plays, rooted deep in folk-lore, and were indifferent to comedy of manners. Even Goldoni, the leading dramatist of the century, could be hissed for not seasoning his lines racily enough. A Roman audience really demanded out and out burlesque, though boos and mockery might be avoided if a piece were resolutely lachrymose. On the other hand it was important not to be tragic. No one was supposed to die on the stage and so the darkest deeds went unpunished at the end.

Three other leading theatres shared the public favour with the Alberti and the Argentina. The Capranica was devoted to light operetta, with funny plots and cheerful tunes. At the Valle the choice was wider, alternating between comedies *all' improvviso* and the gay musical works of Cimarosa and Piccini, with their inter-ludes of ballet. It was famous for a five-hour programme lasting until midnight, which was very late for those days.

Lastly came the Tor di Nona, a thriving comedy house that had managed to live down a bad start. When newly opened in 1745 it was honoured by a private visit from Benedict XIV and the director had taken advantage of this unwonted favour to put the words *indulgentia plenaria* over the entrance, implying that he enjoyed the protection of the Church. He had to remove the misleading inscription at once and apologize publicly for the blunder, since ecclesiastical toleration of the theatre was then of a very grudging kind. Fourteen years later the feeling was still so strong that in 1759 Clement XIII forbade the clergy to go to the play at all. But such restrictions lagged far behind the ways of the world and his successor, finding them impossible to enforce, repealed them. From that moment onwards the drama in Rome had the freedom of the city and all the theatres were keenly patronized by priest and prelate. The cardinals themselves attended, even after the Pope had said he wished they would not do so. *Abati* would play in the orchestras and special tickets were always available for men of the Church, who often reflected little credit upon her. 'I have seen,' says de Brosses, 'dandified abbés in a public theatre with four thousand people there, attracting the attention of notorious courtesans'—a fine evocation of the free, gallant Italian ways to remind us that we are dealing with contemporaries of Casanova.

This cursory revue would be incomplete without some note of the beloved marionettes. Their most popular theatre was that in the Palazzo Fiano[1] but many little stages also catered for the craze. Puppet shows were given on improvised trestles in the open air—several competed for attention in the Piazza Navona—with the people crowding round to watch Cassandro and mock at his mis-fortunes. This mythical personnage, one of whose adventures formed the subject of each playlet, united in himself all the charac-teristics and minor foibles of the Roman-born Italian. Mad on music, he played very badly and sang out of tune; his ideas as a new-rich burgher were idiotic and inflated; in love, he forgot how old he was and the pretty girls made a fool of him; stubbornly

---

[1] Its puppets were so cleverly made that they seemed like life-size beings. Only when a giant climbed into view and was the boy who snuffed the candles, was their real scale apparent.

looking after number one, he always came off worst. So oblivious were the audience and so naïvely self-opinionated that they never recognized their own stupidities in his. Dominated by that old spirit of disrespect, they preferred to interpret Cassandro's tribulations as a criticism of authority. Layman as he was, he wore for them the red cap of a cardinal or a prelate's purple stockings. And, as the puppets furnished an indistinguishable blend of satire and social comment, who shall say that they were wrong?

Let us, in imagination, follow an eighteenth-century Roman to one of the great opera-houses. Tickets were not sold at the entrance but obtainable from the manager inside and prices varied with the success of the piece. There were no permanent companies; a manager would rent a theatre and engage singers, scene-designers and orchestra for any opera he decided to put on. His financial arrangements, by the most incredible persistence in miscalculation, were in every case unsound and bankruptcy was a foregone conclusion, however well he did. Another impresario then took his place, with another company. As a result, each theatre would present three or four operas in the season, between November and Lent. These were all new productions, for revivals, as we shall see, were never given.

In 1765 a visitor named Samuel Sharp noted in his journal, 'It is the fashion here to regard the theatre as a place for meeting people and paying social calls. Instead of listening to the music they all laugh and talk as though they were at home. I had heard of this Italian habit before leaving England, but never imagined they took it so far.'

Theatres in Rome were indeed more than mere places of entertainment. They were combined drawing-rooms, marts and exchanges. In the huge, finely decorated auditorium, society occupied the boxes and the middling and lower orders the benches in the pit, but from floor to ceiling manners were the same. Bad manners, too, for noise and disorder reigned supreme. This was more than any normal buzz of conversation before the curtain rose. Here people cursed and shouted at each other, they attracted attention by waving handkerchiefs or twirling hats and coats on the end of canes. They argued and quarrelled and threw their arms about and generally tried to see who could make most din. There was an indescribable hurly-burly of varied and extraordinary utterance: piercing shouts, strident laughter, exclaimings and feminine chatter, farcical sneezing and coughing. The gifted mimics gave a continuous programme of cat and bird noises, applauded by everybody round. Those not actually in full cry would be having picnic meals on the benches, limiting themselves not at all as to food and drink, nor to what one observer alludes to as 'the consequences'.

Any hope that the babel would end when the curtain went up was doomed to disappointment. There was no ensuing calm and tumult accompanied the performance through, a tumult the operas of Italy might have been written to promote. For if literature declined in this century there was a brilliant revival in music, with marked developments especially in music for the stage. Melody, in which Italy was to lead the world so long, was dominant and composers abandoned the old ways to concentrate on creating opportunities for their singers. The chief result was that the action of an opera ceased to be of interest while the audience waited for the grand aria, the ritual culmination of every scene. There were still lengthy and tedious passages of recitative between these showpieces, but no one dreamed of listening to them, except perhaps the devoted nucleus we have observed, peering over the score by the light of candles which their neighbours usually did their best to extinguish. The remainder paid no attention to what the actors were intoning on the stage, turning instead, in the pitch-dark auditorium, to the pleasures of loud and lively conversation. They conversed about anything and everything. Lovers pledged their vows, rakes made advances to young ladies, business was settled and anecdotes exchanged. Occasionally the unheard and unhearable music might come under discussion, when things grew more serious. While some condemned it and bawled insults at the performers, others praised it and exaggerated arguments broke out between the opposing parties. These debates would electrify the whole house until all present were shouting and gesticulating at once, 'the most cautious old *abbé* as violently as any young man'. Then the aria began. It was listened to in sudden, reverent hush, although the stamping and clapping would start long before it was over as people now yelled applause and complimentary verses at the soloist; 'sad,' thought Bergeret, 'for anyone who was sensitive to noise or wanted to hear what came next.' For the frantic acclamations and echoing cheers—almost maniacal, another witness found —went on long after the favoured singer left the stage, continuing

161

well into the next recitative, which was accorded no more attention than its predecessor.

In the case of divided opinion, the audience split into clamorous rival factions with a deafening hubbub of mingled cheers and booing. Sometimes an artist's supporters would anticipate hostile reaction by applauding all the time he sang and not a note was audible. Quite often the singers appealed directly to the public on some point of criticism or quarrel with the composer. It could be an absurd method of settling things, and Carlo Bandini has this charming tale:

'At the first performance of an opera of Buranello at the Argentina one of the soloists saw fit to murder the finest aria in the piece with a rendering that made a mockery of it. The maddened composer shot from his music-stand and on to the stage and thus addressed the audience: "The aria you have just heard is one I never wrote; this brute doesn't know how to sing it. To show you what I mean, I shall now attempt to sing it myself." This he did, and they applauded him. The soloist then countered with a cry of "Gentlemen, I never liked that aria, but I can do it better than he can. Listen!" Whereupon, he brought the house down by singing it very well.'

Not that things always ended quite so amicably. The cast might have to make their exit under a barrage of assorted missiles—rotten pears were very popular. And the spectators, too, might be in danger from the cast. This extract from a Roman notebook offers food for thought:

'At the Capranica they [the actors] had got a stack of tiles and stones on the stage, ready to throw at anybody in the audience, as they did last year.'

The construction of contemporary musical drama contained yet another element of uproar. There was no place in it for the choruses and ballets of traditional opera, but it presented instead a succession of marches, sacrifices, ceremonies and, above all, mimic combats. These activities, entirely unconnected with the plot, were the affair of a host of extras. Armies 150 strong would take the stage in the wake of mounted captains whose real horses were seldom properly trained in trotting to the music. Fierce warriors waged

162

epic battles in such chaos that friend and foe were, from the front of the house, as one. The louder and more muddled the mêlée, of course, the better the audience liked it, seeking to add clamour to clangour with hellish screams and frenzied stamping of feet.

The ceaseless alarums from the pit almost prevented those seated in the boxes from following the play at all. This did not, however, matter very much since they were not greatly interested in it, whatever it might be. They had come, not to hear an opera, but to spend the evening in pleasant company. A hostess took her box by the year and considered it somewhere for entertaining, like an extension of her drawing-room at home. The theatre was an occasion for visiting, every box a small centre of elegance, charm and amorous intrigue where the men came to woo the ladies and the ladies to show off their jewels and finery. Talk was of business or politics, there were friendly suppers and ice cream. The corridors outside buzzed with the servants carrying refreshments to and fro.

There was gambling too, sometimes for heavy stakes. The boxes were easily adaptable, for the owners had furnished them luxuriously and curtains and draperies could be drawn close to shut the occupants from view. The chairs were not in rows but set round a table and etiquette demanded that each gentleman in turn sit by the hostess. When the box was full and someone else came in, whoever had been there longest left his place at her side and all the others moved up one. The stage they all ignored, unless it were to lend an abstracted ear to an aria when conversation dwindled.

During this century the Church was not to rescind its decree against the employment of women as actresses, singers or dancers in any theatre of the Papal States. This was in part a moral measure, for it was thought that artistic talents might well increase the lure of feminine attractions. The Romans could justifiably have found this over-cautious, but they did not really mind. Steeped as they were in tradition, they always remembered that women had never been seen on the classical stage, where masks were used in any case and beauty was of no account. The first actresses in fact appeared in 1550 but the innovation did not last and no more were seen until that curious interlude, about 1670, when Christina of Sweden constituted herself patron of the cultural life of Rome, with particular attention to the theatre. Under the severe pontificate of Innocent XI (1676–1689) the ban came into force again with sterner penalties than ever.

Female roles were taken by *castrati*, that ambiguous order of beings mutilated, as their names proclaimed, for the sake of the dulcet voices that were the glory of Italian opera and the joy of listeners for many a generation. The Church opposed the practice in principle but did nothing to stop it, requiring, at most, that castration should be voluntary. Since the operation was performed on seven- or eight-year-old boys who could not possibly foresee its consequences, this proviso was useless, and the children were in any case the victims of parental greed. No concern was ever expressed about the surgeries where castrations were done and at least one establishment near the Vatican boasted, with some justice, of official protection on a signboard saying 'Pope's Chapel Singers Castrated Here'. The attitude of the popes themselves may be gathered from the story that one of them, petitioned by a *castrato* for leave to marry, noted in the margin of the document, '*Che si castri meglio*'—'They should castrate him better'.

The 'sacred capons', as the revolted Stendhal called them, had good, sometimes wonderful, contralto or soprano voices in addition to other feminine characteristics. With the walk, gestures and carriage of women, their equivocal state gave them a whole armoury of fascinations which they employed frequently, complacently and with great success, against men. As a French visitor observed,

'They have hips, buttocks and bosoms and plump round necks; you could mistake them for real girls. And even their fellow-countrymen have attempted, occasionally, to mistake them indeed.'

And not their fellow-countrymen alone, if we may credit Montesquieu in his *Voyage en Italie*:

'There were two little *castrati* at the Teatro Capranica when I was in Rome, tripping about in dresses, the prettiest things I ever saw. Their names were Mariotti and Chiostra and they would have started the least likely of men on the road to Gomorrah. A young Englishman fell madly in love with one of them, believing him to be a woman, and they kept him dangling for a month or more.'

We hear also of another *castrato*, the *prima donna* of the Teatro delle Dame, whose looks, rather than his talent, set the whole town by the ears. His figure was nymph-like in its well-made corset, his bosom second in form and beauty to no woman's; in fact most of the havoc the odd creature wrought was due to his bosom. 'The tender, modest way he cast his black-eyed glances like favours over the boxes was enough to ravish every heart.' Some of the *castrati* complicated things still further by dressing like churchmen. Casanova, sitting with his friends in a café on the Via Condotti, saw a pleasant-faced young *abaté* come in whom he judged, by his hips, to be a girl in disguise. But it was a famous *castrato* named Beppino della Mamana, who proceeded to make highly improper suggestions to him.

The *castrati* were much sought after and openly entertained, even by the cardinals. How extraordinary it is that a tête-à-tête with a *castrato* was allowable under a régime which found it wicked to sup with a pretty girl from the opera! Rome rang with outrageous gossip about these youths and the aspirants for their expensive favours, but the vice was generally regarded with indulgence. It was known as the *peccato nobile*, the sin of gentlemen.

All this interest in the 'virtuosi' and their doings bred in them an insufferable conceit, to the exasperation of theatre managers and composers who bore the brunt of every whim over cuts and alterations in scripts. The stage-management, too was called upon for all manner of fancy additions, as one refused to make an exit unless he had a horse or another claimed that an ascent into heaven was essential to improve the effect of his aria.

In the small private theatres of the princely palaces all the petty papal regulations were duly observed and the embassies, too, conformed out of courtesy. Only the Spanish Embassy, in 1782, actually presented an opera with a real leading lady, a bold and scandalous departure. Women were not seen upon the Roman stage until the French came with their republic *per ridere*.

The eunuch singers had the voice and demeanour to sustain illusion, but it was otherwise with the dancers who took female roles. The masculine character of the *castrati* was weakened by sundry modifications, but the men who danced as women were real men and such they remained, even when professional habit made them to some degree degenerate. Disguise would have been difficult in any case for they were obliged by the police to wear unsightly short breeches of black velvet under the abbreviated skirts in which they usually appeared and these garments, visible at intervals as they curvetted about, robbed them of all femininity. Their beards, too, were something of a problem. Chins grew noticeably darker by the end of the evening, despite the pre-performance shave, and there would be disconcerting allusions ('Zaire's just shaving', for instance) to the ballet-heroine herself. And when her hero kissed the ballerina's hand it was a gnarled and hairy paw that she extended. As someone said, 'You had to be Goethe and come from Germany to find that sort of travesty amusing.'

As for the dancing of these men of masquerade, it was all flailing limbs, acrobatic pirouettes and great bounds from one side of the stage to the other. Choreography was in the doldrums for want of women executants and ballet by no means so important as it had become in France. Italian opera did not really need it; the dancers were seen only in obscure interpolated pieces that had nothing to do with the plot and drew from the audience the boisterous reception noted above. In two pithy sentences Montesquieu disposes of such talent and of the taste of the Romans for these antics: 'They have the most awful dancing and they think it wonderful . . . Since they lack a notion of what dancing is and confuse it with jumping, they believe that whoever jumps highest must be best.'

It is all very odd when we remember the pleasure that all classes took in dancing themselves. For people danced everywhere in Rome, with perfect grace and even, occasionally, with admirable technique.

CHAPTER EIGHT

LETTERS, ART AND VISITORS

LITERATURE AND LITERARY ACADEMIES

From a literary point of view the eighteenth century was one of decadence in Rome and there were no Romans among the leading figures in Italian literature. The poet Alfieri was a Piedmontese, austere, rough and harsh. Goldoni, who gave to comedy the buoyancy of life itself and left us vivid sketches of contemporary manners, came from Venice. So, too, did Gozzi, with his attempted revival of the art of impromptu comedy. Of the great authors only Metastasio, 'the Racine of Italy', was a child of Rome and his Greek-sounding name a version of the typically Roman surname of his father, who had a small grocer's shop in the Piazza della Vallicella. Romans thought little of writers born anywhere else and did not understand them. Goldoni himself, the foremost comic dramatist of Italy, failed here. The literature that pleased this individualistic city must be reared beside the Tiber.

Unhappily, and always excepting Metastasio, such literature was a poor sort of product, its mediocrity only emphasized by a quite astonishing prolixity. Everyone wrote sonnets and tragedies, from magnates like the Chigi, by way of cardinals and monsignori (specializing in epithalamiums and elegies), to unemployed lawyers and unconsulted doctors, not to mention the horde of minor clergy who plunged in enthusiastically with plays of intrigue. But their amateur comedies materialized as clumsy farce, the tragedies were comic and the country poems and idylls hopeless doggerel.

An illusion of intense literary activity was nevertheless produced, for these shoddy Pindars and their pseudo-Theocritus friends banded together in the mutual admiration societies known as Academies, 'sonnet-mongers,' it was said, 'meeting to read each others' nonsense'. The Academies, some of them venerable institutions, bore fantastic names: gli Umoristi, i Virginali, gli Uniformi, gli Ordonati. Each of these conclaves had a badge and rules of its own and its own hierarchy of pompous titles. Some bestowed upon their members names to fit the general picture: Pampano, Agresto,

Mosto and Uva—Messieurs Vinebranch, Verjuice, New Brew and Grape—all belonged to the Accadèmia dei Viticultori, innocent of all connection with grape-growing.

Dupaty encountered such bodies in Florence and pronounced, 'In Florence there were four academies. They had no function, they were just four academies.' The same and more was true of those in Rome, for they did not even indulge in the sterile intellectual gymnastics to which Florentine labours were directed. There the themes were frivolous but the discourse erudite; a discourse heard in Rome would be so much vapouring mish-mash. The main purpose of a Roman academy was to hear the members read their insipid poetasting and acclaim it as the product of genius. The audience needed all its tolerance and all its patience, too, for these recitals were monotonous to a degree, uttered in a bizarre, psalmodic cross between speech and song that sounded completely unnatural and made the whole thing unintelligible.

Enthroned above all other academies in Rome, their arbiter and exemplar, stood the Arcadia, or Accadèmia degli Arcadi. Though founded in 1689 by habitués of the salon of the Swedish Queen Christina to 'wage war on bad taste', it quickly and assiduously set about the practice of bad taste on its own account. Its self-appointed task was the purification of Italian poetry, for which purpose it nurtured a sort of parody of Platonic idealism and modelled its style not only on Petrarch but on the least admirable of his imitators. This, it said, was the renaissance of the Renaissance, and the result was a strained ingenuity and a wildly artificial fashion of presenting life and emotion, at variance with the spirit currently dominating the rest of European literature.

Each member relinquished his own name and adopted that of some Arcadian shepherd. These literary would-be shepherds met on the Janiculum to stroll by the road above the Tiber discussing art and ethics. They liked to encourage poets and prided themselves on discovering new ones. On taking up some second-rate Petrarchan aspirant they would praise his genius to the skies and pay him much unmerited honour. One case must be excepted, that of the silver-tongued child they found in the streets and who was to become Metastasio, but it was seldom they displayed such flair. The only two poets they crowned on the Capitol have left no memory behind them but that of their absurd pretensions.

In 1725 they honoured a Sienese bard named Bernardino Perfetti who first composed at twelve months and wrote a sonnet at the age of seven. Petrarch had received his laurel garland in 1341 and the Arcadians would have liked this coronation to be equally impressive but they made it, unfortunately, a parade of all that was spurious in their society. The proceedings had an air of travesty despite the great train of cardinals, the velvet-draped stands full of alluring ladies and the presiding likeness of the Pope, who had sent his portrait by way of representative. One after another the learned harangues poured forth, alternating with Arcadian poetical affusions. The central figure, wearing his laurel circlet and accompanied by the music of guitars, made impromptu verses for over an hour on the Glory of the Colosseum. It was long, boring and rather silly.

The other lyric coronation of the century was that of a Florentine lady-poet whom the Arcadians had welcomed to their collective bosom under the pastoral name of Corilla Olimpica. This particular shepherdess produced no written word. Her talent, one much prized at the time in Rome, was for improvisation. In a stupefying poetical flood, Corilla improvised on all known subjects. She had even done so in honour of Casanova though without managing to seduce him, being altogether less remarkable for grace and beauty than for her command of language. She also squinted, a slight disadvantage which, although supposedly shared by the goddess of love herself, put the gay Venetian off. The fact that she was over fifty, too, would explain his cold reception when she wooed him with her muse.

Corilla had her great day on the Capitol on August 31, 1776, in the huge Sala degli Orazi e Curiazi hung with brocade and cloth of gold. Dressed in white satin and enveloped in a star-embroidered cloak, she took her place upon a purple throne before a distinguished audience that included the Duke of Gloucester, brother of George III, then travelling in Italy in search of stirring sights. She received the laurel crown from the Roman Senator, together with the usual plenteous tribute of poems composed by the Arcadians. She replied at length, taking as her theme the Glory of Rome. The generality treated this extravagant homage for what it was worth, and when the heroine emerged from the Capitol to drive home in the Senator's state carriage she was greeted by a volley of catcalls and escorted on her way by the rude jeers of a populace sadly indifferent to poesy. The redoubtable Pasquino added his biting epigrams to the popular verdict and the shower of derision made Corilla and the Arcadians appear so thoroughly preposterous that the Academy itself succumbed soon afterwards. France was not the only place where ridicule could kill. Corilla's triumph, however, even though it ended in buffoonery, was to give Madame de Staël material for 'Corinne'.

Happily, the intellectual life of Rome was not limited to the farcical academies. There were many small groups of genuinely learned people meeting to discuss their productions. As well as the picture galleries and the rich collections of sculpture and inscriptions attracting connoisseurs from all over the world the city was excellently endowed with libraries. The Vatican library was justly famous and every convent had its own. Augustines, Jesuits and Dominicans all competed to collect the greatest number of rare books and manuscripts. In the palaces of prince and cardinal the shelves were filled with treasures.

It would be wrong to remember the footling literary academies and forget the valuable work of the Accadèmia dei Lincei, which took as its province the natural products of the earth. Founded in 1603, it was in its heyday in the eighteenth century and did much to forward the study of physical sciences. Every great noble had his own 'cabinet of curiosities', while the Farnese gardens on the Palatine afforded a wonderful ground for study, for the botanical garden created there, largely through the Accadèmia dei Lincei, contained plants of the rarest species from all parts of the world.

ARCHAEOLOGY

Although the ancient monuments of Rome were so neglected this was not because the eighteenth century took no interest in them. Their sad state was due to a very long period of disregard and age-old habits of indifference, but the neglect and indifference applied mainly to the visible remnants of the classical world; about what was still buried in the soil, under the turf and flowers and bushes, there was enormous curiosity.

Every man of culture—and any man with pretensions to culture —took an interest. Yet archaeological fever led only to the making of shallow digs without plan or method and the hauling forth of statues, bas-reliefs and fragments of any sort that could be put in a gallery of antiques. The century's real mania was for collecting. The popes, who considered it their duty to bring to light their city's glorious past, had a veritable passion for the work and throughout the Settecento embellished the Vatican museums with mosaics and statuary. The cardinals, every one a Maecenas by tradition, showed equal enthusiasm. Rich foreigners on their long Roman visits would find their time best spent and their expeditions most usefully directed in the search for 'marbles'. They all longed to discover, on a site or at a dealer's, some classical object to take home as a memento of their travels. For many, as for many cultivated Romans, the ardours of the chase were increased by a praiseworthy desire to learn all they could about antiquities.

All this investigation bore much fruit, certainly as far as enriching the galleries was concerned, but there was, at least in the first half of the century, nothing scientific about it, for all the investigators were in fact amateurs. They delved in the ruins and took away their treasures with no thought of any light these might have cast upon the original structure of the buildings. This aspect meant so little to them that when the Duke of Parma's antiquaries laid bare the great hall of the Flavian Palace and removed the finest objects to adorn the Farnese collections, they were to bury the imperial mansion once more underground. They did not even trouble to make a record of the layout, which was not to be established until the excavations paid for by Napoleon III, 150 years later.

But an important discovery towards the middle of the century would bring a change of attitude. When Charles III of Naples came into his Farnese inheritance and transferred the famous collections to his own capital, he gave to Rome the fragments of the city plan engraved in the reign of Septimius Severus. These had lain neglected in a cellar, but when exhibited at the Capitol Museum furnished the archaeologists with their first real, valid notion of Roman topography at the height of the Empire. With this sure foundation they could give positive aim to their studies, while at the same time they were beginning to adopt empirical methods. Such methods had spread to archaeology by way of the natural sciences and history and excavators now wished to discover, from the few remaining elements, what an ancient building looked like. The possibility grew that, allowing for mutilations, alterations and additions, they might arrive at some idea of the remains as the toga-clad inhabitant once knew them. Before this the four academies which concentrated on Roman monuments had been, like all Roman academies, working in the clouds, their feelings running high on subjects of doubtful historical value, such as the arrival of Aeneas in Italy. But with the finding of that first plan of Rome and with the new developments, their researches were directed to more important ends. A new body, the Accademia della Storia ed Antichità Romane, founded by Benedict XIV, gave a healthy impulse to the labours of the 'antiquaries'. Archaeology as a science was not yet born, but the taste for archaeological learning was becoming established at Rome.

It received new lustre from 1755 onwards, from the first excavations of Pompeii and Herculaneum, buried seventeen centuries before under the ashes of Vesuvius. The site of the two Campanian towns was found quite by chance, but the digging, though on a small scale until the beginning of the nineteenth century, yielded much information about the ancient Romans, their public and private lives, their art and architecture. From these discoveries the Neo-Classical movement would be born, but they meanwhile encouraged the passionate interest in excavation at Rome and many wonderful works of art came to light. Only the most famous need be mentioned here. In 1748 the great red granite obelisk was dug up which Augustus brought from Egypt to serve under the Empire as the gnomon of the sundial in the Campus Martius and which stands today in the Piazza Montecitorio; in 1765 the celebrated Mosaic of the Doves was added to the Vatican collections; and excavations in a vineyard near the Porta San Sebastiano revealed the tomb of Cornelius Scipio, father of Scipio Africanus. It dated from 300 years before Christ, was among the oldest remains of the Republican era and caused such a sensation that the most elegant ladies in Rome felt impelled to go down into the trench and scrabble the damp earth with milk-white hands.

But the vogue for the Antique, though it re-established Rome as the artistic capital of Europe and drew most gratifying visits from painters, noblemen and crowned heads, stripped her in the end of a large part of her artistic inheritance. She had been once enriched with the loot of Greece and of the East; then she was plundered in her turn by the Byzantine Emperors, since whose time not a century passed but she had been, to a greater or lesser degree, picked over and despoiled. And of this pillage none was more thorough than that she suffered from foreigners in the seventeen hundreds, with the English proving greediest of all. It was not for the gentler climate and the glorious past they came, but to take home what their homes most lacked—works of art—and to this end they organized a regular export system. Their example was followed by the Swedes. Gustavus III, wishing to create a museum of sculpture in Stockholm, filled it with Roman work through the good offices of his consul Francesco Piranesi, son of the engraver, whom he had appointed solely for his archaeological flair and business ability. In the same way Catherine the Great secured the help of the sculptor Cavaceppi in adding to her gallery of antiquities and the Elector of Saxony and Frederick the Great made similar arrangements. The French cut a less exalted figure in the auction, for they could not bid so high. The Grand Duke Leopold I bore off to Florence most of the treasures from the Villa Medici on the Pincio, and we must now go to the Uffizzi to see Niobe and her Children, the Wrestlers, the Sleeping Hermaphrodite and many other masterpieces. The most grievous loss of all was when the King of Naples removed the main items from the Farnese collections, notably the Farnese Bull and the Hercules, the Venus Callipygos and the colossal busts of Antoninus and Vespasian. Four hundred and twenty-two items were sent away to Naples and narrowly escaped falling into the hands of Algerian pirates in the course of the journey.

The Romans did not stand aside and watch this plundering as uninvolved spectators. Some, by offering their services to foreign collectors, helped the process on. Others strove to make good the gaps by means of fresh discoveries. In this they were imitated by the popes themselves, whose zeal led to the formation of new galleries, such as the Museo Pio-Clementino in the Vatican, with its Gallery of the Candelabra, its Halls of the Greek Cross and of the Muses. The pontiffs went to all lengths to improve these collections, buying antiquities and urging princes and cardinals to give up those they possessed to the Vatican. And more than anything, they dug. The Roman earth must have been rich indeed to yield such finds, for official operations were conducted with a languor that even the Romans found surprising. One of them, observing Pious VI's cherished excavations in the Forum, noted 'the gangs of convicts making a show of digging in the ruins, looking for more ruins, under orders from two or three louts in uniform, carrying canes and quite as lazy as their workmen'.

DEVELOPMENT OF THE PLASTIC ARTS

The art of an age is the portrait of an age. In the preceding centuries the spell-binding effusion of the Baroque had made plain the great resurgence of religion and the Papacy, but now the Holy

See was diminishing under the pressure of 'philosophy'; every day the kingdoms of the world cast their shadows longer over Peter's throne. It was the beginning of the artistic decline of Rome. Elsewhere there was to be no quarrel between the new doctrines and art of a splendid kind, but Rome embodied ideas utterly opposed to those of the Enlightenment. Her history had not prepared her for coming to terms with materialism, nor with any feeble brand of spirituality, and so the break-up of the old humanism was felt more deeply here than anywhere. Atrophy weighed the Eternal City down. Her art was exhausted, she had no life to breathe into new work. Her architects, painters and sculptors could be derivative, no more.

And yet every country in Europe and even most of the Italian centres had produced a very definite Settecento style. In France, particularly, it developed from lofty, Louis XIV majesty to all the involvements of rococo, though without arousing the admiration of the Romans. They would copy the French in dress and manners, not in art; the spirit of French art in the eighteenth century was not in tune with a priestly court, however worldly the latter may have grown. The Baroque, fashion and reflection of its own period, had fulfilled the ancestral leanings of a whole people, had been the ultimately Roman manifestation of Roman art, the classic Roman style. And to it Rome was to remain faithful when its creative energy failed and the vital spark went out of it; even when it grew tamer and less weighty, even when it strayed, with bizarre linear refinements, back to Borromini. For the first two-thirds of the century architects and decorative artists persisted with their 'hackneyed, out-of-date creations in the Baroque mode', and the sculptors tried vainly to recapture Bernini's airy crispness. Is it therefore, so surprising that the decadence of Roman art is, at this period, so cruelly obvious? Sculpture has become facile modelling, the painting is skilled but flaccid, for even the best artists thought of nothing but the money they earned 'doing English portraits by the dozen'. The Accadèmia di San Luca, watching over the plastic arts, was no better than the poetic and literary lyceums whose fatuities we have already noted.

Neo-Classical reaction came with the last third of the century and was a foreign importation. Its progenitor was Winckelmann, that immigrant to Rome from Brandenburg who was said to make such 'incredible efforts to become Italian by sheer force of imagination.' In a famous sentence he summed up the tendencies of the new school :'The one way to grow great and, if possible, inimitable, is to study the Ancients.' He saw no point in wishing to surpass the Laocoon or the Farnese Hercules, for they were the perfect expression of beauty. An artist could seek the sources of inspiration nowhere but in the works of Antiquity, since in them were united 'the various rays of beauty scattered and divided in the vast domain of nature'. They were, moreover, 'nature herself, transposed and purified'. It followed that he disapproved the study of the living model and recommended 'disassimilation', by which he meant the search for ideal form stripped of all individual character.

This new school, whose theorists so far outshone its practitioners, this new religion as it might almost be called, had its pontiffs too. They foregathered in the luxurious villa at the Porta Pinciana where Cardinal Albani lived like a prince of the Renaissance. There could be seen the famous 'Parnassus' ceiling painted by Raphael Mengs as a manifesto of the Neo-Classical aesthetic. It is a cold, literate composition which exactly demonstrates the spirit of the school while fixing its bounds inexorably. The third Renaissance was to remain a pale and frozen thing, incapable of begetting rich artistic life. A lamentable inferiority complex led these Roman painters to follow fashions from the world outside, although their hearts were not in the pursuit. Flatness and banality invaded all they did, in the name of a modernity whose principles they never thoroughly understood. It was the Trevisan sculptor Antonio Canova who was to be the real champion in Rome of the theories of Mengs and Winckelmann. Canova stormed the heights with his first work, was ranked with Michelangelo for his second and officially installed as the divinity of art. In his hands sculpture became plastic once again, a matter of form, that 'told no stories and composed no dramas' such as the Baroque had presented for the last 150 years. And yet how obviously the art that replaced Bernini's lacked his movement and his mettle and his overflowing energy! Canova's reputation, undeserved and inflated as it was, lasted a long time but now he strikes us only with the chill of lifelessness. His acknowledged masterpiece was that celebrated marble in the Casino Borghese of the Princess Pauline in her would-be abandoned and seductive attitude; and yet who today feels tempted to offer her half-naked person any but the most respectful homage?

Even if they did not produce creative artists of their own in the eighteenth century, the Italians claim to have formed many foreign ones, by dint of giving them Rome, with all its intellectual stimulation and the models it provided. Every European artist of note certainly made his Roman pilgrimage and a number lingered here. They were honourably received, all the palaces were open to them and they could live in contact with the great works there displayed; and yet their achievement is only in slight measure the product of Roman culture. Italy seems to have brushed by them, leaving them untouched. It was in Paris that there came to birth the graceful, delicate art we find in the pictures of Watteau, Boucher and Fragonard, the sculpture of Falconet and Bouchardon.

Later, when the miraculous finds at Pompeii had led them to study the antique world, the artists did not turn for inspiration to those discoveries on the slopes of Vesuvius. They turned to Rome, its stored collections, its rows of columns and blocks of ruined buildings. Rome came to be considered the ideal place for study and learning. We must remember, however, that it was an international, non-Roman movement which made this use of Rome, and that the stiff, unanimated art it so often produced ran absolutely counter to the whole character of Roman art throughout its history.

And yet there was much that the painters could usefully learn when they came to see the ruins and to draw from Michelangelo and Raphael. In spite of temporary decline, Rome was in many ways far in advance of the other great cities of Europe. Her treasures of archaeology made her a world centre of art and the light she shed was brilliant as in her glorious days. She imbued these artists with her classical serenity. They were kindled, too, with the flame that touched the earliest humanists and ready to echo Goethe's cry when he entered the Eternal City and recognized his adoptive country there—'Only now do I begin to live.'

This period opened with Rome adoring the most hallucinatory extravagances of the Baroque and she fell as it continued into a bog of learned solemnity; and yet there remain from it things which recall the great tradition and afford us charming glimpses of the old papal city. First and foremost there is the Trevi fountain, built in 1762 by belated followers of Bernini. It may not be a masterpiece, this gay, fairytale cascade with its surging decoration like an echo of the tumbling, noisy water; but its festive mythology, its mock-heroic verve and the enormous *joie de vivre* it conjures up are a timely reminder, to a century just beginning to suspect the fact, that all Roman magnificence, in that final flowering of ancestral tendency, was meant to be enjoyed. From the eighteenth century too, dates the monumental stairway rising from the Piazza di Spagna to the Trinità dei Monti church. This was built in 1725 with money left by the French ambassador Etienne Gouffier and the French architect François de Sanctis composed its landings and balustrades on an elliptical design that recalls the colonnade of St Peter's. The 137 steps, with their two corbelled terraces, seem to wave one gracefully down towards the city, with all its domes and towers and bell towers, spread below.[1]

It is from this period too that we inherit a work which, if not the most poetical ever inspired by Rome, is certainly the finest evocation of the spell she cast—the engravings of the Venetian Piranesi. He was the most spirited artist of the century and in his *Vedute di Roma* and *Antichità Romane* the old stones live again. We see the lichen and the cypress shadows and the people walking about. A shepherd drinks from the basin of a fountain, a carriage drives across a small piazza and leaning their elbows on a column stand a gentleman in a tricorne hat and a lady in a panniered dress. Minute exactitude and an almost incredible profusion of detail combine to bring it all to life. Out of the simplest things emerges real lyric feeling. Modern realism and the frenzy of romanticism may well both stem from Piranesi. He it was, in any case, long before Chateaubriand who usually takes the credit, who recognized the poetry of ruins.

Despite occasional flashes of brilliance the eighteenth century was, then, a period of decadence in the major plastic arts. The minor arts, on the other hand, flourished. The artistic conscience is written large upon every object out of every workshop of the time. A recent Settecento Exhibition held in Rome in 1959 displayed a wealth of arts and crafts, and for every branch of them a mass of documentation astounding in the mastery and ingenuity revealed. It was above all fascinating to see how these workmen fell

[1] The Spanish Steps are French property for which the city of Rome is a tenant paying a peppercorn rent.

Whoever makes that noble climb will be rewarded by a view of which Ferdinand Buc wrote, 'It is beyond belief. So many picturesque elements all at once recall those composite landscapes the eightenth-century artists loved to make up because nature was never dramatic enough for them, and to which they were always adding things. But what could they add to this? It is the stupendous back cloth for some operatic stage that is the actual city of Rome.'

in with the general development of artistic taste. The goldsmiths, for instance, abandon their decoration *alla bernini*—that is to say, Baroque—and grow gradually less ebullient, ending up with geometrical designs that foreshadow the Directoire style. Collectors may wish to note in passing that a Roman silversmith stamped his work with a seal reproducing the sign of his shop or studio while, as all over Europe, the standard of the metal was guaranteed by an official imprint, the *bollo camerale*, with the two keys of the Holy See beneath the papal basilica. In spite of often overloaded designs, the silversmiths produced delicate objects, beautifully decorated by the cunning use of precious stones, bronze and silver work.

Church ornament was woven and fashioned in many of the studios and it, too, evolved along the same lines. Instead of the old exuberant, overall effect the trend, under the new ideas, was towards elegance of detail. The subtlest graduations were obtained in gold-thread embroidery, as in the dyeing and weaving of silk.

One very practical art was that of tapestry-making and the studio at the Ospizio di San Michele was to have a great vogue. At the century's end the weavers, like everybody else, paid homage to the fashion for Antiquity, drawing inspiration and subject-matter from the classical world.

Several potteries were to be found in Rome, grouped as usual in the same district, which in their case was that near the Porto di Ripa Grande. Here they enjoyed, and wrangled stubbornly over, various privileges from the Pope. Filippo Coccunos brought the process of porcelain-making to Rome in 1761 and in 1785, still in the Ripette district and still with papal privilege, Volpato opened a factory specializing in the reproduction in biscuit ware of motifs from classical sculpture. This he must have made in quantities, for you may still find triumphal arches, obelisks and columns bearing his mark in Roman curio shops. He had, too, many imitators doing the same kind of thing privately and the miniature monuments were the standard tourist souvenir.

Another delicate art that flowered in Rome in the eighteenth century was that of the *biglietti da visita*, or visiting cards. These were employed exactly as are modern visiting cards, but were exquisitely decorated with charming pictures, painted or engraved, in which the perceptive might read some allusion proper to sender or recipient. The tradesman's *biglietto* was a useful advertisement and would include his price-list, but even so was neither commonplace nor drearily functional. The artists worked with a light, imaginative touch that could make the little picture cards delightful and their book-plates, too, are usually attractive.

MUSIC

The divine inspiration may have passed from the painters, sculptors and poets of Rome, but for music the eighteenth century was, in its second half especially, what the days of Michelangelo and Raphael had been for the plastic arts. It was touched by the same creative flame that had, throughout the glorious history of the Eternal City, so mightily kindled all the other arts in turn. The chief glory now was melody, a glory which was to spread all over Europe, with an influence particularly compelling and enduring in the south, justifying Stendhal's remark that 'Cimarosa's style suits the southern races and is beyond the comprehension of fools'. The greatest melodic composers of this century filled Italian music with the 'themes' that were to make opera-goers and worshippers in church alike stamp their feet for more.

The main centres of music were the Sistine Chapel and the Congregazione di Santa Cecilia. The other Vatican chapels provided organ music, but at the Sistine part-singing was unaccompanied. The performers were world-renowned and, as upon the stage, included many *castrati* for the female roles. The Sistine had a jealously guarded private repertoire. Reproduction of its scores was forbidden and to avoid any leakage no notes might be taken during concerts. Mozart caused a sensation in 1770 when, at the age of fourteen, he reconstructed Gregorio Allegri's *Miserere* from memory after a single hearing.

The Congregazione di Santa Cecilia had, for its part, succeeded in gaining control of all the instrumental music, sacred or profane, in Rome. No orchestra might give a work in any church or theatre without its permission, granted only when players and conductor came up to its required standard.

The taste for and knowledge of music was very widespread and concerts were held almost everywhere in the city. Every church was itself a concert-hall and we have seen how numerous were the operas staged. No society reception was complete without music and some of the nobles had real theatres, capable of seating several hundred people, in their palaces. One such theatre, belonging to Cardinal Pietro Ottoboni, was the scene of the memorable musical contest between Handel and Scarlatti, when the result for the harpsichord was undecided but Scarlatti had to acknowledge his rival's superiority on the organ.

Not only local, but foreign composers, too, added their quota and still they could not satisfy the unending musical appetite of the public of Rome with its constant demand for new work. It was a highly critical public. Poor offerings never survived and even good ones were granted only a brief career. Anything over two years old was automatically hissed and since work by a dead composer was inevitably damned it was pointless to put it on. 'There are two kinds of music in Italy', as a visitor said, 'the old and the new, and the Italians will not tolerate the old.' This greed for novelty, common to the whole country, was most noticeable in Rome and much astonished Montesquieu, who wrote,

'How extraordinary that the French, fickle as they are, should have clung to their music, that they still love their old tunes and Lulli's operas. The Italians are always wanting new music, their operas are always new. Is it perhaps that their music is more likely to produce new developments?'

We need scarcely add that this eternal cry for something fresh kept the composers, as Jean François Revel says, 'in an astounding fever of invention'.

They were well served by a galaxy of admirable interpreters, both singers and instrumentalists. There were numerous schools of music in Rome where foreigners—Boccherini among others—came to perfect their art. Every convent had such a school of its own and in the homes and orphanages musical education was of the first importance. Sometimes, indeed, it was the only form of education given and among the girls' hostels were veritable conservatoires where the white-clad orphans were instructed in 'the most sensual music in the world'.

It was surprising that such teaching should be dispensed so freely, for in 1703 Clement XI had forbidden the study of music and singing in convent schools. His reasons, more noteworthy than his ban, illustrate a frame of mind that was to prove long-lived in other spheres. Learning music, explains the 1703 edict, tempts females from 'the modest ways that become their sex so well', distracting them from more useful avocations. Mention is also made of the

danger to which the 'melodious creatures' expose the men, lay or
clerical, who coach or listen to them.

But as more and more people grew to love music these embargoes
grew less and less determined until at last its study was accorded
the freedom of the nunneries. Operas even were performed there,
with nuns in male costume for the men's roles. When Bergeret went
to one, called *La Donna Stravagante*, he noted, 'They acted it
convent-fashion. Need I say more?'

The Church, as we have seen, never so far unbent as to allow
the appearance of women on the public stage and so, although
female voices were tremendously admired, the great women
singers in Rome could be heard only in private houses. One of
them, singing at her home near San Silvestro in Capite during 1734,
drew crowds that blocked the street with carriages whenever she
gave a concert. Women might also take part in the serenades which
admirers would arrange under the balcony of mistress or betrothed.
The serenade was a favourite eighteenth-century compliment,
prompted at times by nothing more exciting than respect. Thus we
read in the Spanish ambassador's journal for August 12, 1717, 'The
abate Chigi had a very noisy [*strepitosa*] serenade performed yesterday under the duchess of Fiano's window because she is depressed
and he wished to cheer her up.'

In the warm weather the Roman night was gladdened by music
and song. 'It is quite usual,' reports Lalande, 'to hear concerts,
singers and choirs in the streets, with tambourines and mandolines,
so that one's evening walks are very gay.'

THE CHAMPS-ÉLYSÉES OF EUROPE

The French travellers who savoured the delights of Roman life
in the eighteenth century all maintain that no one but a naturally
jaundiced person could be discontented in that marvellous town.
One, when reproached by a friend for lingering far too long,
replied, 'You must learn never to believe people who say they are
leaving Rome. It is so pleasant here, and so agreeable, with so much
to see and see again, that no one ever actually goes.'

Here is the explanation; this is why the enormous stream of
visitors came pouring into a city so full of treasures of all
kinds. Great men with great trains of servants, obscure voyagers,
artists finishing their studies, ordinary middling folk with a liking
for beautiful things, priests seeking out their Mother Church,

endlessly they hastened to these encircling, sacred hills. And how many, intending a short stay, settled here for life. They would realize one day that here, where they had come as sightseers, was their real native land and that they neither could, nor wished to, leave it any more. An obvious case is that of Seroux d'Agincourt, the great French nobleman world famous among bibliophiles for his *Fermiers généraux* edition of the *Contes* of La Fontaine; coming for what he meant to be a short pilgrim-visit, the Eternal City seduced him and he never went away. He became an untiring explorer of the catacombs and died in Rome soon after having had the bust of Poussin placed in the Pantheon. He is buried in San Luigi dei Francesi.

Even those who merely passed through without settling here were fascinated and always retained what Goethe calls a dear nostalgia for Rome, for Rome which was at that time the magnetic pole of Europe. The faithful saw here the centre of their faith, the home of Christianity that Paul V had dreamed of and where the popes who came after him had made the ceremonies ever more dazzling and built their close-packed churches. To artists she was as Mecca to the people of Mohammed, offering 'the truest, the most vitalizing synthesis of the whole varied heritage of the human race' (Maury and Percheron, *Itinéraires Romains*). There was no more enchanting spot where sophisticated or leisured wealth might linger, or find more of life's refinements. Rome was in fact the Champs-Élysées of Europe. Refuge of dethroned monarchs, of artists and of poets, here everyone was free to follow his own bent in peace. 'Life,' says Abel Bonnard, 'did not revolve round money.' The learned nibbled away undisturbed at the accumulated wisdom of vast libraries, the talkers held forth over their ices in the café, the pious embraced the images of saints. Chafed with delay, ambitious men watched the mitre or the hat they longed for drawing nearer; there, for artists to draw and mantled in greenery, lay the Colosseum. God was to be loved, for this was Rome, and women, because this was Italy. Foreigners grafted their own national characters upon the serene non-curiosity of the unastonishable natives. They came to Rome to live 'at one remove from the present day'. And Rome, bathed in her glorious light, shed upon them all that soothing equanimity that was her own special gift.

Life was entertaining and delightful in this engaging place, Rome was a good-natured city whose people, like their history, were full of contradictions; a city of songs and laughter and a few amicable quarrels, of plashing fountains and the sound of bells, of long files of seminarists and passers-by who never seemed to hurry, where pomp and misery met and blended together; a city benignly harmonious beneath the surface disarray. And from a loftier viewpoint there was, indeed, the synthesis of civilization wholly perceptible, without discord, to the mind. Here life and art were one and the same, the intellectual horizon was limitless and shabby thinking was impossible. And all the stimulus to mind and spirit was augmented by that clear and splendid light, the shining sky that kept 'its youth, its freshness and its early radiance' all day.

It must be added that not every visitor was drawn to Rome by religion, attracted by art nor fascinated by unfathomable charm. Many came quite simply because to do so was the fashion. No one could hope to qualify as a man of parts anywhere in Europe who had not travelled to Italy and lived at Rome. Such voyagers were haloed with unquestionable prestige on their return and were so well aware of their new superiority that when the Dilettanti society was founded in London in 1750 no one might join who had not made a sufficiently long stay here; those who had merely passed through were ruthlessly excluded. All over the continent these freemen of the Roman life showed the same tendency to flock together. A few moments' talk were enough for recognition. 'They exchanged a masonic handshake, like men who had loved the same woman at some years' interval and shared an equal kindness from her.' So Edmond About described the devotees of this new faith who, numerous as they were by the nineteenth century, are even more so now. Anyone who has known the place long enough to feel the spell wishes only to return, as though some part of himself were left behind him there. Goethe is for ever the spokesman of that longing, who found in Rome the great illumination of his life and when he had to leave did so in dread of never seeing her again. That grief was always with him. 'I have not spent an entirely happy day,' he wrote as an old man, 'since I crossed the ponte Molle to come home.'

In their own way, all travellers shared his feelings, as their letters and memoirs prove. We cannot here give even a brief list of that bewitched brotherhood; it would involve reprinting the Almanach de Gotha and the Artists' Yearbook for every land in Europe. Kings and princes came to Rome in plenty, some in their own proper persons, others with the not always successful shelter of assumed names. Joseph II of Austria was the Comte de Falkenstein, the Duc de Chartres and his wife were known as the Comte and Comtesse de Joinville and the heir to Russia passed as the Comte du Nord. The King of Sardinia, the Archduke Ferdinand, the Archduchess Maria Christina and the English Duke of Gloucester, travelled privately but under their real names. When the Revolutionary storm broke over France Rome was to be the goal of all the most distinguished *émigrés*. Throughout the century she was, indeed, that strange hostelry where, in *Candide*, Pangloss dined one night with the six strangers and 'perceived to his great surprise that all of them were kings'.

Longer still, and quite dazzling, would be the list of writers and artists who were Roman pilgrims. Mozart was only fourteen when he came in 1770 and so small that they had to lift him up to kiss St Peter's toe. To the wonder of all, as we have seen, he wrote from memory a perfect score of Allegri's famous *Miserere* and Pope Clement wished to see the marvellous boy. But instead of scolding him for breaking the rules the Pope offered compliments on his talent and loaded him, we are told, 'with graces and favours'.

The two-year stay that Goethe made in Rome was to stamp him for the rest of his life. As well as the great ruins, he loved the cool *trattorie*, especially that in the Piazza Montanara where an Italian girl began an idyllic liaison by tracing the time in a clumsy scribble on the wine-dabbled table to fix their rendezvous. He left such insubstantial evocations of Faustina that she has been thought a symbol only, or some transferred, idealized image of his German love, Christiana Vulpius. But she was real and very much alive, daughter of a Roman tavern-keeper, and with her the poet of the *Roman Elegies* took his carefree pleasures with characteristic eagerness. Goethe relates the episode as follows in the fifteenth Roman Elegy:

'Never should I have gone with Caesar to the shores of the distant Britons, though Florus would have persuaded me to the wineshop easily enough, for I hate the northern fogs more than any busy band of fleas in the south. Oh, wineshops, my happiest thoughts go out to you from now on, *osterie* as the Romans rightly call you, for today you have brought my love to me. She came with her uncle, whom she so constantly deceives in order to see me. Our table was here, with the simple Germans sitting round us, and the child found a place near her mother, opposite to me. She pulled the bench round and manœuvred so cleverly, until I could see her neck and half her face. She was talking more loudly than Romans usually do. She spilled and let fall the glass and as the wine ran over she began to trace wet rings on the wooden table-top. She wrote her name and mine, intertwined. I followed, greedily, as that small finger wrote and she knew that I was watching. At last she made a Latin five and put a stroke in front of it. When I had seen it she drew circle after circle to efface letters and numbers, but that magic figure four remained fixed in my sight. I sat still and kept silent. Half in delight and provocation, half in desire, I bit my burning lip until it bled. How long it was, still, until nightfall, and then four more hours to wait . . . !'

Almost all the great French artists spent long periods in Rome, from Fragonard and Hubert Robert to Houdon, who lived at the French Academy while working on his colossal St Bruno for Santa Maria dei Angeli.

The worlds of art and finance in France were seized with a driving urge to see Rome in the second half of the century. Madame de Pompadour began it. She had her brother, M. de Vandières, appointed *directeur général des bâtiments* in 1749 and, 'wishing him to gain the knowledge indispensable for the exercise of his duties', sent him for two years to Rome with the architect Soufflot and Cochin the engraver. In their wake the great collectors, the *Fermiers généraux* and everyone else who could afford to indulge a whim, set out for Italy, with attendant artists to ensure better value for their journeying. It was thus that Hubert Robert came, first with the *abbé* de Saint-Non and later with the Comte d'Hestenheim, and thus that the *trésorier-général* Bergeret engaged the companionship of Fragonard in the mistaken hope that the painter would hand over the sketches he made, by way of reimbursement.

It was in great part due to the French painters that the most majestic things in Rome, 'her pavement of ruins and the solitudes around her', came to be appreciated. This poetic feeling for ruins was something quite new, something that, with the exception, already mentioned, of Piranesi, may be said to have originated in France; it grew up together with the 'melancholy that is hardly found in her literature before Rousseau'.

The two most famous adventurers of their time, too, gave Rome the benefit of their presence. Here Casanova enjoyed some of his easy conquests and Cagliostro imported that faintly demoniac aura that pursued him wherever he went. When the States General were meeting at Versailles he caused a great stir by making sensationally successful experiments in magic at a reception in his house on the Piazza Farnese. Before the eyes of all present he caused the stone in Cardinal de Bernis' ring to increase in size; and in the reflected lights of a carafe of water he beheld Louis XVI beset in his own palace and the monarchy of France in deadly peril. Sitting in the audience Louis' ambassador managed, we are told, a somewhat constrained smile.

Rich foreigners, whose money filled so many pockets, always arrived to a great welcome, with a spate of fantastic rumours running before them to all the shops and inns. Speculation as to their probable advent could be premature, however, as happened in 1704. In that year report spoke of a very important person who was expected to settle in Rome. No one less than the Queen-dowager of Spain, thought some; a son of the Russian Czar, said others. This person would be taking the entire Palazzo Farnese and the newly-furbished Farnesina too. Accommodation for 400 horses was called for in Trastevere and Fontana drew up plans of the sumptuous stabling for them. When excitement had reached fever-pitch an individual named Pagni was arrested and the thunderbolt fell: the important person did not exist and Pagni had spread and fostered the whole thing for his private amusement. It was not the only occasion on which the credulous Romans fell for a similar tale.

There were few inns where the wealthy foreigner could be lodged in suitable style. The old splendour had gone from the 'Albergo del Orso' where Montaigne once stayed and the 'Sole' that had welcomed Ariosto. Now the great people who came for any length of time settled in furnished apartments in the Via Babuino or round about the Piazza di Spagna in a district which had the advantages of independence as well as its own attractions. It was ruled, in effect, by the Spanish ambassador who maintained an efficient police-force there and saw to it that his diplomatic exemptions ensured good order and pleasant circumstances for the visitor. One notable result was that the prostitutes, hounded away in the rest of the town, were still in this privileged quarter allowed to pursue their trade in peace.

More and more inns and family *pensioni* were opened, in avoidance of papal regulations and sure of plentiful clients from abroad. They had commonplace names and no great pretensions—'The

Golden Lion', 'The Golden Head', 'The Eagle', 'The Falcon', 'The Moor', 'The Five Moons', 'The Star' and so on; none was luxurious. Casanova says that one called 'The City of London' was the most comfortable, an opinion no doubt due to his more than friendly welcome from the landlord's daughter Teresa, a very young girl whose youth he respected—most abnormal behaviour for this normally unhesitating seducer. 'The Monte d'Oro' was reputed among the best hotels in the Piazza di Spagna, although de Brosses claims they fleeced him there. 'The Monsù Pio' had the best food but so many rowdy artists frequented it that the less vigorously disposed went elsewhere. At any of these places a good meal cost from five to ten *paoli*. As for furnished rooms, they were very cheap; Alfieri rented a complete palace on the Via Viminale for ten Roman crowns a month. One could hire a carriage from six in the morning to eleven at night for six *paoli*. The stay in Rome was not expensive.

Cafés in great numbers sprang up to satisfy the luxurious requirements of rich and fashionable customers and now they began to cover their walls with looking-glass and gilding. At first the leading café was the Veneziano on the Corso, consisting of four shops with an *entresol* above. The Caffé degli Specchi opened in the Piazza Colonna, then Petracchi's, Cappretari's Bagnoli's and Pastini's. There still exists in the Via Condotti one of the cafés founded at this time, the famous 'Greco'. Being so near the Piazza di Spagna, the Caffé Greco attracted a splendid clientèle. Goethe went there, and it was to know Wagner, Liszt, Mendelssohn, Rossini, Schopenhauer and Bizet, being still an artistic rendezvous in the nineteenth century. Gorani gives us interesting details on these cafés and tells us that 'Six *baiòcchi* will buy a pyramid of ice cream, three times bigger than you get in Paris and much nicer. The waiters are most exquisitely polite.'

To steer them round the monuments of Rome the foreigners enlisted the help of *ciceroni*. There were many *ciceroni* available but they brought only superficial knowledge to their task and never hestitated to produce a thumping lie if facts should fail them. Many of the howlers that contemporary travellers put into their own accounts may be laid at the door of such inept and unscrupulous informants.

Just as strong as the desire to see the ruins was that to take away souvenirs of them and frenzied artistic bartering was the result. 'Modern Rome,' said Montesquieu, 'is selling the ancient bit by bit.' Often the professions of dealer and artist were combined. Sculptors and painters would display all sorts of antiquities in their studios—vases, statues, figures and rare marble sarcophagi—and then declare that though not, of course, in business, they were willing to let these objects go for reasonable prices. One such astute character was the son of Piranesi himself. Many artists, however, were content to sell only their own productions and since they produced a good deal, to satisfy the rich clients, a mechanical quality sometimes creeps into their work. But it was a prosperous era for painters and engravers and their views are hanging now in many an old house in England and Germany, to show us aspects of the Eternal City and picturesque details of her life, as truthfully recorded in the light of common day. They may not be the finest pictures in the world, those Roman views, but they are charming, all the same.

CHAPTER NINE

HISTORY

THE DOWNWARD PATH

The eighteenth century began unhappily, for in 1703 Rome endured one of the worst disasters of her history. The Tiber, overflowing after heavy rainfall, turned the streets as far as the foot of the Trinità dei Monti into canals. There had been serious floods before, and it was not the first time that people had taken boats in the Piazza di Spagna, but what made this more dreadful was its accompaniment of violent earthquake. The shocks went on for fifteen minutes and brought down houses in the flooded areas, destroying whole streets and burying the inhabitants under the debris. When the water subsided it left a foul deposit of slime and evaporation caused grave epidemic. No crops survived the flood and shortage of food, sickness and the ruin of so many homes brought terrible suffering.

The catastrophe in fact did as much moral as material damage, for some questionable situations arose from the great charitable impulse for the relief of victims. Churchmen of all ranks had opened their doors to girls made homeless by the earthquake and to young women widowed by the epidemic and, according to report, good works were covering a multitude of evil deeds. These doubts were so persistently expressed that the Pope took alarm and published a Bull: the prelates must part company with the young persons sheltering in their palaces, and any such without families of their own were confided to the care of good women and fed at the public expense. These measures, together with the noticeable—not to say precipitate—speed with which they were put into effect, lent all too much colour to the unpleasing rumours.

Hostile opinion made much of the incident, at home as well as abroad, and the authority of the Holy See was affected at a time when its influence was almost everywhere beginning to decline. Those Christian princes of Europe whose states were still within the fold were paying less attention to the community of essential interests that bound them to the Papacy; it would not be long before they were entering into alliances with and giving aid and comfort to its enemies.

The pontificate of Clement XI, beginning with the Jubilee of 1700, spanned twenty-one difficult years. The Pope was successively in conflict with the Emperor Leopold II, who erected the Prussian duchy into a kingdom under a new, Protestant dynasty; with Spain, which sent his nuncio packing from Madrid; and with the house of Savoy. A large section of French opinion was alienated by his famous Bull Unigenitus against the Jansenists, a measure which served only to embolden them and help to spread their doctrines. The Church in France, weakened by the fratricidal war between the bishops and the Jansenists, secretly opposed by Madame de Maintenon and soon to be made a mockery by the sceptical libertines of the Regency, was also suffering the initial rounds of a literary attack that aimed at undermining the whole structure of Christianity and of society itself. Fontanelle's *Histoire des Oracles* and Bayle's *Dictionnaire Historique et Critique* had appeared not long before the election of Clement XI, like a prelude to the sterner blows that were to come from Jean Jacques Rousseau and Voltaire. 'Philosophy' was on the march.

Clement's successor, Innocent XIII, reigned only for three years, from 1721 to 1724. Saint Simon says he owed the Papacy to having promised to leave the Jansenists alone and to make a cardinal of the Regent's pander, Dubois; and certainly on both these points he bowed to the wishes of the French court. Persecution of the Jansenists ceased and the *abbé* Dubois received his hat in 1721, becoming with that honour a member of the Council of Regency, and first minister soon afterwards.

Benedict XIII (1724–1730) was a simple Dominican, unlearned and of austere habits, who accepted his throne only at the insistence of the General of his Order. He ruled the Holy See with the simplicity of the earliest Vicars of Christ and would go out, poorly clad, to visit convents and hospitals. His charity was boundless, but his very self-effacement smoothed the path for unsuspected schemers in his own household and for all those who abused and drained the papal Treasury. After him came Clement XII (1730–1740) who was no better statesman, a Pope who cherished the highest intentions and let himself be forced into yielding points that damaged the authority of the Church. It was from him that Elisabeth Farnese, the Queen of Spain, wrested a cardinalate for her seven-year-old son. Despoiling the Papacy had developed into a game that any court could play.

Benedict XIV, who came to the throne in 1740 and reigned for eighteen years, was not the man to combat this sort of thing. We have seen already how much goodwill this Pope created in the sphere of human relations by his liberality, culture and love of the arts. His intelligent administration increased the charitable resources, the beauties and intellectual treasure of his capital. He rebuilt the church of Santa Croce in Gerusalemme and opened a broad avenue to link it with the Lateran. He restored and embellished Sant' Apollinare and San Martino ai Monti; he rescued the ancient mosaics of Leo III's triclinium by preserving them in a tribune behind the Scala Santa. He was a good, kind man with a delightful personality. He had a gentleness, tolerance and moderation that put him permanently in the giving vein. Consequently, as a Pope, he was appalling. Where his predecessors had stood firm he allowed foreign powers to encroach on his authority, winning the friendship and embarrassing compliments of the Grand Turk in the process. Worse, his liberalism led him to make concessions on points of doctrine which in the long run were fatal to the Papacy.

The French Revolution can be considered as no spontaneous eruption. Long before it broke out there had been signs enough to put the least apprehensive mind on guard. The philosophic movement was alarmingly widespread by the middle of the century, yet Benedict XIV never recognized what threats it held for every principle he existed to defend. He opposed to the rising tide of novel ideas the most pitiable of barricades. In 1751 he repeated Clement XIII's measures against Freemasonry, though without any machinery for making them work; half-heartedly he condemned the 1753 edition of Voltaire. But he remained too fond of peaceful conciliation to make any resolute stand against the *philosophes* and their propaganda. Certainly they never enjoyed his approval, even though Voltaire dedicated *Mohamet* to him[1] and he gave Montesquieu a dispensation from the Lenten fast. He was, of course,

[1] To assess Voltaire's sincerity with regard to Benedict XIV one need only compare two quotations. For the Pope's portrait he sent the lines

Lambertinus hic est, Romae decus et pater orbis,
Qui scriptus mundum docuit, virtutibus ornat.

Lambertini the pattern of virtues,
He writes that the world may read,

(*Continued overleaf*)

indulgent towards them—he was fundamentally an indulgent character—and it is a fact that he came to be popular with the philosophers and even with Protestants. But how can it be proper for a pope, whether willingly or not, to stand security for the enemies of his Church?

Rome, supremely detached from what went on beyond her boundaries, remembered only the very real virtues of her Lambertini Pope and the warmth of his good nature. No pontiff in history can have been so sincerely mourned. How popular he was may be gathered from the astonished exclamation of Count Rivera that when he died, 'Marvel of marvels, no one, not even Pasquino, has anything bad to say of the late Pope'.

Clement XIII came after him and the main event of his reign (1758–1769) was the defence of the Jesuits against the Catholic powers demanding their suppression. The voice of the Papacy meant little enough in the councils of Europe; in inter-European struggles it would cover its weakness with affected neutrality. Some resources, however, it still had, despite its apparent straits and the losses of the past two centuries; but it acted nowadays only through its famous militia, that Society of Jesus where alone was found such liveliness and ambition as Holy Church could muster. The 25,000 members of the Society were spread all over the globe. Their schools were many and successful and they offered wonderful education, facts which drew down upon them the double opposition of lay universities and rival teaching Orders. All the monastic Orders, too, were jealous of the Jesuits and in the end it seemed that their most influential enemies were lodged in Rome itself. They had, moreover, a conception of philanthropy which called them across mere human frontiers in the service of human need and which, conflicting with narrow, national patriotism, had more than once given pretext for their being treated as the forces of a foreign power.

But above all they threatened Protestantism and Jansenism and were natural and determined adversaries of the *philosophes*. When

---

With the whole wide world his children,
The glory of Rome indeed.

At the same time, practically by the same post, he was writing a disrespectful letter to the Marquis d'Argenson about the Holy Father: 'I have just received a portrait of the chubbiest old Holy Father . . .' (August 10, 1745).

Voltaire said that 'nothing can be accomplished against infamy until the Jesuit Order is destroyed' he was paying them the finest of compliments. And d'Alembert, improving on this theme, wrote,

'The hardest part will be over when philosophy is freed from these grand grenadiers of fanaticism and intolerance. The rest are only Cossacks and Hungarians, they will never stand up to our regular troops.'

The Society of Jesus, then, regarded as the strongest shield of Catholic doctrine, was the inevitable target of assault upon the political power of the Church, for what blow could reach the heart of that ancient unity until its defenders were wiped out? Protestant, Jansenist and *philosophe* drew together to pour combined and contradictory volleys upon them. The attack was open for all to see and only a close alliance of throne, nobility and Church could have repulsed it. And this was the moment, when such an alliance was most vital and most painfully missing, that the house of Bourbon chose to ask the Holy See for the suppression of its holy train-bands. As d'Alembert admitted in a letter to Frederick of Prussia, it was asking a great deal:

'They say the Pope is needing a lot of persuasion to do away with the Jesuits. I am not surprised. Suggesting the destruction of that gallant militia to a Pope is like suggesting to Your Majesty that he disband his guards.'

After the event the soldier-king was to extend the comparison, saying, 'It is like the treaty the wolves made with the sheep, forcing them first of all to give up their dogs. You know what happened.'

But before this stage was reached the attack upon the Jesuits assumed the aspect of a veritable Unbelievers' Crusade; the crusade against the men of darkness, it was called. They were accused of terrible misdeeds and the far-fetched charges were dug up from the times of the Wars of Religion. In every land the wretched indictments were fomented. Their very achievements counted against them, since their crime lay precisely in successful work and devotion to duty. Any faults and errors of individuals were visited on them all.

The Society had no intention of bowing before the storm, nor of compromising. It had conquered empires and had kings for

193

penitents, through its missionaries it had ruled the world; it considered its fate as inextricably bound up with that of the Papacy and, recognizing no master but the Pope, believed him too deeply indebted ever to abandon it. This, however, was gravely to misjudge the pressure which the Catholic States, leagued secretly together, could at the time bring to bear upon the Holy See. Linked by their own Family Pact, the four Bourbon realms Spain, France, Naples and Parma, stood in the forefront of the crusade. The Pope protested ceaselessly against their onslaughts but his personal allies, the Venetian and Genoese republics, and even Austria, deserted him one after another. Meanwhile unbelief, under the impetus of the 'enlightenment', had ceased to be a drawing-room sensation and was spreading to the masses. 'The enemy of all good,' said Clement XIII, 'has sown the bad seed in the Lord's field; the tares have flourished and threaten to choke the harvest.' He had no defence but heartrending and ineffectual outcry against the forces of evil and blow after blow was to fall upon the Society of Jesus.

The King of Portugal, in whose domains the Jesuits were numerous and powerful, expelled them and the persecution began. Cruel restrictions imposed by the King of Spain augured badly for their future in the Peninsula. Then France in her turn joined the inglorious pursuit and here the rising tide of scepticism and the stinging darts of the *philosophes* made themselves felt more than anywhere else in Europe. 1761 saw the publication of Rousseau's *Nouvelle Héloïse*, to be followed a year later by his *Contrat Social* and *Émile*, while parts of Voltaire's *Philosophic Dictionary* were circulating among the chosen. Madame de Pompadour joined with the modernists, for she had accounts to settle with too-scrupulous confessors and wished to be seen in the ranks of action. The Duc de Choiseul laid secret plans to confiscate the possessions of so well-endowed an Order, hoping thus to divert attention from the need for reform.[1] The court was trusting that the event might make enough noise in the world to divert the public mind from the currently unsuccessful war. Louis XV alone, retaining what Sismondi calls 'the fears and precepts of devotion', sought ways and means of saving the Society as he clung, against wind and tide, to that close alliance binding throne and altar. But the failure, largely through English machinations, of a bank in Martinique

---

[1] The historian Sismondi tells us that these possessions mostly disappeared as the result of sequestration or misappropriation, leaving the Minister of Finance without the funds he had been counting on.

established by the Jesuit Father de la Valette, served as pretext to overcome his opposition. On August 6, 1762, a decree of the *Parlement* condemned the Order and securalized its members, requiring their expulsion and the sale of all their goods.

As though at a signal, the whole pack was unleashed. The persecution spread from country to country with incredible speed. Accused of no crime, adored by the common people, they were expelled in turn from Mexico, Peru, Chile, the Philippines and the kingdom of the Two Sicilies, and at last in 1767 Spain most brutally drove out her Jesuits. The police herded them like criminals into ships where they lay crowded together for weeks in such dreadful conditions that the ordeal killed many of them before they reached Civita Vecchia.

The Pope, rebuffed on all sides and bereft of aid and allies, had watched with anguish in his heart the banishment of his faithful soldiery. But when Ferdinand of Parma too expelled them the old pontiff reacted very strongly to this insult from a vassal of the Church. On January 20, 1768, he excommunicated Ferdinand de Bourbon and deprived him of his duchies of Parma and Plasencia. It was a bold course to take with Louis XV's grandson, the nephew of Charles III of Spain, the cousin of the King of Naples and Maria Theresa's future son-in-law; Clement XIII was awaking by his actions the old investiture quarrel with the Bourbon princes. But it was seven centuries since the German Emperor had made his journey to Canossa and now temporal sovereignty declared against the spiritual and made its chosen victim once again the Jesuits, blaming them for the extravagant claims of the Papacy. Peremptorily it demanded the suppression of the Order.

Now the Bourbons were requiring the same thing as the *philosophes*, who ought to have repaid them better. They were wanting, as Louis Veuillot put it, to see 'a blameless religious body erased from the book of the Church by the hand of Christ's own Vicar. This they desired and this they had and the sons of St Louis were to know no more victories in that century.' They did not obtain their wish immediately, nor did they obtain it from Clement, whom death saved from draining the cup they proffered him. Rumour said that he was poisoned and this may have been true. He was certainly assailed with mysterious pains on February 2, 1769, and died in unexplained convulsions. Officially, he succumbed to 'the bitterness of his position', the kind of roundabout phrase that can throw a useful veil in awkward circumstances.

THE SUPPRESSION OF THE JESUITS AND THE LAST ACT

The conclave that met on the death of the Pope was entirely dominated by the grievous Jesuit problem and Cardinal de Bernis played a leading part in all the trickery and stratagem that packed the three months of its duration. The aim was to make the Sacred College elect a pope to suit the anti-Jesuit courts of Europe and so itself destroy the Order. These courts cannot have been wholly successful in their manœuvres, for the new Pope was a Franciscan, had been an intimate of Clement XIII and might have been expected to favour the Jesuits, to whom he owed his hat. And yet he had already dropped one or two remarks which might be taken as implying that 'Francis had strength to kill Ignatius'. When still a cardinal Clement XIV had in fact said, loudly enough for Paris and Madrid to hear, 'the time is come for kings to be obeyed, for their arms stretch far beyond their frontiers and their power can overtop the Alps'. Harassed into it by the Spanish envoy, he had also declared, before the conclave met, his belief that 'the tiara might, in due form and conscience and so far as prudence and justice might allow, abolish what the tiara had created'. Had the Pope been making a promise—which was hardly the case—his election would have proved a fair example of simony, and yet his words were read as a promise by the over-agitated parties on both sides in the struggle. It was claimed that the various governments, eager to see the Jesuit question finally disposed of, had adopted the speedy means of buying votes for Cardinal Ganganelli, having first obtained written assurance of his co-operation. Needless to say, light has never been cast upon this dubious affair.

We may add, without claiming to shed any new ray, that little in the character of Clement XIV can support the quite unwarranted imputations that stain his memory. He was a humble and charitable man, frugal and studious in his ways; a man of moderation. One of his teachers had once said of him, 'It is not surprising that he loves music, for everything about him is harmonious.' He was perhaps the man to reconcile the rights of the Papacy and the demands of the courts of Europe. His words already quoted, and on which such serious accusations were based, should be taken as an expression of his profound desire for compromise and understanding, the praiseworthy wish to bring back peace and union to Christendom. He is exonerated, above all, by the long lapse of time between his supposed promises to the Bourbons and his action against the Jesuits. He took in fact four years to decide, years of hesitation and heartsearching. He had also to resist pressure, daily renewed, from the Spanish ambassador, who not infrequently indulged in supplementary threats. 'If we cannot succeed through mildness,' this terrible man would say, 'we shall try force.'

There was not only this pressure from the powers. There were prelates too, won over by questionable means to the kingdoms of the earth, to add their serpent voices. Wherever he turned, whatever he listened to, he found someone ready to ensnare him and in the end the unhappy man, old and ailing, yielded to all the cabals and to what he thought were the demands of a situation that was probably too complicated for him. True to the ingenuous Franciscan spirit, he dreamed of restoring the Church to a primitive simplicity and was obviously deficient in practical sense and knowledge of the way things worked. There were gaps in his political education which left him powerless to thwart the intrigues that surrounded him. He knew only how to procrastinate, how to suggest unacceptable compromises, how to make interim gestures, like the closing of the Jesuit College in Rome, how to meet threats with 'nonsense and volubility, a torrent of meaningless words'. When at last he framed the fatal Bull and submitted the text to the Spaniards he disputed their suggested additions at length. He drew out the negotiations with feigned sickness and prolonged sojourns at Castel Gandolfo; he increased the number of religious retreats and was of course unavailable while they lasted. He was giving the Jesuits time to parry the coming blow. But they were lost. Not even from the Empress of Austria had they anything left to hope.

On July 21, 1773, the Pope, with the newly-signed Brief that suppressed the Society of Jesus before him, heard all the bells of the Gesù ringing in the novena of St Ignatius. Sadly he bent his head and said, 'They are not ringing for the saints, but for the dead.' The Bull *Dominus ac Redemptor* was published on August 16th. Up to the last moment the Pope, a prey to remorse, had tried to withdraw it but he had let the Spanish ambassador have the document and a special courier was already on the way to Madrid.

The papal Brief, in the most explicit manner, annihilated the Order throughout the world, closed its schools and its foundations, cancelled its statutes and revoked its privileges. Yet the doctrine, ways and discipline of the Jesuits were uncondemned. No reason for their suppression was given beyond royal complaint and the need for accord with public opinion. Nevertheless, their houses were occupied by papal troops and their General and other high dignitaries imprisoned in Sant' Angelo.

The Church's enemies hailed the dissolution with rapture. D'Alembert wrote to the king of Prussia:

'Everything is in a rosy haze. I see the Jansenists dying quietly next year after bringing the Jesuits to a violent end in this. I see toleration established and the Protestants recalled, I see the priesthood married, confession done away with and fanaticism uprooted without the slightest trouble.'[1]

Clement exclaimed, 'I am lost,' when he signed that Bull. And indeed he fell immediately into a singular state of agonized prostration. He sobbed incessantly and wandered through his palace like a lifeless creature, sunk under the weight of grief. He died, in great suffering, on October 2, 1774. His death had been foretold as a judgment of God, and as though to confirm the rumours of assassination his body decomposed too quickly for the face to be shown and his funeral had to be held with none of the customary ritual.

The Jesuits were naturally accused of having had him poisoned and once more it was the Protestant Frederick the Great who took their part. 'The body was opened,' he told d'Alembert, 'and not a trace of poison found. But the Pope blamed himself for having sacrificed such an Order as the Jesuits at the whim of his rebellious children. Towards the end of his life he was edgy and depressed, which helped to shorten his days.'

It was at this juncture that the menace of revolution declared itself in France; it was inevitable when the *parlements* were recalled, less than two months after Clement XIV's death. Now the very powers they had employed against the Church were to be let loose against the Catholic governments of Europe which still persisted in trying to extend the victory they had gained.

The conclave to choose the new Pope was divided between the party of the monarchs and that of the *zelanti*, standing for the defence of papal prerogative. Five months the holy gathering spent

---

[1] Oddly enough, Prussia ignored the papal ban; her Jesuits were not disturbed and it was in her territory that the Order would be born again. Frederick foresaw as much when he wrote to Voltaire on July 9, 1770: 'The good friar at the Vatican is less peevish than they think. I really can't complain of him, he is leaving me my dear Jesuits when they are being persecuted everywhere. I shall cherish the precious seed and one day, when people want to cultivate such a rare plant, I shall give it to them.'

in ravelling and unravelling the plots and plans by which each side tried to lay its hands on the tiara. The Holy See might have been vacant for ever had not Cardinal de Bernis contrived the election of Giovanni Angelo Braschi in the belief that he had deserted the *zelanti* for the French interest. 'The new pontiff's reign,' he reported home, 'will show the court whether it was his face I saw before his elevation, or a mask.' The Spanish ambassador, for his part, was said to have used 'the fairest prostitutes in Rome' as a means of urging a declaration from the Holy Ghost.

Various assessments have been made of this Cardinal Braschi who became Pius VI. He seems to have combined two quite distinct personalities. One was that of a strikingly handsome man (he was popularly known as *il Papa bello*), tall and strong, lordly in bearing and strong as a horse. But he had one vice, and that was vanity. He wished to be loved and to be wondered at; he played the part of Great Pope and saw himself as Leo X or even Julius II. 'A vain and empty head' he has been too severely called. He was simply rather vain of his own noble features and rather dazzled by the lot that had fallen to him. Later he was to offer an impressive resistance to the greedy ambition of France and he died in exile 'with the dignity befitting a bishop and saintly resignation'.

He showed his less admirable side in his first years as Pope. For all the world as though the times were right for such retrograde behaviour, he acted like some pontiff of the Renaissance, some spendthrift trifler who relied on charm alone to solve problems more serious than he knew. He even brought back the palmy days of nepotism, summoning his nephews to his side and providing one of them with a brilliant wife to queen it over Roman society. For this couple he raised the huge Palazzo Braschi as a proper setting for their allotted ceremonial part, vaster and more magnificent than anything built by popes in the spacious days. Pius VI liked complimentary inscriptions to himself and doing things that would perpetuate his name, but he did not build solely for his own glory. His cherished and untimely ambition was to restore to the Eternal City her lustre of the Renaissance. He gave St Peter's a great sacristy by Marchionni, and to do so pulled down the Temple of Venus which Michelangelo had said it would be sacrilege to touch. This gift was followed by that of two large clocks for the façade and the big bell known as the *Campanone*. He laid out the Giardina della Pigna in the Vatican; he decorated the Hall of the Muses and inaugurated the Cabinet of the Masks, both in the Pio-Clementino Museum, a foundation of Popes Clement XIII and XIV, which he extended in princely fashion. It owes its splendid staircase, too, to Pius VI. He beautified many of the squares of Rome, raising the ancient solar obelisk in front of the Montecitorio palace and another, from the gardens of Sallust, before the church of Trinità dei Monti.

His most useful enterprise was the draining of the Pontine marshes, a task in which many popes had followed in the footsteps of the censor Appius Claudius and the Emperor Augustus, none with much success. Pius VI devoted himself entirely to the vast, ungrateful undertaking and was often seen in that noxious country-side, urging on the workmen and discussing plans with engineers on the spot. About 1,500 acres of barren land were reclaimed and the ancient Via Appia, laid bare in the course of the digging, restored and made fit for traffic once again. Now workshops were being opened at the same time in Rome, sheds for woollen weaving and the *conservatorio* which the Pope founded on the Janiculum, soon to become famous for its perfect damasks. The Roman popula-tion-figure of 165,000 was the highest of the century and never had the Eternal City welcomed so many illustrious guests—the Emperor, the Czar, the King of Sweden, the sons of the King of England. But none of this, alas, spelled a golden age for the Papacy. On the contrary, difficulties crowded in, for with the French Revo-lution 'philosophy', triumphant, aimed openly at the downfall of the Roman Church. 'Take good care of your Pope,' said Cerutti to a member of the nuncio's suite in Paris, 'he will be the last.'

Pius VI was not cut out to be the hero of such a conflict. His feebleness had appeared in his handling of a dispute with Austria in the early years of his reign. Then, in the naïve conviction that he could placate Joseph II by a persuasive manner alone, he had gone in person to Vienna. It was a fatuous move, led to a humiliat-ing check and severely damaged the spiritual prestige of the Holy See. In answer to the activities of the revolutionaries in Paris *il Papa bello* could produce nothing but pathetic and entirely fruit-less protests. To this bleating accompaniment the clergy were put under civil authority in France and the hierarchy and discipline of the Church were overthrown, her religious Orders abolished, her property nationalized, her priests first imprisoned and then massacred. In such circumstances his appeals for concord were a puerile mockery, showing clearly the state to which he was reduced.

There was only one moment of relief on all this downward path. After the flight to Varennes the rumour spread that Louis XVI had been successfully rescued by the Marquis de Bouillé and was on the way to Italy. Rome was in ecstasy at the news and huge crowds surrounded the French Embassy. They beat the drums and let off fireworks and shouted *Vive le roi!* They took the horses from Cardinal de Bernis' carriage and dragged him through the streets. The whole town was given over to rejoicings. Only the art students at the French Academy, notorious Jacobins, held aloof and were said to have planned a charge on the cheering people under the Embassy windows.

After Louis XVI's execution Pius solemnly condemned the horror of the deed, sobbing as he did so. He realized at last how futile were his protests. 'I see terrible misfortunes coming,' he declared, 'but I shall have nothing to say. To speak in such times of trouble and disturbance can only make bad worse.' And into this mute disapprobation he retreated until the Revolution established itself and proclaimed a republic in his very capital and dismissed the Vicar of Christ to his death in ignominious exile.

THE REPUBLIC 'PER RIDERE'

The first storms of revolution had been ignored here when they broke out in Paris. From the greatest prelate to the scum of the streets, the Romans regarded the new thinking as so much moonshine. 'Monsù Voltaire', as they called him, was a lunatic. One blenched a little on mentioning his name, and made an immediate, precautionary sign of the cross, but there was no fear of his doctrines spreading. People were far more taken up with the trial of Cagliostro and the progress of the Pope's important public works. If there were revolution in France, if the peasants fired the *châteaux* and the Paris mob stormed the Bastille, these were just the quirks of a nation gone temporarily astray. This attitude was reinforced by the presence of the many courtiers who, removed by the turn of events from Versailles and waiting, as they thought, until the cloudburst was over, had come to visit Rome, as all right-thinking persons should. They asked no more than to pass the time agreeably and the social season of that winter of 1789 was the most brilliant ever seen.[1]

But the Revolution, having swept king and nobility away, found the priests too in its path and dealt hardly with them. The blows it

[1] Among the many elegant French ladies Mlle de Coigny was much admired; she was later André Chénier's 'belle captive'.

levelled against the Church, and which evoked those vain complaints of Pius VI, were resented by the Romans, first as affronts
to their faith and then as attacks upon their welfare. The Treasury
in Rome suffered from the nationalization of Church property in
France; it suffered from the confiscation of the papal territories of
Avignon and the Comtat Venaissin;[1] it suffered most of all from
the drying up of tribute to the court of Rome from Church and
people beyond the Alps. This affected the whole population and
there were mob demonstrations from time to time, with cries
of 'Long live the Pope!' and 'Long live religion!' The *émigrés*
were hailed with rapture and when the royal sisters, Madame
Adelaide and Madame Victoire, arrived in 1791 they were received
at the Porta del Popolo with proper ceremony as Daughters of
France and their procession turned into a sort of Ancient Roman
triumph.

The citizens, near to considering the revolutionary French as
devil-possessed, were in no frame of mind to swallow the provoca-
tions offered them on their own doorstep in 1793. The Republic
had been proclaimed on the previous October 21st and when
Pius VI failed to recognize it the Convention sent threatening
envoys to him. These men, Hugon de Basseville and La Flotte,
fulminated at the Pope, who refused to listen to them, and their
behaviour was a challenge. They walked about with tricolour
cockades in their hats and had the statue of Louis XIV torn down
by the art students; they removed the portraits of pontiffs and
cardinals from the Academy and hung up pictures of the grimmest
republicans in all history instead. The answering crop of sonnets
that went round the cafés and salons further inflamed the situation.
The town boiled over with insulted pride, 'the men of Trastevere
looked with bloodshot eyes'. The Convention's two emissaries had
meanwhile taken down the shield with its carved fleurs-de-lis from
the embassy pediment to make way for their republican insignia.
This happened on the morning of January 13, 1793, and they
appeared on the Corso for the afternoon parade in a carriage
flaunting revolutionary favours and with their own and their
servants' headgear stuck with tricolours. It was asking too much of

[2] The Comtat Venaissin had been ceded to the Papacy by Philippe le Hardi,
King of France, in 1272. Avignon had been papal since 1347, when Clement VI
bought it from Joanna of Provence, Queen of Naples, and the sale was ratified
by the Emperor Charles IV. Such venerable title should have been beyond all
question and scenes of murder and 'all kinds of horror' accompanied the
reunion of these lands with France.

the hot-tempered Romans, who took fire at once. They shouted abuse and soon the stones were falling 'in showers' on the coach. The alarmed coachman made a sudden swerve into the Via San Lorenzo in Lucina and a successful dash for the courtyard of the Palombara Palace, which was then the Embassy. But he was followed through the gates and with people so quick to violence the Frenchmen were obviously in danger. La Flotte escaped their rage, but Basseville, who confronted it, had a razor-slash from a barber in the crowd and died next day.

The Palombara Palace and the French Academy were sacked and the whole incident was celebrated as a glorious affair in Rome. Not a poet withheld his ode or sonnet, nor a musician his cantata. It gave rise to a whole literature on the subject of popular justice exercised upon the Church's foes. On the Corso an inscription not far from the scene of the killing gave thanks to the Madonna for the victory.

The Convention, from which the severest reprisals might have been expected, was silent. Basseville was made a Hero of Liberty, his son adopted by the nation and that was all. The generals of the Army of Italy received emphatic orders to exact resounding vengeance for the assassination and unofficially instructed to ignore it. This was not the moment, with Louis XVI newly dead and the allied sovereigns about to take up the gauntlet, for sending troops to central Italy.

For three years France barked and never bit and while the respite lasted the Romans could safely pour scorn on the government in Paris, the Pope display his settled opposition, stigmatize the murder of King Louis and shelter the royal aunts and the most active émigrés. But when the forces of the Republic began to win battles all illusions fled. General Bonaparte took command of the French armies in Italy and thereafter nothing could stop them. Soon they were menacing the Papal States and Pius was thankful to sign a truce, while privately determining to avoid the heavy terms it laid upon him: five hundred rare manuscripts to the victor and a hundred works of art as well as his twenty millions in ready cash. Such a clause had never figured in a diplomatic document before and did so now because the revolutionaries so crammed their heads with Roman history. Burning to imitate at all points the heroes of Antiquity, they recalled how Rome had marched away with the artistic treasures of Greece. Bonaparte himself, who knew his Plutarch off by heart, took pride in the role of Marcellus and could have quoted him as 'carrying the finest pictures and statuary from Syracuse, to show first in his triumph and afterwards as adornment for the city'.

Marcellus, however, was not even a memory to the Romans of the eighteenth century and all their pride was roused by these demands of the French. Ferdinand de Navenne, the historian of the Palazzo Farnese, wrote:

'To judge by some of the popular demonstrations the subjects of the Church were eager for a chance to fight the soldiers of the Republic and the clergy did their best to inflame patriotic feeling with appeals to heaven to support the Holy See. In September a huge procession went winding from the Aracoeli to the Vatican with societies and brotherhoods bearing emblems of public mourning and repentance. Men walked barefoot, halters round their necks and arms outstretched to form a cross; some violently beat their breasts. The holiest relics and consecrated images were meanwhile shown to the faithful. Signs and marvels multiplied, whipping excitement to the highest pitch. Nothing but the approach of French troops could dissolve the artificial ferment or recall the shepherds to the dangers threatening their flock.'

Pius VI had now come to terms with the court of Austria, but Bonaparte had not taken long to penetrate his evasions. Declaring war on the Pope, he overran his garrisons with ease and left him no choice but to purchase peace by the penitential Treaty of Tolentino. This exacted twenty-one millions of money and an enormous quantity of pictures and works of art, and the treasure-houses of Rome were ransacked to fulfil it. Over the Alps went the golden chalices and the marbles out of the museums, 'the old imperishable glory' of Italy. Every convent and church had to contribute, not even excepting San Luigi dei Francesi, which gave twenty thousand crowns' worth of gold plate.

The Roman people took this treaty bitterly to heart. They hated more than anything to see the excommunicated French plenipotentiaries proceeding across the town in state to the Vatican, where the Pope received them with incomprehensible politeness. Bonaparte had appointed as ambassador his brother Joseph, now installed at the Corsini Palace with a large military household. The aristocracy were fearful of provoking the new masters and welcomed them effusively; the Duchess of Braschi presented the

Roman ladies to the ambassadress and balls were given in honour of the Republican envoys.

It was the briefest of honeymoons, for the hostility of the common people never weakened. They knew only so much as they were told, but by instinct they understood far better than the Curia what the French were really going to do. The Republic intended to overthrow the Pope, and they knew it. Bonaparte's proclamation from Milan had been clear as daylight: the French, friendly to all peoples and especially so to the descendants of Marcus Junius Brutus, of Marcus Decimus Brutus and of the Scipios, were coming to make the Capitol itself again, honourably to set up there the statues of those heroes who once brought it fame and to reawaken the Roman people from centuries of degrading slavery. The Directory had given its spokesman a very explicit plan of campaign: 'You will reinforce all those who consider it time that papal rule was finished with.' No one could frame more direct orders to organize revolt.

Were they carried out? It is very probable they were, for a faction was quickly formed, drawn mostly from those parts of Italy which were trying, with French help, to drive out their own rightful sovereigns. Openly encouraged by France, these agitators staged a demonstration on the Pincio on December 28, 1797. They were soon dispersed by papal troops, went for assistance to the Palazzo Corsini and were caught there by the Pope's dragoons. In the clash that followed a young general named Duphot was shot in the heart while attempting to intervene and killed on the palace steps.[1]

This murder, which probably happened by mistake and certainly in such confused circumstances that nobody could say whose fault it was, meant that the measureless sacrifices of Toletino had been in vain. General Berthier, commanding the Army of Italy, received orders to march on Rome and avenge the insult to the honour of France. His men were deployed on the slopes of Monte Mario on

---

[1] The report to the pontifical authorities suggests that this intervention by Duphot was something more than Joseph's despatches might lead us to suppose. Seeing a corporal and four soldiers loading their firearms under the Porta Settimana he had, in fact, brandished his sword and advanced upon them shouting, 'Long live Liberty! Courage! I am your general!' with the rioting mob behind him. The corporal, whose name was Marinelli, fearing that the general would disarm him, responded with a volley and Duphot fell at the first shot. As we have seen, French sympathies were all with the republican faction in Rome, whose plans had been known some days before. Several of them were arrested and Joseph's only criticism is that they had chattered like women and acted like babes, behaviour in which he failed to recognize Brutus, or any other hero of old. (*Letters of Joseph Bonaparte*, vol. IV, p. 144.)

February 10, 1798. Next day they occupied Castel Sant' Angelo and all the key points of the city. The troops of the Pope were disarmed and his cardinals arrested or removed. Ten days later Pius, who had never ceased to protest at the violation of his rights, was deposed and taken into Tuscany by force, and then to Valence in France, where he died the following year. He was eighty-one and his reign of twenty-four years was the longest since St Peter's. He had asked to be allowed to end his days by the Apostle's tomb. 'People die anywhere,' rejoined the officer, a Swiss Protestant, arresting him.

According to the French newspapers of the time, Rome was now in the grip of revolutionary mania, with a crowd in the Forum planting a liberty-tree and hoisting a cap of liberty on top, and the hills re-echoing to liberating cries 'unheard for four centuries'. How inspiring, wrote the Paris *Moniteur* on Nivôse 14, year II, to behold a great people extinguishing the Vatican thunderbolts as with the same hand they raise the altars of liberty once more upon the Capitol. In Bonaparte's opinion, no more was needed to light the fires of liberty but the memory of ancient Rome. Only Berthier, actually on the spot, was realistic. 'I have seen here nothing but the most profound dismay,' he wrote, 'there is no trace of the spirit of liberty at all.' The popular movement was in fact so disunited and so unspontaneous that it was hard put to find anyone to petition for a republic and the French general hastily bestowed the liberty of Rome upon a handful of hired agitators who were the only persons asking for it. Five lawyers as hastily drew up an act recording the people's newfound sovereignty and Berthier then made a solemn entry to the sound of fanfares. Like a triumphing Roman he went to the Capitol and there, wreathed with laurel and standing in front of Marcus Aurelius' golden horse, he gave one of those flamboyant speeches for which all the revolutionaries had such a happy talent. The horse was wreathed in tricolours.

Rome was now to see all the egalitarian raree-shows, 'all the farrago of the civic fêtes of the year II'. Patriotic altars, trees of liberty, republican processions, nothing was spared. Ribbon-bedecked, the busts of Cato, Lucius Scaevola and Brutus presided over every celebration. Save as derisive onlookers, the citizens disassociated themselves from all such frolics. Those taking part were either the French or 'the friends of the French', folk from Lombardy or Naples brought in to dress the stage.

For the Romans, long used to the great papal ceremonies, obviously saw these burlesque displays as nothing more than a huge joke. They were offered a Fête of the Federation, modelled on that held in Paris, and saw St Peter's square filled with a sorry straggle of girls dubiously disguised as vestals, and pasteboard allegories fit only for a carnival. On July 17, 1798, the archives of the Inquisition were ritually burned in the Piazza di Spagna, together with the Golden Book of the Capitol, the official register of the patriciate. A large number of supernumeraries gathered round the pyre for this occasion, got up as Roman historical characters in borrowed costumes from the Teatro Alberti. The fire was lit by immodestly disgarbed youths with idiotic wings on their shoulders and the climax disclosed an altar complete with naked lady—Truth—rising from the Ashes of Superstititon. The massed audience on the Spanish Steps whistled heartily. Objects were thrown.

The pageantry usually took place in the Forum or the Colosseum. Here, in the ancient Flavian amphitheatre, they paraded Pompey's statue and gave a considerable rendering of Voltaire's *Death of Caesar*. Then there was the Fête of the Perpetuity of the Republic, at the Temple of Antoninus and Faustina. In honour of the martyrs of liberty a commodious stucco sarcophagus had been placed before the Constantine Basilica and round it were grouped young girls with green garlands, while the supernumeraries, in appearance fanciful though Roman, struck heroic attitudes. All the French-employed painters manage to ignore the fact that these absurdities earned more catcalls than applause and to present them in the guise of splendid spectacles, acclaimed by large, enthusiastic crowds. In the Napoleonic Museum in Rome may be found a delightful collection of their misleading records.

Once masters of Rome, the French set about organizing a new State on the ruins of the papal power. They went to no undue pains to be inventive: the Roman constitution of 1798 was a pale copy of the Directory. It had consuls, tribunes and togaed senators, all of whom spent the time in abject quarrels while their wives were wrangling over the best apartments in the Quirinal and the Vatican. Like their Parisian colleagues, they plotted against each other, indulging in makeshift orgies of wine and women the while. Sheltering behind the façade of government, French generals and commissaries exercised a collective dictatorship that bore every appearance of anarchy. The five chief generals fell out continually, three or four claimants fought a war of insults for any post of

importance and every official of this peculiar republic was surrounded by 'a shoal of courtiers, harlots, Jews and odd-job men
from all corners of Italy'.

Obstinately, the commons refused to catch any republican spark.
There was for them little danger in persistent hostility, but more
prominent people ran a greater risk. They were quite aware that
high places attract thunderbolts and they were poor candidates for
martyrdom. It was for such interested reasons that a section of the
Roman aristocracy rallied to the French. The deserters included
the Sforza and Santa Croce families and the whole Borghese clan.
There were cardinals found to renounce the purple and one, the
Pope's own Vicar, to sign himself 'citizen Somaglia'. Revolutionary
fashions penetrated the upper reaches of society. Men wore panta-
loons with coats of red or blue and cut their hair *à la Titus*; elegant
females were seen at parties, and even out walking, draped in light,
clinging tunics. Priests and devout persons crossed themselves, and
the lower orders guffawed, as they went by.

Licentious plays were acted and now women acted in them.
Cicisbei were no longer the only escorts available; the French
officers invaded their territory and husbands, used as they were to
cavalieri serventi, still looked on indulgently. 'These were days,'
says Ferdinand de Navenne, 'of which ladies and officers alike long
retained most happy memories.'

But things were very different for the working class, who were
in every way put out by the régime. They could not grow accus-
tomed to the new names for old streets and districts, nor to the
ridiculous republican calendar that robbed them of their Sundays
and gave them only one day's rest in ten. The familiar Roman
coinage was replaced by *assignats* and the cost of living rose in
consequence. As the cardinals went into exile and the convents
were shut up the unemployed, always dependent on providers, saw
the bread snatched from their mouths.

More, the revolutionaries applied themselves shamelessly to the
pillage of Rome with official levies, semi-official searches and the
most usual method of plain confiscation. 'Men invested with public
office enter the wealthiest houses and remove all they find there.'
So ran the report of 200 French officers who met in the Pantheon
solemnly to denounce the brigandage of their own commanders.

The Directory took its fair share of the spoil. One of its agents,
a former Oratorian priest named Daunou, was told to send 500
packing-cases to Paris, filled with stolen treasures from churches

and museums. It was even hoped that he might be sending the column of Titus, but this project he declined on the grounds of expense. There was systematic rifling of palaces, churches, sacristies and the houses of the middle class. The writer Paul Louis Courier serving in Italy has left us a picture of Rome bled white by the extortions of his fellow-soldiers; and even his inventory of her wretchedness omits what her people felt was worst of all—the hounding of their religion and the blasphemy that assailed them from every hustings.

And yet, more than these profanities perhaps, the Romans hated the Jacobins for challenging their dearest traditions. The talking statues had been daubed red as a sign of disgrace, but still their bitter dialogues went on. 'What is the weather like?' asked Marforio. 'Weather for thieves,' was Pasquino's reply. They were infuriated when the French painted the bronze angel above Castel Sant' Angelo with their national colours, placarded him as 'the Liberating Genius of France' and stuck a cap of liberty on his head.[1] By tradition the seated bronze statue of St Peter, for which St Leo I had melted down an image of Jupiter, was always hung with rich pontifical emblems for the feast of Peter and Paul on June 29th. When the Republic broke the tradition in 1798 the anger of the people of Rome was such that they were forced to restore it on the next occasion.

The murmuring soon turned to violent protest. On February 26, 1798, there was rioting in Trastevere. It was quickly subdued[2] but was the signal for serious unrest throughout the Roman province. There followed the risings, the surprise attacks, massacres, and isolated murders. Then repression, bloody and brutal.

By the time the King of Naples, taking advantage of Bonaparte's withdrawal, came to free the Papal States, the citizens were in open rebellion. The French troops prudently evacuated the town and he, who was to restore the Pope and overcome the Revolution, was welcomed in to scenes of transport and delirium. The French were back in force before the cheers had died away. He retired unceremoniously after only twenty days of jubilation, leaving the town in their hands and the people to digest the discovery that

[1] The French imprisoned in Sant' Angelo those who refused to pay the war-levies and forced loans, anyone who destroyed trees of liberty or spoke against the new régime. The object of this was to give the former papal stronghold a bad reputation and a Parisian named Communeau was tried by court-martial for kindness to prisoners when he was in charge there.

[2] Twenty-two people were executed on the Piazza del Popolo.

their 'saviours' too, had garnered into warehouses such marble and canvas as had so far escaped plunder and were prevented by sudden flight alone from sending it to Naples.

Reinstated, the republic lasted only a few months. It collapsed when the French, defeated in Northern Italy, their lines of communication threatened, left the city on September 29, 1799. She was abandoned to a Neapolitan occupation and the terrible reaction pictured so vividly in *Tosca*.

The eighteenth century was dying. This book has been, perhaps, some evocation of the old theocracy, the Rome of the *Ancien Régime* that died at the same time.

BIBLIOGRAPHY

ABOUT (Edmond): *Rome contemporaine,* Paris, Michel Lévy, 1861.

ADDISON (Joseph): *Remarques sur divers endroits d'Italie par M. Addison pour servir de supplément au voyage de Mr Misson,* Paris, 1722.

ANGELI (Diego): *Storia Romana di trent' anni (1770–1800),* Garzanti, 1945.—*Le Cronache del Caffé Greco.*

BAC (Ferdinand): *Promenade dans l'Italie nouvelle,* Paris, Hachette, 1935.

BANDINI (Carlo): *Roma al tramonto del Settecento,* Naples, Renosandron, 1922.

BARTHÉLEMY (Abbé J. J.): *Voyage en Italie,* letters to the Comte de Caylus, ed. A. Serieys, Paris, 1801.

BERNIS (François Joachim de): *Lettres et Mémoires du cardinal de Bernis,* ed. Fr. Masson, 2 vols. Paris, 1878.

BERTAUX (Louis): *Rome,* 3 vols., series 'Villes d'Art célèbres'. Paris, Renouard, 1913.

BONNARD (Abel): *Rome,* Paris, Hachette, 1931.

BORGHESE (Daria): *Vecchia Roma,* Gherardo Casini, 1955.

BOTTA (Carlo): *Storia d'Italia,* 15 vols., 1832.

BRIFFAULT (Eugène): *Le Secret de Rome,* Paris, Boizard, 1846.

BROSSES (Charles de): *Lettres familières sur l'Italie,* ed. Yvonne Bézard, 2 vols. Paris, 1931.

BURNEY (C.): *The Present State of Music in France and Italy,* Milan, 1771.

CALLARI (Luigi): *Luci ed Ombre della Roma papale,* Rome, 1944.

CAMPOMARZIO: *Roma,* Tipografia Agostiana and Libreria internazionale modernissima, 1939.

CATALOGUE of Exhibition, 'Italian Painting in the Eighteenth Century', Paris, 1960.

CAYLUS (Comte de): *Voyage en Italie (1714–1715),* ed. Amilda A. Pons, Paris, 1914.

COCHIN (C. N.): *Voyage pittoresque d'Italie,* Paris, 1751.

COINDET (John): *Histoire de la Peinture en Italie,* Geneva, 1849.

COMTESSE DE ——: *Souvenirs de Voyage* (Anon.), Lille, Lefort, 1856.

CONCARI (Tullo): *Il Settecento*, Milan, n.d.

COSCI: *L'Italia durante la preponderanza straniera*, Milan, 1879.

COYER (Abbé Gabriel François): *Voyage d'Italie et de Hollande*, 2 vols. Paris, 1775.

DAL PANE (Luigi): *Il Tramonto delle corporazioni in Italia*, Milan, 1940. — *Storia del lavoro in Italia dagli inizi del secolo XVIII al 1815*, 2nd. ed. Milan, 1958.

DANDOLO (Comte T.): *Roma ed i Papi*, 5 vols. Milan, 1857-8.

DUPATY (Jean Baptiste): *Lettres sur l'Italie*, Le Cointe et Durey, Paris, 1824.

ESPINCHAL (Comte d'): *Journal d'Émigration*, Paris, Librairie académique Perrin.

FOCILLON (Henri): *G. B. Piranesi*, Laurens.

FUGIER (André): *Napoléon et l'Italie*, Paris, Janin, 1847.

GASPERONI (Gaetano): *Settecento italiano*, Padua, Cedam, 1941.

GEOFFROY (A.): *Études italiennes*, Armand Colin, 1898.

GOETHE (Wolfgang): *Italianische Reise*, vols. XXVIII and XXIX of *Works*, Stuttgart and Tübingen, 1827-1842. — Trans. by J. Porchat (*Works*, vol. IX), Paris, 1878 and M. Mutterer, Paris, 1931.

GOLDONI (Carlo): *Mémoires pour servir à l'histoire de sa vie et à celle de son théâtre*, Paris, 1787. — *Opere teatrali*, 44 vols., Venice, 1788-1795.

GORANI (Joseph): *Mémoires secrets et curieux des cours, des gouvernements et des moeurs des principaux États de l'Italie*, 3 vols. Paris, 1793.

GOURNERIE (Eugène de la): *Rome chrétienne*, Paris, 1867.

GREGOROVIUS (F.): *Promenade en Italie*, Paris, Hachette, 1894.

GROSLEY (P. S.): *Observations sur l'Italie et les Italiens données en 1764 sous le nom de deux gentilshommes Suèdois*, 2 vols. London, 1770.

HAYWARD (Fernand): *Les Deux Derniers Siècles de la Rome pontificale (1769-1870)*, Paris, Payot, 1928. — *Histoire des Papes*, Paris, Payot, 1942.

HOUSSAYE (Henri): *Athènes, Rome, Paris*, Paris, Michel Lévy, 1879.

LABAT, O. P. (Father Jean Baptiste): *Voyages en Espagne et en Italie*, 8 vols. Paris, 1730.

LAFON (Mary): *Rome ancienne et moderne*, Paris, Furne, 1854.

LALANDE (Jérôme Lefrançais de): *Voyage d'un Français en Italie fait dans les années 1765 et 1766*, 8 vols. Paris, 1769. Pub. anonymously. 2nd enlarged ed. Paris, Desaint, 1786.

LANFREY (P.): *Histoire politique des Papes*, Paris, 1860.

LEROUX (Marcel): *Rome–Paris*, Hachette.

LESSER (Creuzé de): *Voyage en Italie*, Paris, Didot, 1806.

LIERDE (Mgr.): *Derrière les portes vaticanes*, Tours, Mame, 1957.

LLORENTE (Juan Antonio): *Portrait politique des Papes*, Rouen, Bechet Jeune, 1822.

MADELIN (Louis): *La Rome de Napoléon Ier*, Paris, Plon.

MANTOVANI (T.): *Il Presidente de Brosses in Italia*, Collezione Settecentesca.

MARCABRUNI (Mario): *La Connaissance de l'Italie d'après Corinne*, Montpellier, Coulet, 1910.

MAUREL (André): *Un mois à Rome*, Paris, Hachette.

MAURY (Jean) and PERCHERON (René): *Itinéraires romains*, Paris, Lethielleux, 1958.

MISSON (Maximilien): *Voyage d'Italie*, 4 vols. Hague, 1724.

MONTAIGLON (Anatole de): *Correspondence des Directeurs de l'Académie de France à Rome*, Paris, 1907.

MONTESQUIEU: *Voyages*, ed. baron de Montesquieu, Bordeaux, 1894.

MORONI (Alessandro): *Vie voci e viandanti della Vecchia Roma*.

NAVENNE (Ferdinand de): *Rome et le palais Farnèse*, Paris, Champion, 1923.

NIBBY (A.): *Itinéraire de Rome*, 1824.

NOLHAC (Pierre de): *Souvenirs d'un vieux Romain*, Paris, Plon.

ORLOFF (Comte Grégoire): *Essai sur l'Histoire de la Musique en Italie*, Paris, 1822.

ORMESSON (Wladimir d'): *Mission à Rome*, Paris, Alsatia, 1956.
— *La Ville éternelle*, Paris, Alsatia, 1956.

ORSI (Pietro): *L'Italie à la fin du XVIIIe siècle*.

PALÉOLOGUE (Maurice): *Rome*, Plon, 1902.

PIOVENE (Guido): *Viaggio in Italia*, Milan, Mondadori, 1957.

PONCHEVILLE (A. Mabille de): *Collines de Rome*, Paris, Librairie Bloud et Gay, n.d.

PORTAL (Emanuele): *L'Arcadia,* Collezione Settecentesca.

POUJOULAT (M.): *Toscane et Rome,* Paris, 1840.

RABANY (Charles): *Charles Goldoni, le théâtre et la vie en Italie au XVIIIe siècle,* Paris, 1896.

RÉGNIER (Henri de): *La Double Maîtresse,* Paris, Mercure de France.

REVEL (Jean François): *Pour l'Italie,* Julliard, 1958.

RICHARD (Abbé J.): *Description historique et critique sur l'Italie,* 6 vols. Paris, 1766.

ROBELLO (G.): *Les Curiosités de Rome,* Paris, 1854.

ROCHÈRE (Comtesse Eugénie de la): *Rome,* Tours, Mame, 1854.

RODOCANACHI (Emmanuel): *Les Corporations ouvrières à Rome,* Paris, Alphonse Picard, 1894.

ROLLAND (Romain): *La Musique en Italie au XVIIIe siècle; Revue de Paris,* August 15, 1905.

ROMANI (Pietro): *Due Secoli di vita romana (Aneddoti, documenti, curiosità)* S. Angelo (1936).—*Famiglie Romane* (1942).—*S. Eustacchio.*—*La Satira nella Roma napoleonica.*—*Pasquino e la Satira in Roma.*—*Raccolta di Pasquinate.*—*Pasquino nel Settecento.*—*Strade e piazze di Roma,* 3 vols, 1939 (Rome, Tipografia Agostiniana and Libreria internazionale modernissima).

ROMANO (Pietro): *Roma nelle sue strade e nelle sue piazze,* Rome, Palombi.

ROUSSEAU (Jean Jaques): *Confessions,* Books VI and VII.

SAVELLI (A.): *Histoire d'Italie,* French ed. by F. Hayward and Albert Falcionelli, Paris, Payot, 1936.

Settecento a Roma (Il): Catalogue of 1959 Exhibition, De Luca, Rome.

SILVANI: *La Corte e la Società romana nei secoli XVIII e XIX.* Rome, 1881.

STENDHAL: *Promenades dans Rome.*

TAINE (Hippolyte): *Voyage en Italie,* Paris, Hachette, 1876.

TIVARONI: *L'Italia prima della Rivoluzione francese,* Turin, 1887.

TORNEZY (A.): *Bergeret et Fragonard,* Paris, May et Motteroz, 1895.

UNTERSTEINER (Alfredo): *Storia della musica,* Milan, 1893.

VAUSSARD (Maurice): *Daily Life in Italy in the Eighteenth Century.* London, Allen & Unwin, 1962.

VEUILLOT (Louis): *Rome et Lorette,* Tours, Mame, 1869.—*Le Parfum de Rome,* Paris, 1862.

WEY (Francis): *Rome, Description et Souvenirs,* Paris, Hachette, 1875.

X.: *Nouveau Voyage d'Italie* (anon.), Hague, 1711.

X.: *Voyage historique d'Italie* (anon.), Hague, 1729.

YOUNG (Arthur): *Voyages en Italie et en Espagne pendant les années 1787 and 1789.* French translation by Lesage, Paris, 1860.

YRIARTE (Charles): *Autour du conclave,* Paris, Rotschild, 1887.

ZELLER (Jules): *Histoire d'Italie,* Paris, Hachette, 1865.

INDEX

The names of individual churches are to be found under the heading Church, of individual palaces under Palazzo, of individual squares under Piazze. n after a number refers to a note on that page.